SOLOMON, Stanley J. Beyond formula: American film genres. Harcourt Brace Jovanovich, 1976. 310p ill bibl index 76-19900. 5.95 pa ISBN 0-15-505400-7
One of the favorite approaches to film criticism in the numerous books currently appearing is the *genre* approach. Solomon's work is another such effort and, while no tremendous accomplishment, better and more useful than many of its counterparts. He selects six categories — the Western, the musical, horror, criminal, detection, and war. While one might quarrel with this breakdown, it is legitimate, and the author treats each category with admirable clarity and intelligence. In addition to his succinct essays dealing with each genre, he has selected good examples of each for further inspection. It is a book that lends itself well to a fundamental course in film criticism.

BEYOND FORMULA

AMERICAN FILM GENRES

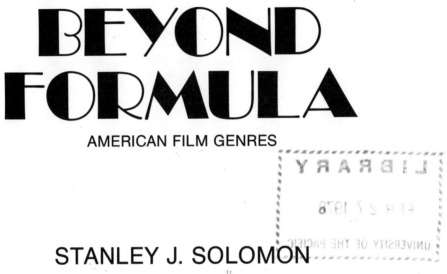

BEYOND FORMULA

AMERICAN FILM GENRES

STANLEY J. SOLOMON

Iona College

HARCOURT BRACE JOVANOVICH, INC.

NEW YORK   CHICAGO   SAN FRANCISCO   ATLANTA

To

Jennifer, Nancy, and Barbara

ILLUSTRATION CREDITS

CHAPTER OPENING POSTERS

page 11: © 1969 Campanile Productions, Inc. and Twentieth Century-Fox Film
Corporation. All rights reserved.
59: From the MGM release *Singin' in the Rain*, © 1952 Loew's, Inc.
111: From the motion picture *The Exorcist*, courtesy of Warner Bros., Inc.
© 1974.
157: The Memory Shop, New York City.
199: © 1974 by Long Road Productions. All rights reserved.
241: © 1969 Twentieth Century-Fox Film Corporation. All rights reserved.

TEXT ILLUSTRATIONS

page 31: Culver Pictures.
35: From the motion picture *Winchester '73*, courtesy of Universal
Pictures.
38: © 1959 by Paramount Pictures Corporation.
45: From the motion picture *The Searchers*, courtesy of Warner Bros., Inc.,
© 1956.
53: From the motion picture *The Wild Bunch*, courtesy of Warner Bros.,
Inc., © 1969.
57: © 1969 Campanile Productions, Inc. and Twentieth Century-Fox Film
Corporation. All rights reserved.
82: Culver Pictures.
85: © RKO Radio Pictures.

*Illustration credits continue on page 310, which is regarded as part
of the copyright page.*

PREFACE

American moviegoers have always been receptive to the notion of genre—the recognizable ordering of narrative patterns to produce related experiences from film to film. The sustained popularity of certain cinematic genres—the Western, the musical, the war film, and so on—over many decades, through changing fashions and new sensibilities, suggests that the patterns themselves rely on characteristic events or actions of abiding significance to many types of mass audiences. No wonder then that writers on film in recent years have tried to account for the mass appeal of genres by comprehensively surveying the details of symbols, images, social contexts, and historical developments in genre films.

As interesting as these studies often are, I find in them all sorts of obstacles to an appreciation of a genre's essential substance. When I am given extensive data about all the typical elements I should expect to find in the typical films, I begin to wonder why anyone would bother thinking about so many commonplace details that are only part of intentionally cultivated reworkings of mediocrity. Of course, from time to time our ordinary expectations of genre films are revitalized by examples of cinematic brilliance that reveal new insights into old routines. My own preference is to concentrate on just such examples—to go beyond formula, beyond fashion and nostalgia, to the heart of a genre's general matter as it figures in the particular circumstances of individual films of considerable merit.

A good genre film works because it is art as well as genre. So much is obvious. Less often noted but equally important, such a film is *of its genre,* and therefore to understand its meaning we must also understand its relationship to a hundred similar minor films, and even to some dreadful films. For this reason, the first half of each chapter in this book describes the relevant categories of a genre, and the second half treats individual works of art within those categories. My ultimate aim is to explore the key associations between the unique elements of a particular work of genre art and the conventions and traditions within which the work exists.

I want to express my appreciation for the help I received from Images Film Company, Hurlock Cine-World, and Films Incorporated in making certain films accessible to me, and in particular I am indebted to Robert Harris, president of Images, who is the most knowledgeable film distributor I know. And of course my gratitude must also extend to those masters of genre who showed me what it was all about a long time ago: Alfred Hitchcock, Fred Astaire, John Ford, Humphrey Bogart, and the Warner Brothers studio of the 1930s and '40s.

STANLEY J. SOLOMON

CONTENTS

2

SINGING AND DANCING: THE SOUND OF METAPHOR
59

The Metaphorical Mode   60
The Procedures of Metaphor   63
Categories of the Genre   66
Filmmakers   68
The Theory of Integration   70
Thematic Integration: *A Star is Born* and *An American in Paris*   74
A Note on the Musical Theater   78

80   *Gold Diggers of 1933* (1933)
83   *Top Hat* (1935)
87   *Swing Time* (1936)
90   *The Pirate* (1948)
95   *Singin' in the Rain* (1952)
98   *The Band Wagon* (1953)
102   *Funny Girl* (1968)
106   *Cabaret* (1972)

3

THE NIGHTMARE WORLD
111

Fears and Horrors   112
The Cinema of Reason and Nightmare   114
The Terror of the Plausible: An Aspect of Science Fiction Films   116
Irrational Terrors   119
Romantic Isolation   122
Some Minor Categories   125

129   *King Kong* (1933)
132   *The Bride of Frankenstein* (1935)
136   *Invasion of the Body Snatchers* (1956)
138   *Psycho* (1960)

viii

4

THE LIFE OF CRIME

157

ix

5

THE SEARCH FOR CLUES

199

6

WARS: HOT AND COLD
241

x

INTRODUCTION

My intentions in this book differ sharply from those apparent in most contemporary studies of film genre. The prevailing attitude of even the most knowledgeable critics and theorists' suggests only casual recognition of the value of genre analysis. I want to promote the thesis that genre study incorporates critical evaluation—that such study need not rely, as it now seems to do, on the more faddish critical tendencies of sociology and of cultural archeology, which often consists merely of sifting and digging among the gravestones of Monogram Pictures.

Popular as genre critiques have become in recent years, the subject still lacks the kind of intellectual grounding in theory that would qualify the genre approach as a plausible category of film criticism. The current level of genre comprehension can be seen from a recent study of film theories:

1

> It is precisely for this reason that *genre* notions are so potentially interesting. But more for the exploration of the psychological and sociological interplay between filmmaker, film, and audience. . . . Until we have a clear, if speculative, notion of the connotations of a *genre* class, it is difficult to see how the critic, already besieged by imponderables, could usefully use the term, certainly not as a special term at the root of his analysis.*

Such attitudes toward genre are common and reflect only a limited approach. Yet the deficiencies of such an approach may denigrate the entire subject, since the kind of criticism that cannot establish qualitative distinctions is of little use in any attempt to understand artistic achievement.

The theory I advocate in this Introduction and will be developing throughout the following chapters starts with the view that the truly typical elements of a genre, both visual and dramatic, are not necessarily the most obvious props and devices shared by bad films and television parodies. Secondly—and basic to the apprehension of qualitative variations within the genre—whatever these typical elements may be, they are not trite, repetitive patterns stored in film studio libraries or file cabinets, but artistic

*Andrew Tudor, *Theories of Film* (New York: Viking, 1974), pp. 139–42.

insights stored in the minds of such filmmakers as Alfred Hitchcock and John Ford.

From these premises evolves my belief that *the most generic works*—the most "typical" works—of a significant genre are, artistically and intellectually, the best works of that genre. The best films never do what certain critics always assert they must do in order to succeed—that is, genre classics never "go beyond the limitations of the genre," but in fact incorporate the generic elements to the fullest degree. Since these elements often include premises basic to a film's artistic strengths, it appears to me that genre study not only permits but suggests analytical approaches to the evaluation of individual works. Ultimately, genre study contributes to our understanding of major films, to our perception of how artists shape their creative materials.

DEFINING GENRE

The problem of defining film genre does not seem very great until one reads the critics. Then what appears to be a genre to one writer becomes a subgenre to another, and what to one is merely a technique or a style becomes to another an identifiable manner of grouping films. In practice, the term *genre* has an almost unlimited number of valid connotations, and all I wish to set down here are the guidelines for the use of the term in this volume.

The identification of groups of films is not at all a matter of preconceived logical categories, but of common practice. I reject some of the common practices only on the grounds that they seem unusable to me. For example, there are books published on "the thriller" and "suspense in the cinema," categories that, from my point of view, are so vague as to include films the public could more easily recognize as belonging to a number of genres more perceptible than those two—for techniques or styles by themselves can tell us little of the content or effect of most films. Similarly, I cannot get a critical handle on a generic immensity now much esteemed, the *film noir*, a classification that includes most of the somber melodramas of the 1940s, mainly on the basis of mood or lighting, though I discuss several of these films under crime or detective genres. Nor do I consider comedy as a genre. Comedy is a mode of presentation, one of three possibilities (along with tragedy and tragicomedy). But having noted that, I can derive no specific cinematic qualities to apply toward a definition to serve as the basis for genre analysis; nor can I conceive of any fundamental characteristics that might relate an enormous

2

number of comic categories to a workable, unifying notion of a genre of comedy.*

For a different reason, I also reject some of the currently popular types of categories that I have elsewhere called "conceptual genres."† By locating a theme or an ideological topic that recurs in a group of films—for example, "politics in film" or "sex in the cinema"—some critics and historians are able to construct genres for the study of certain attributes that seem to me less cinematic than sociological. With the virtually unlimited possibilities that confront a critic willing to write on such a popular theme of the day as "images of women in the cinema," a random selection of twenty films would produce generalizations hardly likely to be closely matched by any equivalent selection. When ideology dominates the critical endeavor, the sense of cinema is ignored—or made less important than it is when studied as a perceivable *art form*, of ultimate importance in and for itself.

The genres discussed here—for the most part the usual ones the public recognizes as genres—are all based on perceptual patterns that filmmakers intend to be observable from film to film, though all of these do not occur in all instances of the genre. (If some element does seem to occur in every memorable film made in a particular genre, then very likely we are confronting an essential aspect of the genre's meaning.) Broadly put, a genre film is one in which the narrative pattern, or crucial aspects of that pattern, is visually recognizable as having been used similarly in other films.

3

Generic cores

Although definitions of particular genres are too often confined to the assembling of characteristics, it seems to me that the defining aspect of a genre is a certain mythic structure, formed on a core of narrative meaning found in those works that are readily discernible as related and belonging to a group. The core can be composed of different sorts of elements. For example, if genre A evolves from the main character's occupation while genre B develops from the visual environment, it might seem that the quali-

---

*To do so, one is forced into the absurd stance of having to devise all-inclusive categories in defiance of common sense, as Gerald Mast does in *The Comic Mind* (Indianapolis: Bobbs-Merrill, 1974): "There are eight comic film plots, eight basic structures by which film comedies have organized their human material. The film shares six of the eight with both the drama and the novel, one of the eight with only the novel, and one seems completely indigenous to the cinema" (p. 4).

†Stanley J. Solomon, "Film Study and Genre Courses," *College Composition and Communication* XXV (October 1974), pp. 277–83.

ties central to A may be so different from those central to B that A and B are not comparable genres. But in fact, genres can be formulated on different bases and still be widely recognized by critics and general audiences as comparable, though distinct, groupings. Genre A, for instance, might be established on the basis of the hero's being a private investigator, while genre B is premised on the action taking place in the West. The source of each is important for the study of the particular genre, but whatever the source, the results are similar: identifiable narrative patterns develop from a core of ideas that in turn stem from the concept "private investigator" or "Western locale."

Neither of these two generic cores would necessarily suggest any particular meaning to us were we questioned about them apart from the American cinema. Yet when considered in the framework of the American motion picture industry, "private investigator" and "Western locale" immediately begin to assume a visual dimension, culminating eventually in a list of attributes. This study, however, does not attempt to categorize, let alone collect, items for such a list. Instead, my concern is to examine the aspects of each genre closest to its essential core, using its attributes only as they shed light on the primary meaning surrounding that core. In other words, I mainly desire to explore the manner in which a genre such as that of the private investigator film takes shape, in terms of the questions anyone might raise about it: Why does a person become a private investigator (a question rarely asked and never answered *in* any film)? What is his implicit attitude toward his work? How does he go about solving the professional problems that confront him? These are matters that spring naturally from the first awareness we have of this particular kind of professional. The mythic structure formulates itself from the premise found at the genre's central core.

It is, of course, quite possible to make a film about a private detective on vacation who falls in love with a woman, marries her, retires, and opens a successful grocery store. But obviously what we mean by the private investigator genre comprehends films about a professional engaged in the work of his profession. Indeed, it is extraordinarily clear that the real-life profession has little to do with the genre's meaning—real-life private investigators do not track down murderers, but take pictures of spouses in compromising situations and provide personal security services. And when a film at last is made entirely from the reality of a private investigator's routine, then a new genre will have been created. In the meantime, the immediate narrative core of this genre remains one in which a highly skilled professional detective is hired to do something, discovers some crime in the course of his investigation, and solves it. This is the basic material. The

implications of that material seem strongly to suggest an underlying mythic structure that reappears in all the memorable works
of the genre.

Narrative patterns and iconography

A good deal of the popular sense of a film genre relates to its
recurring elements, including dialogue patterns (for instance, the
ironic repartee of the private eye), rather than to its underlying
structure. These characteristic images are sometimes referred to
as the *iconography* of the genre, but those who employ the term
do not always seem to realize that iconography means the images
or visual symbols *that represent something else*. That something else is the deeper reality that justifies genre art. Those
genre enthusiasts who refuse to go beyond the literal surfaces
they enjoy so much—the contorted faces of monsters coming
alive in laboratories, the shootouts between sheriff and badman,
the private detective mocking the police—reveal an infinite patience for small variations, but they surely seem out of touch with
their own sensibilities. We sometimes identify very strongly with   5
genre situations and heroes, and such films may become significant to our perception of our world. But if the unexamined life is
not worth living, as Socrates said, then perhaps the unexamined
genre is not worth loving.

In this book I deliberately avoid systematically surveying the
iconography of any genre, the repeated visual characteristics and
motifs that serve to identify, in the public mind, both the best and
the worst films of a genre. There are, in most cases, essays on the
subject that supply more of such details than would suit the
purposes of a book primarily concerned with the implications of
the narrative issues. Furthermore, I am uncertain about too
many aspects of what other writers sometimes bring forth as the
typical evidence of a genre—all the way from the decor of costume
drama to the dialogue of a Western. If my generalization is true
that the most typical genre film is likely to be the best genre
film—not for its surface properties, but for its artistic statement—
then probably there are not enough "best" films or close-to-best
films in any genre to justify a survey of iconography that would
hold true of the lesser, but numerically greater, films in the same
genre.

For example, in a memorable sequence from Francis Ford
Coppola's *The Godfather* (1972), the displeasure of a crime family don with a defiant movie producer, who is unwilling to give a
part to one of the don's friends, leads to a rather gruesome scene
in which the movie producer wakes up one morning to find the
severed head of his horse in bed with him. Now this particular

method of persuasion had never, to my knowledge, been seen in a film before, so it cannot be claimed as a bit of conventional scenic design in the gangster film. Yet without taking anything away from its horror and originality (and artfulness, because it shows at once the crudeness, violence, and omnipotence of the mob), the sequence belongs crucially to the conventions of the gangster genre. In the genre's heyday, the 1930s, the mob that wished to make its power apparent would "bump off" someone or break up a rival distillery or nightclub. But the element of psychological warfare—gaining a point by proving to a holdout that the gang can reach him and destroy him—is entirely common elsewhere in the genre. The image of the horse's head becomes an icon of the genre.

A listing of all common iconography would consume much space and not be worth the effort. What I prefer to do is discuss those patterns of action most interesting to me because they have appeared in the most interesting films of the genre—rather than analyzing iconographic images from dozens of minor films that lie beyond the scope of this book.

6   I am open to the argument that every convention, no matter how seemingly minor, helps us to comprehend the nature of a genre. But I believe that at this point in the study of cinematic genre, less attention has been paid to understanding the major narrative patterns than to the elements of iconographic design. For instance, it seems to me at least theoretically possible to make a successful Western without a pistol (that is, an icon), but not to make a good private eye film without the detective coming across as highly moralistic and honest (that is, a pattern of meaning). Failure to understand the pattern (as distinct from the iconography) of any genre—for example, to underestimate the integrity of the private eye—leads to a lot of poor genre films, by filmmakers who think they are being original when in fact they have simply failed to grasp the materials at hand. Much of would-be genre parody is merely self-parody by those who have never understood the nature of the genre they think so suitable for ridicule.

Genre and originality

There remains one more element essential to a definition of genre, and that is the matter of originality. The final criticism offered by those who do not respect genre art is that there is implicit in all genre works, except for the earliest examples, a lack of originality.

Genre, as partially defined in the preceding discussion, has much to do with the familiar. But there is a difference between the reproduction of familiar patterns and outright repetition—the trademark of lesser films, whether they belong to a recognizable genre or borrow from many. Everything depends on how genre filmmakers, who we assume are skillful to begin with, handle basic story structures, conventional environmental factors, and the conception of major characters. If they want merely to repeat the surface elements that have recently proven successful—to vary them with, for example, some new styles of murder, but to retain the essential thrills that brought audiences to the theater the last time—then such filmmakers are exploiting the blatant imagery of the genre, but, contrary to creating genre art, they are merely reproducing genre formula. To achieve genre art, filmmakers must be committed to exploring new facets of the familiar setting, elaborating on their insights into the mythic structures of the genre. For above everything else, genre is a convenient arrangement of significant human actions that can be returned to, over and over again, to provide new understanding of basic human motivations or needs. Genres may originally be derived unconsciously, by accident. But the patterns are repeated on purpose because other filmmakers see, in those first films of a genre, latent possibilities for the reinterpretation of human conduct in archetypal situations.

GENRE AND POPULAR CULTURE

A too-easy association is often made between film studies based on genre and film studies based on popular culture. Popular culture studies describe, categorize, and analyze in regard to the sociological and psychological phenomena apparent in films. In contrast, genre criticism is concerned with the traditional values of art as they happen to appear in a group of related works. For the purposes of popular culture, any well-worked-over genre that is still current is as worthy of study as any of the genres selected for this book, presumably chosen on the basis of artistic merit. But to dismiss popular culture as a serious scholarly pursuit because, for its purposes, *Love Story* is sometimes just as important as *The Birth of a Nation,* is to neglect the aspect of it that is indeed analogous to genre study: the search for underlying patterns that can relate a particular cultural or artistic experience to some universal truth about human nature or the society we live in.

I believe that the widespread insistence on regarding generic patterns as either artistically indiscriminate or as detracting from the artistic value of individual films is based on a simple failure to discern what those patterns really are. To assert that the worst examples of the Western film are the most typical—the most generic—works of the genre is to confuse genre with formula. Formula, indeed, it can be argued, is the essence of almost all the longer studies that purport to analyze and classify genres. And it is in the large area of formula that genre study and popular culture analysis may overlap, the latter expounding a view that the frequent reappearance of a formula in itself denotes sociological significance. Yet no one wants to defend the value of a particular film just because it purposely exploits a current formula. Such films usually convey no esthetic quality, since the general formula itself attracts all the attention. In contrast, genre study probes beneath surface details for whatever dimensions of meaning adhere to the patterns manifest in the individual example. Whereas exponents of popular culture seek to reveal a category, students of genre explore the ways in which the category illuminates particular films.

Until the relatively recent growth toward respectability of popular culture studies, few critics had written on the theory of genre without conveying a sense of suppressed laughter, or at least condescending amusement, at what the masses found entertaining. Among the first to write with perception about the subject as it pertains to film was Robert Warshow. He treated genre as an important manifestation of a psychological aspect of mass culture that deserved analysis because of what it revealed about all of us. In this sense, he functioned as a precursor to all popular culture studies that aspire to serious analysis in our day. Warshow's approach was to make a generalization about society and to link it to a popular film genre's narrative pattern, thereby making a lucid connection between a general cultural idea or condition and its manifestation in popular art.

There is, however, one negative aspect of Warshow's methodology—although of course he cannot be blamed for instituting it—and it is the process of generalization, which is probably indigenous to genre criticism. It makes sense to generalize when one's subject matter is a group of films that have reproduced a certain formula, even though individual works within the group show marked differences. The problem with later critiques of genre—all of them more detailed than Warshow's two famous essays on gangster and Western films—is that often the generalizations have counted for everything and the comparisons have verged on the absurd—true in a *general* sense, but preposterous in regard to *many specific genre films*. Yet generalizations about genre are essential or else there can be no analysis of a category in the first place. The problem is really one of defining a basis for such generalizations, and here again the issue seems to me a matter of separating the popular-culture approach from the esthetic analysis of narrative art. The critical endeavor that strives for an all-inclusive approach to a massive body of popular works is dealing virtually by definition with popular culture, regardless of the author's specific intent. And at this level of criticism, certain formularizations, as they apply to the innumerable works of passing interest—films of the day—if they have any validity at all may help us to deal with chaotic data as we receive it from contemporary trends in our culture. This kind of approach helps us to classify, and therefore comprehend, the ordinary and the mediocre—works that defy extended esthetic analysis because they are intended to be meaningful primarily or entirely on the level of popular entertainment. I do believe that popular entertainment must be studied and its impact understood, but I am more interested in the admittedly narrower question of how genres within a certain form of popular entertainment—motion pictures—affect the artistry of certain films that are to my way of thinking far better than ordinary. Genre in the cinema, as elsewhere, surely provides refuge for much mediocrity, but it also provides us with much art, and it is this aspect of genre that concerns me in this study.

9

1

THE WESTERN AS MYTH AND ROMANCE

The Western is probably the major American film genre in terms of endurance, quantity, and perhaps quality. Many of its major subgenres were formed in the silent film era of Broncho Billy Anderson, William S. Hart, D. W. Griffith, and Tom Mix, and have retained their influence until today.* In recent years the Western has gone into a decline, as evidenced by the number of anti-Westerns that have been made, including Andy Warhol's *Lonesome Cowboys* (1968), Robert Downey's *Greaser's Palace* (1972), and Mel Brooks's *Blazing Saddles* (1974). This decline is probably temporary, however, since the Western embodies certain key myths of our culture and so is not likely to remain out of fashion for long. Still, even if no new serious Western is made for a decade, the great quantity of Western films turned out through the years and the impressive number of quality Westerns will insure that the genre's artistic heritage continues to be critically appreciated.

LANDSCAPE

The Western genre has been so prolific that several of its subgenres are no doubt larger than most of the other genres discussed in this book. What relates all these different categories—the unifying factor in our comprehension of hundreds of films as a genre—is a sense of place. The Western is primarily a genre of location, but richer than other such genres because the location—which varies from vast landscapes of rocky ridges to

---

*In their encyclopedic survey of the genre, *The Western from Silents to the Seventies,* revised edition (New York: Grossman, 1973), George N. Fenin and William K. Everson devote seven chapters to the major filmmakers and stars of the silent-era Westerns. For the most part, the conventions of the genre formed sixty and seventy years ago remain recognizable today, although modifications in the form and iconography have been and still are part of an expanding tradition.

forts to Indian reservations to towns seemingly built on a single street—immediately circumscribes the kind of action that will occur. The location with almost equal rigidity suggests not only plot but characterization. If we are shown, for instance, a barren, craggy terrain, we assume that the people who ride over it triumphantly must themselves be fairly rugged. At the same time, we can also assume that others less rugged will be victimized by the same environment (by robbers of stagecoach or train, perhaps) and will be forced to accept or actively seek the protection of those who will defend them (a cavalry escort, for example). If the environment expresses a kind of toughness and primitiveness that seems to foster a law of survival of the fittest, then we normally would expect some Western characters to present a bullying aggressiveness and criminality.

The rural locales, furthermore, are generally sparsely populated, except in films where cavalry hordes converge on a tribe of outnumbered Indians. Lack of population and the accompanying lack of industry make the sources of wealth few: banks, cattle ranches, and stagecoaches, for instance. These sources are constant temptations to that portion of the populace prone to live by violence because, banded together, these people represent enough power to grab up the wealth through daring or force. In defense, the citizenry forms a nominal, usually weak-spirited opposition group. This group gathers around the solitary defender, the sheriff or marshal who, in any Western environment, performs his duties despite numerically greater opponents but nevertheless manages to survive on strength of character as well as ability. Similarly, as an outpost of civilization, the fort, surrounded by gathering tribes, occupies in a broad sense the same position in a film about cowboys and Indians as the sheriff does in a lawless town.

The nature of Western locations tends to breed an environment of threat and counterthreat, in which conflict along sharply delineated moral lines is all but inevitable. To some, the moral issues joined in such an atmosphere are too simplistic, especially since they are seldom explored at length. It is true that right and wrong are meant to be apparent, and the characteristic laconic dialogue is hardly likely to lead to the articulation of moral problems. But the Western is a great genre because the issues it deals with are clearly embedded in the cinematic qualities of the films. We see the given premises and they are hard to argue with. The constant challenge of the landscape urges a consistency of response to typical situations and chance meetings with strangers, for there is never time to calculate all the degress of danger in an unfamiliar place. Naturally, Westerners tend to develop codes of behavior to cope with most of their ordinary

13

interactions with those not well known to them. The codes are easily ascertained, since both heroes and villains seem to understand them. Indeed, sometimes the outmaneuvered or overmatched hero can taunt his otherwise unethical enemy into hand-to-hand combat—the democratic way—with the outlaw relinquishing an advantage because the code of the place seems to demand it. When codes are violated, when someone is shot in the back, the villain is quite aware of his vileness and his motives for it (cowardice, revenge, and so on). The location further determines the moral perspective by inviting sudden violence and the accompanying necessity of perpetual preparedness. Thus, one ought to know how to act in a perilous situation. And therefore, if one is so prepared, the probability is strong that his whole life is patterned in a certain way, evident in a certain style. We are continually impressed by the fatalistic, melancholy, and serene deportment of many of the Western heroes played by John Wayne, Randolph Scott, Gary Cooper, and James Stewart on their way to one more deadly encounter.

14   The environment, of course, suggests a good deal about the roles of women as well. Only a few notable films depict women in control of events (as Joan Crawford is in Nicholas Ray's *Johnny Guitar* [1954]) or in a position of command (as Marlene Dietrich has in Fritz Lang's *Rancho Notorious* [1952]). More typically, the action—raids, robberies, shootouts, and so on—is taken up with men's pursuits, almost as if women were ancillary to the plot. And sometimes the location can supply a sense so unduly masculine that the men seem to exist on an animal level. Thematically, the function of women in the Western is to humanize the situation by providing a necessarily feminine role—not primarily as victims requiring masculine help, but as bringers of civilized thinking to a brutalized environment, especially through an insistence on the value of human life. Although they frequently offer tenderness, consolation, and devotion, women are only attractive to the Western hero when they prove to have an independent toughness of their own.

The special qualities of the Western landscape often affect our awareness of main characters' personal histories. In the Eastern locale, the metropolitan existence allows characters to arrive and immediately be assimilated into the environment, their appearance often informing us of nothing more than their present occupations. But the arrival of the hero or villain in the Western setting immediately prompts discussion of who he is, where he came from, why he left. Sometimes no great mystery is implied, and yet much of the film is spent on speculation: is he a retired outlaw, a bounty hunter, a revenge seeker? The answer to such speculation supplied in the film is often nothing more than a hint that the hero has lost a loved one (wife, brother, father—less commonly, I think, a mother, though Jesse James in Henry King's *Jesse James* [1939] did lose his). But even this little biographical information seems quite necessary, for the individual stands out in the Western landscape—on the plain as he rides alone or in the bar when he asks for a whiskey (or a glass of milk).

For a simple contrast to this use of personal biography, consider a well-known urban film such as Alfred Hitchcock's *The 39 Steps* (1935). The film begins with the hero wandering the streets of London for amusement and entering a music hall. We see that he is a visitor from the way he takes in the sights, and later we learn that he is a Canadian. We never learn anything else about him; he apparently knows no one in London, but for all we can tell he may not know anyone in Canada either. He's just one of a million tourists. Hitchcock even omits any mention of his occupation, his interests, or his place in society (in the literary source he is an engineer). Nothing matters in regard to the hero's past; life in the city demands only an intent awareness of the present.

15

Now of course it sometimes happens, in an urban film, that we need to know the hero's past. But in a Western we must have a constant interest in it, for when we encounter him the character stands at a critical point in his career. He may have changed a good deal from what he was, and that change itself may have occurred a long time ago, but the plot line will force him to confront his former self. Henry King's *The Gunfighter* (1950), which Robert Warshow has examined in terms of this quality of the inescapable past,* provides an archetypal example of this pattern of confrontation, as does Anthony Mann's *Bend of the River* (1951), in which the reformed badman must evolve into the heroic good man or be drawn back to his old ways—a typical issue of many good Westerns. In the genre, nevertheless, character formation often seems to have been fixed before the film begins, and what we are therefore introduced to is a rather grim, fully experienced, mature man confronting some crisis situation that is not entirely new to him. The landscape will establish the arena for the reenactment of certain events, but almost always the mere surface action is meaningless unless it has some bearing on what the character has been through, similar situations he has faced earlier in his career, and whether he handles matters any better now. Similarly, there are the historical Westerns in which

---

*Warshow's classic study "Movie Chronicle: The Westerner" is included in his book *The Immediate Experience* (New York: Atheneum, 1970), pp. 135–54.

the predicaments grow out of larger social problems not solved in the past such as the relations between the Indians and the representatives of the government.

The interrelationships of landscape, characterization, and the past are natural to the genre. The basic locale is either a form of the primitive settlement (the town, the lonely ranch house) or the wilderness itself (the mesas and valleys), which includes the temporary encampments of cattlemen, as in Howard Hawks's *Red River* (1948), and pioneer wagons that represent mobile outposts of civilization, as in John Ford's *Wagonmaster* (1950). Both types of locale are associated with the endless attempts to overcome the hardship (sometimes brutality) connected with nature in its untamed form. Yet almost never is the elemental aspect of nature a primary threat to the humans playing out their dramas within it. Much more common is the essential neutrality or passivity of nature. In a common form of the showdown gunfight, both hero and villain find cover behind the mountains' massive rock formations. Nature, if not exactly indifferent, tends to be fair in its hostility. It represents the constant factor of life—eternal past, present, and future. With settings of this sort, the genre is readily susceptible to themes linking the individual's past and future to a present event.

16

Since the most elemental dramatic question posed visually by the genre has to do with the human ability to survive in this primitive environment, the particular battle of hero and villain is only one more piece of evidence of the eternal myth of humanity's struggle to bring civilization to the wilderness. Those virtues constantly needed for survival must therefore be part of the hero's characterization. Among those virtues are competence in the face of danger, courage, determination, and endurance, and so the past experience of the characters is often the crucial factor for their survival. The Western is not notable for visual surprises. We usually need to be prepared for the outcome of events, and this is another reason why the characters' past is put before us. In Mann's *Winchester '73* (1950) we may be surprised to learn, late in the film, that the hero and the villain are brothers, but it is an inevitable surprise, since we know that something in their past has made them enemies—a fact that is visually apparent from the beginning. It would have been a surprise for the genre if the evil brother had killed the good brother in the final shootout and gotten away scot-free, but the genre excludes that sort of possibility.

The possibilities really appropriate to the genre tend to be clear-cut, in keeping with the conventions of the landscape. Thus the dramatic conflict, though it may contain finely shaded ambiguities of moral responsibility and guilt, is always overtly clear in the confrontation of good and bad characters. Refinements made by the best filmmakers usually affect the development of the conflict rather than the nature of the conflict. No filmmakers, presumably, would want to tamper with the landscape, and therefore the most suitable kinds of conflict for those locations seem to have been fixed long ago.

MOVEMENT

Since so many of the essential genre characteristics result from the implications of landscape and the types of people that inhabit particular environments, it seems quite natural that many of the basic structures of the genre are based on movement.* A terrain with inhospitable, stark, natural elements immediately creates in the viewer a sense of the obstacles that would make it challenging for people to get from one location to another. But the fact that people are there in the first place indicates that a movement toward a destination, beyond the film's environment, is basic to many Western films. The impediments of robbers and Indians are logical extensions of the alien nature of the locale.

17

Some of the most basic structures of the leading Western film categories include the motif of the perilous journey: it appears in the form of settlers moving their wagons through Indian country, stagecoaches moving through robber territory, a marshal or bounty hunter attempting to bring a captive to justice, or cattlemen moving a herd. These types of plot contain situations of tension, usually in which the hero or heroic group is outnumbered or at some disadvantage. In these situations, the environment makes it seem unlikely that the hostile threat can be averted, even when the threat is something much less obvious than flying arrows. Many Westerns have turned on the question of how the lawman will bring in his prisoner; often the prisoner is simply waiting for the lawman to fall asleep to take revenge or just to escape. (And we have seen the fake sleeping bag made up to look like the hero not only in the worst of films but in great works like Ford's *The Searchers* [1956].) Movement from place to place often takes purposeful form in films about the building of railroads across the West such as Cecil B. DeMille's *Union Pacific* (1939). Films dealing with the transportation of gold (Sam Peckinpah's *Ride the High Country* [1961]) or the herding of cattle a long distance through dangerous territory (*Red River*) involve great risks not only from the environment but from

*See John Cawelti, *The Six-Gun Mystique* (Bowling Green, Ohio: Bowling Green University Press, 1971), pp. 40ff.

thieves or rustlers, ready to employ violence for considerable financial gain.

The idea of movement *without* specific destination is also common in certain subgenres. The outlaw gang, for example, may have specific places to go for robberies, yet it is not really a special place they ride to but a general goal; all towns to them are more or less equal. The subgenre of outlaws on the run is, again, usually structured around no particular place, but around the desire to get away from a particular place. An exception is "the border," a common destination in such films, which is geographically specific enough. Another typical kind of unspecified location appears in the subgenre of revenge heroes. Such heroes set out to find a person or group, but usually they follow random leads with no clear implication of the eventual locale.

With all the possibilities for cinematic movement that are built into the genre, it is sometimes surprising to realize that movement from place to place is not absolutely essential to the Western. Although location is at the heart of the genre, the location in a given film is not necessarily a traversable one. There is, after all, a sense of imposing immobility in the Western landscape. Many times the dramatic action of a Western concerns the arrival of a hero or a villain, a new sheriff or an outlaw, a settler, a retired gunfighter, a mystery figure. Although the character may not remain in the new location permanently, the film will concern itself with the conflicts that arise in the basic environment of that one location.

18

THE ROMANCE OF THE WEST

That the Western is not a realistic portrayal of a historical period is evident to most writers on the subject. Yet the genre does not depart radically from the generally realistic tradition of the cinema, nor does it forego the privilege of dealing with authentic history: the settling of the West, the spread of democracy and commerce, and the real-life outlaws, sheriffs, and other historical figures who existed during the period within which most Western films take place—from the end of the Civil War to the early part of the twentieth century. The genre conveniently simplifies social issues and historical complexities, not for purposes of propaganda (the issues are usually dead ones as far as the viewer is concerned), but for reasons of art. The Western has emerged as a major American cinematic genre less for the historical information it embodies than for the opportunities its landscape provides to depict the kinds of conflicts and characterizations that major filmmakers have seen as artistically important.

Yet if the cinema Westerner is no true character out of American history, he is still a creation out of our past, a figure of American romance. An irrepressible adventurer in touch with some purer reality than remains today, the Westerner resists the kind of cultural impermanence that still affects us. He does not represent a naive reaffirmation of the natural man, for frequently we encounter him midway through life, his present condition fixed by past experiences. As a wandering or traveling figure not usually tied down by occupation, he often, out of necessity, forms temporary affiliations. These associations may not last, leading him eventually to reject his surroundings and community and resume his previous undirected life style. Sometimes his newly formed associations are worth his commitment, in which case he often indicates a willingness to sacrifice himself helping others. His philosophy is generally fatalistic; his own death, which sometimes happens in the genre, comes as no great surprise to him. He dies well.

In general, romance narratives are set in the past, sometimes in remote locations. The Western neatly exhibits both qualities. The era of the Western is not simply one hundred years back in American history, but a fictional time when civilization looked distinctively different from the way it does today. This concept of time has much to do with the Western's setting in or around desert wasteland or uncultivated terrain. The Western does not deal objectively with historical time or authentic place, though some casual attempt is frequently made to establish at least a town's name. "Most of the following is true" is the insert title preceding the opening of George Roy Hill's *Butch Cassidy and the Sundance Kid* (1969), but the assertion does not change the fact that the film has little relationship to actual history, and Hill knows this. We may be curious about the real Butch Cassidy after seeing the film, or about the real Judge Bean after seeing John Huston's *The Life and Times of Judge Roy Bean* (1972)—which offers a similar assertion of its historical realism—but Butch and the Judge are, quite obviously, romantically heroic projections of Paul Newman's laconic characterization. They do not bear the same relationship to truth that we hope to find elsewhere in film biography, even in musical comedy biography. General Custer, Billy the Kid, Geronimo, Calamity Jane, Wyatt Earp, and Davy Crockett have no historical authenticity within the genre, but merely legendary names. Similarly, there is no development of historical issues in this romance genre. Time is abstracted and made merely an aspect of environment, or setting, fixed and immutable as the mountains and valleys of the landscape.

The appeal of the Western genre to filmmakers probably lies in the chance to return to fixed premises and their accompanying

19

themes because widely understood conditions and materials make it possible to establish quickly all the necessary circumstances of conflict. The dramatic conflicts that the genre's framework supports are diverse and permit more variations than any other major genre. Jim Kitses briefly summarizes these possibilities as "complex variables":

> The romantic mainstream that the Western took on from pulp literature provided it with the stately ritual of displaced myth, the movement of a god-like figure into the demonic wasteland, the death and resurrection, the return to a paradisal garden. Within the form were to be found seminal archetypes common to all myth, the journey and the quest, the ceremonies of love and marriage, food and drink, the rhythms of waking and sleeping, life and death. But the incursions of melodrama and revenge had turned the form on its axis, the structure torn in the directions of both morality play and tragedy.*

There are of course many additional motifs relevant to the situation of a character in a clearly definable location, bound only by the slender surface requirements of historical facts. (For instance, he ought to ride into town on a horse rather than drive up in a Cadillac, but as we see in Martin Ritt's *Hud* [1963], even the Cadillac can be absorbed into this genre. Perhaps riding into town on a camel would be fatal, though.) Then there are certain attributes of the hero—competence and reserve, among others— that fit in immediately with the premise of place and the anticipated situation. For instance, though the hero is rather quiet, he can never simply be thought of as inarticulately stupid. Filmmakers can rely on the audience's acceptance of a figure of romance as at least somewhat intelligent, his aloofness explainable in terms of his past, which has led him to an attitude of world-weary sadness over previous failures or unfulfilled possibilities.

And of course the Western towns that often provide the environment are themselves located primarily in the imagination of the filmmaker. They possess no economic reality. The bank we observe, and the miners' supply store, could hardly subsist on the number of residents capable of using them. Towns of one street, or bigger towns like Dodge City with perhaps two streets, now exist collectively in our imagination: stable, barber shop, sheriff's office, bar (the only crowded, urban-like area in the West), and brothel. (The brothel has always been there, if only glimpsed in passing, until recently when commercial pressures on filmmakers have begun to make this locale prominent in a genre that habitually resists the lure of the sensual; e.g., Peckinpah's *The*

---

*Horizons West, Studies in Authorship in the Western Film (Bloomington: Indiana University Press, 1970), p. 20.

Ballad of Cable Hogue [1970], Robert Altman's *McCabe and Mrs. Miller* [1971], and Gene Kelly's *The Cheyenne Social Club* [1970].) The towns suffice for settings, but not for depicting society in any stage of development. The thematic purpose of the Western town is to exclude the outside world and to provide a plausible gathering place on which to focus. The Western town typically is neither an outpost of civilization nor a stand against it, but instead a backdrop to conflict or adventure.

THE LONELY HERO

The image of the man on horseback receding into the horizon or drawing nearer from a great distance is commonplace in the Western. This recurring image, the loneliness of the long-distance rider, appears frequently to combine, in a very picturesque form, the condition of a man's life with the landscape upon which he is fated to carry out his destiny. It is not, of course, merely a physical image of the hero, but a symbol of the separateness of his life from others. Considered only as titles, Budd Boetticher's *Buchanan Rides Alone* (1958) and *Ride Lonesome* (1959) are more characteristic of the genre than Ford's *Two Rode Together* (1961). But the use of all three titles indicates how widespread the concept of loneliness is as a commonly understood condition of the hero in a Western. And when the concept of loneliness is thought of in a somewhat broader connotation—not as an absolute but as a relative term, meaning "apart from the larger social context"—it can extend to small groups: Peckinpah's *The Wild Bunch* (1969) or the single coach driving rapidly away from pursuing outlaws or Indians, or—the once-primary image of the genre —the lonely covered wagon caravan moving slowly across the desert.

21

In those Westerns emphasizing the separateness of the hero, a kind of primitive, usually unexplainable, psychology operates. Writing about Ford's *The Searchers,* Joseph McBride and Michael Wilmington take note of the motif's psychological implications:

> It was not, of course, the first Western to criticize the basic assumption of the genre—that the solitude of the hero, because it is an instinctive revulsion against the hypocrisy of civilized society, is *a priori* a good thing. In the decade before *The Searchers* appeared, a whole rash of Westerns were made in which the hero's solitude was presented as socially unjust *(High Noon)*, wasteful *(The Gunfighter)*, callous *(The Naked Spur)*, insane *(Red River)*, or impossibly pure *(Shane)*.*

*"The Prisoner of the Desert," *Sight and Sound* (Autumn 1971), p. 212.

I do not think that the depiction of the hero's loneliness was ever generically an implicit good, for all too often the character's aloofness from society is not a result of any conscious decision on his part. Sometimes it is he who has been rejected by society, as is the case with the renegade or rebel hero. But even in those circumstances where the hero chooses to renounce the permanent company of others, it is just as much a sign of personal failure as a matter of superiority. What often, in fact, makes the genre so richly suggestive is the appearance of such a hero—a man of proven superior qualities who wanders solitarily about, only casually employed (a gunfighter or bounty hunter, after all, does not work most of the time), whose outward traits of nobility, courage, strength, and skill are balanced by some sinister secret—or some deep hurt—that he has not psychologically conquered.

Quite likely the Western hero is maladjusted to society, resenting any sort of crowding, for his stature and distinction are hardly ever a result of skills of camaraderie. If he is respected and liked by people who have known him in the past, they seem called upon to vouch for him, for indeed his separateness, his reserve, indicates some sort of instability—sometimes even criminality—that might alarm the ordinary people of the community the hero has temporarily joined. On a few occasions, notable for occurring in good films (*The Searchers*, *Red River*, and most gunfighter films, in fact), the hero's brooding aloofness does suggest a neurosis that might be dangerous to him or to other people. Strong, silent, and unwilling to make overtures of friendship, some of the lonely but virtuous heroes (the stereotype established by Gary Cooper in Victor Fleming's film *The Virginian* [1929]) seem most concerned with effecting a presence even within the crowded bar. They stand out there too—not because of size but because they radiate strangeness and unsociability.

Although the Westerner is commonly an isolated figure, a man apart from society, much is made in the genre of various forms of community. Other genres may take communal relationships for granted, but the Western evokes a genuine feeling for whatever fleeting moment of communal relationship there may be. There are, for example, the evening campfire groupings, which often afford meaningful revelations of character, as in Hawks's *Rio Lobo* (1970). Sometimes they are sentimentally overused, sometimes just an occasion for a song in the minor Gene Autry and Roy Rogers subgenre—and blatantly parodied with exuberant vulgarity in *Blazing Saddles*—but they often suggest a brief humanizing period in the hero's otherwise violent existence. In most respects, the community built on longlasting relationships such as a town or a large, well-run ranch does not attract the lonely

22

Western hero, the perennial voyager. But the hero's chance meeting of characters who are part of some established community can frequently provide a key sequence for the comprehension of his secret yearnings, as in *Bend of the River,* where the ex-badman-hero meets a caravan of settlers.

Within the genre only one communal relationship endures as an integrated social unit, proud of its separation from the hostile elements encroaching on its environment—and that is the Indian community. Always seen as a small wandering band, even in those instances when several Indian nations joined together to battle the expansionary white society, Indians were for decades the standard villains of the genre. Victimized by this longstanding stereotyping, the Indian community as portrayed in motion pictures functioned primarily as a primitive force of the environment, evincing an irrational threat to the white man. From Raoul Walsh's *They Died with Their Boots On* (1941), glamorizing General Custer's last stand, to Arthur Penn's *Little Big Man* (1970), a definitive debunking of that incident, the public's attitude toward Indians can be seen to have changed—though generally Indians are still not well understood, nor have they totally lost their movie roles as a mysterious, if not exotic, people. In the mainstream of the genre, the cultural differences between white and Indian societies were depicted as unbridgeable; and not surprisingly, the function of the Indian community has been limited to incidents of violence, with a few major exceptions such as Ford's *Cheyenne Autumn* (1964). There have been, however, a few other films in which the usual, simply integrated Indian community is examined in terms of individuals: Robert Aldrich's *Apache* (1954), Samuel Fuller's *Run of the Arrow* (1956), Delmar Daves's *Broken Arrow* (1950), and, most impressively, Abraham Polonsky's *Tell Them Willy Boy Was Here* (1969). In these cases, the motif of the tormented Indian brave establishes a pattern equivalent to the genre's typical depiction of an isolated or alienated hero.

The family unit—or, usually, the breakup of the family unit—is a common structural device in the genre (e.g., King Vidor's *Duel in the Sun* [1946] and Mann's *The Man from Laramie* [1955]). The hero is essentially someone without a family, either literally an "orphan" in the world—a man deprived by some violence of his family—or a man hunting or being hunted by his family (as in Boetticher's *Horizons West* [1952]). The Western is not entirely conducive to the love story, and though there are happy endings in Westerns, often the hero will ride off, depositing the woman someplace else. (In Boetticher's *Comanche Station* [1960], the woman is returned to her blind husband, who does not appear until the end of the film.) Heroes occasionally

23

have wives and children, but the family unit is not often crucial to the action, and the wife's role is sometimes limited simply to offering conservative advice.*

The essential isolation of so many Western heroes is a matter that goes beyond the depiction of the family and the community to the creative nature of the genre as a romance account of man confronting his destiny head-on. The reasons for the separateness of the hero, as noted, are only vaguely described. Apparently, the ultimate motive for this persistent quality stems from the deepest aspect of the character's nature which, as far as I know, has never been described by any character in the genre. Yet the truth seems to be that the Westerner deliberately patterns his life as a solitary romantic, a wanderer, an isolated human being ultimately beyond the understanding of everyone else. Although this quality is partly a matter of his personal romantic style, the Westerner has to believe in his own uniqueness—and as far as we observe within the context of any typical film, he does differ in kind from those he encounters. He exemplifies a romantic philosophy that does not motivate others, a philosophy that permits others to recognize, and sometimes distrust, his singularity. Although often maladjusted and suffering from nostalgia, he is also preeminently a man of the present, capable of doing the right thing when others panic in confusion. And he does everything without flinching or boasting, displaying the determination and confidence that make the audience expect success. Ever since John Wayne as the Ringo Kid made clear his intention to shoot down the three vicious Plummer brothers waiting for him in Ford's *Stagecoach* (1939)—despite the prediction of all observers that he would be killed—we have known that the hero could overcome the odds by imposing his own image of greatness and inevitable victory even upon his adversaries, who thereby become psychologically distraught and prepared to lose. Wyatt Earp could not have gotten out of the O.K. Corral were he merely some unknown sharpshooting citizen. To project his invincibility on the brain of an enemy is the ultimate skill of the hero.

The romantic imagination of the Westerner endows him with the advantage of a noble style, but that style is maintained at the cost of true companionship or community life. He cannot be among equals unless he admits the possibility of equals, and to do so might diminish his own sense of uniqueness. Like a true romantic, he never shuns ordinary mortals simply because they are unheroic. He is solitary because he is different, not because

24

*Warshow remarks of the hero: "If there is a woman he loves, she is usually unable to understand his motives; she is against killing and being killed, and he finds it impossible to explain to her that there is no point in being against these things: they belong to his world." "Movie Chronicle: The Westerner," p. 136.

he insists on his own superiority. He might, in fact, consider himself socially unsuited to the community and consider his life style deficient in various ways, though he does not seem ready to abandon it. In any case, he is not commonplace, and is not about to settle for an average existence when the romantic call to adventure prompts him to move on.

SHERIFFS AND MARSHALS

The sheriff of a territory and the marshal of a town are among the most common character types to appear in the Western. Their portrayal affords virtually unlimited variations ranging from the buffoon to the hero, from the amiable father figure to the corrupt politician (in the service of the town's real power, the wealthy rancher, who literally owns the man and his office). The sheriff or marshal usually has status in pioneer society, his power generally coming directly from the people, who need him as the symbol of law and order. Thus, his stature usually reflects the kind of community he represents. If he is corrupt, chances are that the 25 town is generally corrupt itself or intimidated by the power structure, of which the lawman is just the pawn. Occasionally, the discrepancy between the heroic lawman and the citizenry is notable. In Fred Zinnemann's film *High Noon* (1952), for example, the citizens have enough time to prepare themselves, yet almost everyone refuses to aid the hero in defending his life and their honor. Cowardice of this sort by the townspeople is much more common than cynicism in those films where no help is given to the sheriff. But there is a comic sequence in *Butch Cassidy and the Sundance Kid* where the sheriff tries hopelessly to raise a posse, with not a single taker in the crowd, while the two outlaws watch in amusement from a bordello porch across the street. When the sheriff stops pleading for a moment, a salesman seizes the opportunity to address the crowd and tries to sell them bicycles!

There are times, of course, when the ultimate shootout between the lawman and the villain does not require a third party. For instance, citizens may not be involved in the very personal animosity that has developed between the hero and his enemy in the course of the film. Often the shootout in a town is between a gang and a small group of lawmen—memorably represented by the endless repetitions of Wyatt Earp, Doc Haliday, and their supporters going down the street to the O.K. Corral. Lawmen who are not themselves corrupt or cowardly can expect, at least once in their careers, to stake their lives against the marauders who wander into town. Another perilous side of the lawman's occupation is to keep prisoners, against threats from either a lynch mob or, more commonly, a family or gang that has announced its intention of freeing the criminal (as in Hawks's *Rio Bravo* [1959]). There is also, of course, the John Dillinger-type outlaw who vows to get away and usually does, with some degree of violence, as in Peckinpah's *Pat Garrett and Billy the Kid* (1973).

Given the possibilities for violence in the setting, the lawman's job is exceedingly difficult, even with the town's support. Strange men accept the position. Their commitments to legality are no more clearly articulated than the devoted cop's dedication in another genre, but somehow the Western lawman takes on an isolated position from the start. It is as if he felt that the continuation of civilization depended on the force of his character, his ability to put down a disturbance in a bar or to convince undesirables that they had better leave town by sunup.

THE OUTLAW AND THE GANGSTER

26 That the Western badman is close kin to the urban gangster seems obvious, at least in the style of presentation that Hollywood did so well and so often in those two scenically dissimilar genres. The critic John Mariani has pointed out to me the interesting parallels between two classic examples of each, King's *Jesse James* (1939) and Penn's *Bonnie and Clyde* (1967)—the influence of the earlier work on the later film is both visual and thematic. King's romanticized outlaw actually is thoroughly sympathetic, very clearly victimized by the establishment interests of ruthless big business, manifested here by the railroad bosses. In Penn's film, Clyde Barrow's rage is more abstractly motivated against similar forces, this time the banks. To justify this rage, Penn shows the environment of Depression America so carefully that we see the collective guilt of the banks as a symbolic force. And thinking about *Bonnie and Clyde* in this way we see, obviously enough, that Clyde's automobile is mainly a modern equivalent for the outlaw's horse, and the dizzying chases, the electrifying escapes, and the accompanying illusions of freedom resemble the generic elements of many Westerns, particularly *Jesse James.*

Yet, having acknowledged the kinship of cinematic outlaws and gangsters, we must account for the significant difference in tone, in style, in archetypal patterns associated with the two genres. If indeed Penn's Clyde Barrow is a displaced Westerner with some of the romantic malaise and most of the moral confusion of Jesse James, he is still closer to John Dillinger, Pretty Boy Floyd, Baby Face Nelson, and the desperadoes of the Prohibition era, and they in turn probably direct descendants of Little Caesar, Scarface, and Tom Powers in William Wellman's *The Public Enemy* (1931). Viewed historically, the real-life twentieth-century gangster may well have descended from Jesse James and Billy the Kid, but the Western and the gangster film appeared at about the same time, and cinematically there is no apparent influence of the one genre on the other—though certainly individual works in one genre influenced films in the other.

Most simply put, the life style of the Western outlaw is entirely different from that of the urban gangster or the modern traveling bank robber. The difference in centuries is crucial here. It is not merely a matter of fifty or sixty years, which, historically, is the greatest length of time separating the criminal eras depicted in the genres; frequently the distance in time is much less. Actually, the outlaw, like the Western hero, inhabits a timeless environment that, for the latter, is only roughly the nineteenth century. In contrast, it is always at a clear point in time (such as the Prohibition era) that the twentieth-century gangster participates in criminal activities. The historical settings make the mechanical trappings of the criminal's trade extremely important: Bonnie and Clyde rely on the machine gun and the automobile, whereas Jesse James relies on a pistol and a horse—the common property, apparently, of every male in his society. This difference characterizes the two genres. Although the outlaw Westerner is evenly matched with his opponents, he is always physically outnumbered by the collective forces of law and order that continually chase him. Thus his success depends on daring and skill. In contrast, the modern robber carrying a machine gun into a crowded bank confronts a number of screaming ladies and an aged bank guard, but his potential for violence in such a situation is overwhelming compared to what the opposition is likely to muster; his success depends on brute force.

Although the gangster and the outlaw are equally doomed by the nature of their occupation, the Western bandit seems inevitably a loser. It is this quality that makes him sympathetically romantic even in those films where his reasons for becoming a criminal are not fully drawn. Often, however, these reasons are crystal clear. When the mother of the James brothers is killed by the crooked representatives of the railroad in their eagerness to defraud her of her farm, the sons are driven to seek revenge. Pushed reluctantly into a life of crime, the outlaw is, nevertheless, often capable of resuming, if only for a brief period, the moral and noble life which he was raised to respect. In other words, aside from their criminal activities, Western outlaws frequently lead virtuous lives and almost never accumulate wealth, no matter how many successful robberies they carry out. They never gain

27

any of the flashy trappings of the city criminal, and oddly enough, their personal behavior seems rather rigid. For instance, Jesse James's love for his wife endures for years after she abandons him, and his ultimate decision to reform is a direct result of his small son's being beaten as part of a game where the boy plays the role of the father. Although the urban gangster sometimes exhibits redeeming virtues, his main motivation for a criminal career is money and power, and his achievements are marked by an increase in the quality of his clothes, cars, and girls (usually in that order of importance).

Since the life of the Western outlaw is dangerous, impoverishing, and desperate, it is therefore safe to assume that he would abandon it if he could—if the reward for him dead or alive could be lifted and if he could secure leniency from the law. Jesse James gives himself up when he is tricked by the railroad's assurance that he will be imprisoned for only five years. He continues robbing only because he is trapped by circumstances. Betrayed by his fate, his options always very narrow, the outlaw faces a career that seems filled with treachery—an existence at the edge of survival. Outlaw films of the 1930s as well as the attempted antigenre works of the 1970s, such as *Pat Garrett and Billy the Kid,* seem always to hang on to that element of betrayal as the irony befitting the outlaw's career.

Appropriately, that career is characterized by loneliness and achievement. Even when he has a gang or a family, the outlaw is pretty much dependent on his survival instinct and his cunning. The robberies themselves are certainly never planned with the detail found in the genre of "big caper" crime films, and even when extensively prepared, the robbery can collapse in a comic fiasco, as it does in Philip Kaufman's *The Great Northfield Minnesota Raid* (1972). Most Western outlaw activities are simply acts of daring. When, in *Jesse James,* the outlaw robs a train, there is some degree of skill in his manner of riding up to the train on a horse, leaping aboard, running the length of the cars to the tender, and single-handedly bringing the train to a stop at the point where his waiting gang can join up—but the whole feat is more a matter of one man's courage than an organizational enterprise.

Given the character of the outlaw, we readily understand why the shooting and killing he engages in fall short of the brutality splayed by the endless bullets of his modern-day urban counterparts. There are very few, and often no, innocent victims of robberies or shootouts in the outlaw Western. Lawmen are shot down, of course, but frequently they are either vicious or criminals themselves; never are they victims of premeditated murder. In fact, when they are good lawmen, they will usually display respect for the outlaw they are assigned to track down. The decent lawman in *Jesse James* cannot fulfill the function of his office by tracking down the outlaw because he admires the good qualities of the outlaw and scorns the immorality of the establishment forces that pursue Jesse.

The moral purity of many Western films, however, cannot be carried over to the Western outlaw film because of the unresolved ambiguity in the conflict between the outlaw's good character and his evil occupation. He does kill people, regardless of whether he does so out of necessity or simply in trying to escape and survive. The tragic undertone of such films rules out the possibility of ultimate escape and reform, as well it should, for the nature of the Western film in general demands an accounting of justice—the criminal acts cannot be forgiven and forgotten just because the outlaws are as charming as, say, Butch Cassidy and the Sundance Kid. The genre presupposes that each outlaw will recognize the finality of his choice. There is no turning back, and no real hope for the future. The outlaw is fated to repeat his crimes until inevitably a fatal betrayal occurs and the outlaw is ambushed on a tip-off, or, as in *Jesse James,* shot in the back while taking down a sign that says "God Bless Our Home." In contrast, the typical gangster ending is far from mere fatalism— if fatalism implies an acceptance of the inevitable. The prototypical gangster—James Cagney in *White Heat,* Humphrey Bogart in *High Sierra,* Edward G. Robinson in *Little Caesar*—when trapped beyond escape will shoot it out, gleefully hoping to take as many hated lawmen with him as possible. The gangster's death is an act of public defiance, and surrender is impossible because his hatred of society encompasses everything. Unlike him, the outlaw dies in a final betrayal that rounds out a life of frustration and disappointment. In a better world, he would have done better things. He might have become a sheriff.

29

STAGECOACH
(1939)

Director-Producer	Cinematographer	Script
JOHN FORD	BERT GLENNON	DUDLEY NICHOLS
Executive Producer		From the story
WALTER WANGER		"Stage to Lordsburg"
For United Artists		by Ernest Haycox

PRINCIPAL CHARACTERS

JOHN WAYNE	ANDY DEVINE	TIM HOLT
The Ringo Kid	Buck	Lt. Blanchard
CLAIRE TREVOR	DONALD MEEK	GEORGE BANCROFT
Dallas	Samuel Peacock	Sheriff Curley Wilcox
JOHN CARRADINE	LOUISE PLATT	BERTON CHURCHILL
Hatfield	Lucy Mallory	Henry Gatewood
THOMAS MITCHELL		JOSEPH RICKSON
Dr. Josiah Boone		Luke Plummer

Length: 97 minutes

30

Although widely admitted to be the most famous and perhaps the most influential of Westerns, *Stagecoach* now suffers from over-familiarity and critical condescension. Aside from that of Philip French, all the recent commentaries touching on the genre dismiss this film, usually for the somewhat startling reason that it is clichéd. This seems much like the student reading Shakespeare with disdain because the author employed so many well-known phrases. Appearing in the middle of a long tradition of cowboy-versus-Indian melodramas—an artistically mediocre subgenre of the Western—*Stagecoach* defined the pattern of conflicts and their relationship to the landscape in a particularly meaningful way. Incidentally, it derived from another popular 1930s genre that consisted of films bringing together a group of diverse people—each person at a critical point in life—in a confining location, so that the arising crises brought the widely varied characterizations into sharp focus (compare Archie Mayo's *The Petrified Forest* [1936] and Edmund Goulding's *Grand Hotel* [1932]). It is only in regard to this "grand hotel" genre it resembles that *Stagecoach* now seems somewhat contrived and literary.

Nevertheless, *Stagecoach* is much more effective as a film than as a richly textured literary script, regardless of how much credit Dudley Nichols is given in the various published versions of the "filmplay." Much more impressive to us today than the Ringo Kid's naive shyness and the film's seven or eight other stereotyped characterizations (which were probably stereotypes

in 1939 too) is the magnificent sense of action that John Ford captured against what became the basic scenery of the genre. Ford envisioned the central dramatic conflicts so clearly that we would probably prefer the film to have been done as a silent picture, worked up from a scenario that did not specify most of the chatter accompanying the coach on its journey from Tonto to Lordsburg.

As a symbol of the pioneering spirit that settled the West, the stagecoach in this film provides a continual visual document of human vulnerability among the pitiless rock formations of Monument Valley. This is uncivilized terrain, harboring enemies of the bearers of civilization—Apache Indians—who appear suddenly with the most intense hostility toward the coach and its passengers. The film offers no specific reason for the animosity of the Apaches, who are led by the notorious Geronimo, though it seems to be understood that periodically the Indians arise like a pestilence to attack the white men. (Ford's view of the Indians in his later films is quite sympathetic and complex, particularly *Cheyenne Autumn* [1964], where the Indians are seen as innocent wanderers pursued ruthlessly by an inferior white man's civilization. In *Stagecoach,* though, the Apaches do not really play a humanized role: they are part of the symbolic forces that inhabit the desert and fight savagely against the encroachment of society upon their domain.) Traditionally, this kind of conflict in the genre seems to represent a challenge for the white race, which seeks to demonstrate that it belongs in the West. The people in the coach must be able to get through the dangerous landscape to prove that they and the civilization they stand for are physically strong enough to conquer the ever-resistant natural order of the West.

William Hart, the first of the great Western stars and directors, remarked about the unreality of Ford's film. He noted that any real Indian raid would have begun not with an attack on the passengers in the coach but simply and directly with the shooting of the coach's horses. This comment surely misses the point of the film, and perhaps of the whole genre, which has never been realistically based. The great stagecoach chase is hardly intended to convey a historical event. It presents us, rather, with a dramatic way of accounting for the critical moment in various characters' lives. The ride from the coach station to Lordsburg seems more a spiritual journey than a mere ambush sequence. The demonic forces that terrorize the characters en route attack in senseless waves of violent hatred, but though the Indians are killed off in regular fashion, there is no possibility of their relenting. Except for the chance appearance of an outside force of greater strength—the cavalry, introduced by the traditional bugle call—the Indians could not be defeated. They ride off when the cavalry arrives, but there is no indication of their destruction or placation. To another coach, at another time, the issue of survival will be raised again.

The film seems to reflect the way people act in a critical time —the good people becoming noble as their capacity for heroism is exploited. Among the stereotypes Ford collects for this great journey through the testing grounds of Monument Valley is Peacock, a whiskey salesman, a family man, extremely mild and generally overwhelmed by the threat. Peacock would much prefer safety to risk, but when the time comes, he does not exhibit cowardice in the face of danger but rises above his natural timidity. Heroic characters such as Ringo are given the opportunity to become noble as well as courageous. At the end, the marshal almost forces Ringo to escape, recognizing a higher justice that rewards heroes—though the original screenplay much more feebly motivated the marshal by having him learn at the end that Ringo was not guilty of any crime. The gambler, Hatfield, who dies in the raid (some white man had to die in return for the numerous Indians killed in the encounter), redeems himself for an ignoble life by his chivalrous conduct along the way and by his courage to the end. His spur-of-the-moment decision to make the trip had itself been motivated by a desire to offer his protection to a woman he admired and respected.

The success of *Stagecoach* established certain conventions of the genre that had been used less effectively before. Although the memorable Western aspects of the film center on the symbolic grouping of civilization aboard the stagecoach and that group's encounter with the Indians, this film firmly implanted in the genre John Ford's vision of an intent hero, a Ringo Kid, dedicated to fulfilling a fated task that seemed to imply his own destruction in its attempt. If the Ringo Kid managed to kill the Plummer brothers he would be imprisoned again (his escape is reported at the beginning of the film); if he failed, the Plummer brothers would kill him. The screenplay does work out a third possibility, but what is important is Ringo's prevailing sense that regardless of the consequences, he must revenge his family and himself. We see that for the moment, his honor is more important to him than his freedom—though at one point in the film he is tempted to escape because of the woman he meets and falls in love with.

Ford's handling of the hero's love relationship has proven to be a popular but not essential element of the genre. Indeed, it was a stereotyped convention of other genres before it appeared here. In this film it is the version of the prostitute inspiring the hero, who is unaware of what she is until later, and then, of course, his sentiment cannot be changed. In fact, the girl, Dallas, is the conventional nineteenth-century good-hearted literary figure, heroic in her own right, who still appears in Western films. However, John Wayne's portrayal of Ringo—his ultimate simplicity, great skill, and determination—became part of the Western hero's characterization that Wayne demonstrated in later Ford films. Although Ford continued to deepen the implications of the hero's psychology and behavior, the Wayne figure itself became probably the dominant heroic type in the genre. But *Stagecoach* remains great not for introducing formulas for a hundred later films that improved upon the basic materials—it stands on its own merit for its large mythic dimensions and Ford's grasp of the essential landscape and themes of the Western genre.

33

WINCHESTER '73

(1950)

Director	Cinematographer	Script
ANTHONY MANN	WILLIAM DANIELS	ROBERT L. RICHARDS
Producer		BORDEN CHASE
AARON ROSENBERG		From a story by
For Universal-International		Stuart N. Lake

PRINCIPAL CHARACTERS

JAMES STEWART	MILLARD MITCHELL	JOHN MC INTYRE
Lin McAdam	High Spade	Joe Lamont
SHELLEY WINTERS	CHARLES DRAKE	WILL GEER
Lola Manners	Steve Miller	Wyatt Earp
DAN DURYEA		JAY C. FLIPPEN
Waco Johnnie Dean		Sgt. Wilkes
STEPHEN MC NALLY		ROCK HUDSON
Dutch Henry Brown		Young Bull

Length: 92 minutes

34

Another example of the genre's capacity to deal with classical Greek themes (and thereby prove the eternal relevance of such material), *Winchester '73* functions within the category of search-and-revenge. In Greek theater, the laws of society demanding that Orestes or Electra revenge the murder of their father produced a psychological case study of characters under immense pressure, trying to prepare for some horrible action. Compared to other major Westerns employing the revenge motif, such as Ford's *The Searchers* (1956) and Fritz Lang's *Rancho Notorious* (1952), *Winchester '73* seems to exhibit much less neurotic tension. Unlike the brooding heroes of those two films, Lin McAdam is usually mild and somewhat self-effacing as he sets about revenging the murder of his father. The father was shot by Lin's brother, who calls himself Dutch Henry Brown.

Very early in the film, a surrogate father figure appears in kindly but powerful Wyatt Earp, who presides over Dodge City as a benevolent despot. Earp sponsors a shooting contest, the reward for which is the great and valuable new weapon, the Winchester rifle. When Lin runs into his brother, his murderous ambition surfaces momentarily, but since Earp has banned the carrying of guns in Dodge City during the contest, the two brothers curb their inclinations to get at each other's throats. Instead, they participate in the contest. Both brothers are expert shots—they were trained by their father—and they display their skills in a match demanding the utmost concentration. The match requires them to sublimate their hatred as they compete for the

prize rifle, which perhaps for them has become a symbol of their father's memory. When Lin wins the contest and receives the rifle from Earp, the father's principles are affirmed—the good son triumphs. Dutch's loss of the contest—in spite of his excellence at shooting—indicates a moral failing in his act of killing the father (though at the time we do not know exactly what Dutch has done to arouse the scorn of Lin). Whatever the precise symbolic value of the rifle, it is clearly important for Dutch to claim the Winchester one way or another. He surprises his brother, beats him, steals the rifle, and flees Dodge City. This scene provides us with a visually explicit reason for Lin's pursuit of Dutch.

The rest of the film's plot traces the way the Winchester passes through various hands. Each person who gains possession of the rifle dies by violence, including Dutch, who gets the gun back before Lin but is killed by Lin in the final shootout. Lin then redeems the Winchester, which has now become a symbol of virtue and the endurance of the virtuous. In the course of Lin's search for the gun, the audience always has in mind this visible goal, which externalizes the psychological conflict. Mann has so successfully implanted a larger symbolic value in the gun that the visualized story does duplicate the psychological course of action.

Other interesting generic elements are embodied in this film. As Jim Kitses has pointed out, other "family" groups are depicted—most interestingly, the cavalry battalion of young men who expect to be wiped out in a few hours by the Indians.* Lin easily fits in with them, their sense of community suggesting another insight into the search for revenge: he establishes the possibility of a new family by throwing in his lot with what seems to be a group of doomed men. There is also a young engaged couple, the hardened Lola and the cowardly Steve, who grow respectable in the best and most traditional sense of the genre— by their reactions to the crises of the environment (also a major motif that Ford employed in *Stagecoach*, and one that significantly established a pattern for the genre).

Evil is embodied in the mad outlaw Waco Johnnie Dean as well as in Dutch, and yet both, though eventually killed by the hero, also embody the virtues of competence and courage typical of Mann villains and not elsewhere common in villains of the genre. For Mann, the villains' physical strengths are psychological alternatives to the strengths represented by the hero. According to the conventions of the genre, the hero is relatively soft-spoken. Lin's aggressive behavior is mainly a result of his circumstances, not of his character. Evil in the Western does not seem to require much explication. It is understood that one brother will turn out good, the other a desperate killer, but the genre rarely probes for the causes of the dissimilarities. Mann, in fact, seems to prefer to indicate the resemblances. The evil figure tends to reveal his nature overtly, seizing by brute force anything he wishes by whatever means he can (as Dutch takes Lin's gun or as Waco abducts Lola). The community is not structured to prevent particular outrages, and thus arises the Western motif of revenge—a hero setting out on a lonely course, determined to right the wrongs committed by individuals who exercise evil power. Here is primitive history as well as primitive myth, which tells us as much about the origins of society as it does about the nature of people under pressure. The hero's duty in *Winchester '73*, for the protection of society as well as for revenge, is to eradicate the evil forces, though these forces share with him certain competencies.

The equality of skills between Dutch and Lin makes it difficult to predict the outcome of their final showdown in the hills, but we are, nevertheless, fairly sure from other evidence in the film that Lin is fated to destroy his brother. To restore balance and order in the community, it is necessary for the evil characters to be shot down, although it is not logically inevitable. Our expectation of the genre, however, creates an emotional basis for such an inevitable outcome. Here the visual symbol of the Winchester is increasingly imbued with moral meaning. As the rifle passes

36

Horizons West, pp. 59–60.

from one unworthy possessor to another, it seems inevitably destined to return to its worthy and rightful possessor. The moral legitimacy of Lin's claim to the gun is validated by his ability to defend his honor and accomplish his mission.

SHANE
(1953)

Director-Producer	Cinematographer	Script
GEORGE STEVENS	LOYAL GRIGGS	A.B.GUTHRIE, JR.
For Paramount	Technicolor	Based on a novel by Jack Schaefer

PRINCIPAL CHARACTERS

ALAN LADD	BRANDON DE WILDE	EDGAR BUCHANAN
Shane	Joey Starrett	Lewis
JEAN ARTHUR	JACK PALANCE	EMILE MEYER
Mrs. Starrett	Wilson	Ryker
VAN HEFLIN	BEN JOHNSON	ELISHA COOK, JR.
Mr. Starrett	Chris	Torrey
	Length: 118 minutes	

37

George Stevens's *Shane* was evidently conceived in terms of an interpretation of the Western genre film as an allegorical battleground for a confrontation between good and evil. Some critics of the film find the concept behind such a presentation annoying, perhaps because, in the classic Westerns by Ford, Mann, Boetticher, and others, the surface realism is kept intact, even when the internal romantic myth that structures the whole experience resembles the much more overt myth in *Shane*. But Stevens chose to heighten the symbolic import of the genre's typical iconography (costume, language, manners, and rituals) by setting his film in an immense, open environment, dominated by the snow-capped mountains of Wyoming in the distance. By continually locating the immediate scene within a vast, calm, rigidly endurable locale, Stevens deliberately and recurringly directs our attention to the genre's mythic dimensions, in regard to the lonely hero, the isolated community, the natural conflict between people and the terrain, and the violent power struggle between the land-grabbing local tyrant and the individual homestead farmers over who will control the territory.

The flamboyant colors and balanced visual compositions of the stylized environment help define *Shane* as an allegory. In other Westerns, the particular story may extend its details symbolically toward a statement about human nature, but this film persistently employs imagery to suggest concrete examples of abstract principles extended into a typical genre story about a range conflict.

Among the film's first images is one of a beautiful stag drinking from a stream. As the stag raises its head, its antlers frame the isolated figure of Shane riding toward us from a great distance. The symbolic representation of the hero as a projection of the peaceful, uninhabited environment compares with the more standardized beginnings of many Westerns in which the hero appears to move across a hostile terrain. Later we see Shane frequently associated with the picturesque elements of nature, as when he works on the Starrett farm, outlined by the distant mountains, or when he rides off toward a "town" that consists of even less than the one traditional street, strikingly dwarfed by its still-uncivilized open surroundings.

Equally important to our understanding of the mythic dimension of the film is the point of view engendered in many of the camera shots of the hero. When Shane first appears, framed by the antlers of the stag, he is observed by the boy Joey, who is surprised and overwhelmed at the sudden appearance of a rider from nowhere. A large part of the film is presented from Joey's viewpoint, emphasizing his increasing awe of the heroic nature of Shane. In fact, on one level, the film is about the ways in which we perceive a true hero and our ultimate inability to find a place for him in a nonheroic society. Thus, when Shane rides off at the end of the film after destroying the forces of violence, we realize that without a special mission Shane has no function in a civilized community, and therefore he resists remaining in a place where he has accomplished his function. He is certainly capable of chopping wood and performing the ordinary tasks of a homesteader, but like most of the genre's heroes, he remains an outsider, unwilling to be absorbed into the domestic or social fabric he has worked to protect.

Shane is also a film of initiation, and as such it emphasizes—though not consistently—Joey's point of view as he discovers in the hero the embodiment of his ideals and confronts the disillusionment of having to abandon them. Joey's concluding shouts to the hero, who is riding off to a kind of mystical reunion with the open plain—"Come back, Shane!"—indicate his regret at having lost the safety and naive reassurance that come from being near his idol, but they also hint at a coming of age. With the establishment of peace and justice in the community, the ideal of heroic endeavor is not particularly desirable. In fact, the community of homesteaders now comes of age too, and must stand on its own. It is important for the boy to learn the truth of his mother's earlier warnings—that Shane was not to be admired too much, for he was not going to become a permanent part of their lives.

Shane himself, like other great loners, recognizes his own role and knows that it is his fate to conform to it. He arrives in the typical, mysterious manner of his type, though there is little doubt that he is an ex-gunfighter. Laconic, self-confident, obedient to the social codes of his day (he is attracted to Mrs. Starrett when he goes to work for her husband but outraged at a villain who suggests such an attraction exists), and generally fearless, Shane is able to walk up to a bar and order "soda pop," to the amusement of the various desperado types frequenting the typical Western saloon. His presence, however, inspires admiration, except for the standard foolish local ruffian who insults him. So determined is Shane to avoid violence that not only does he leave his gun at home when he goes into town, but also walks away from the ruffian's first challenge. (Of course, this villain is defeated in their next encounter.) Although Shane hopes to avoid

39

violence, a basic concept of the genre is that the man of ability will take the necessary steps to preserve justice in emergency situations. When the homesteaders are about to be driven off their land by Ryker and his henchmen, Starrett tries to rally the honest people to stay on, but it is clear that only a forceful defense of their lives and property can hold the group together. Soon after Wilson, an ace gunfighter hired by Ryker, kills one of the homesteaders, we realize that the impending confrontation of Wilson and Starrett would end in Starrett's death. Thus, Shane, true to his destiny, takes over by subduing Starrett and going to the rendezvous that has been deceitfully arranged by Ryker. At this showdown Shane outshoots Wilson, Ryker, and another gunman—knowing that by his very act of saving the community, he forfeits a meaningful place there. This example of the genre reaffirms the essential isolation of the hero, even amid nostalgic regret evoked in his admirers at the very moment when he determines to abandon his temporary resting place in the civilized community.

40

JOHNNY GUITAR
(1954)

Director	Cinematographer	Script
NICHOLAS RAY	HARRY STRADLING	PHILIP YORDAN
Producer	Trucolor	Based on the novel
HERBERT J. YATES		by Roy Chanslor
For Republic Pictures		

PRINCIPAL CHARACTERS

STERLING HAYDEN	SCOTT BRADY	WARD BOND
Johnny Guitar	The Dancing Kid	John McIvers
JOAN CRAWFORD	MERCEDES MC CAMBRIDGE	JOHN CARRADINE
Vienna	Emma Small	Old Tom
ERNEST BORGNINE		BEN COOPER
Bart Lonergan		Turkey Ralston
	Length: 110 minutes	

Nicholas Ray's critically admired but iconographically peculiar film conceals its generic patterns under a surface that is part melodrama, part comedy, and sometimes (unintentionally?) part camp—a mixture not readily appreciated by an audience that expects the conventional format of the Western. Most unusual is the final shootout, which takes place between two women. In contrast, early in the film, the first "showdown" encounter between hero and antagonist in front of the bar (the standard arena for such battles) concludes not with drawn pistols or exchanged blows, but with the Dancing Kid saying to Johnny Guitar, "Can you play?" and Johnny responding with "Can you dance?" As the hero immediately proceeds to strum his guitar, the Dancing Kid grabs the film's female villain, Emma, and leads her in a lively dance!

Nevertheless, the generic structure of the film is not jolted by the unusual imagery because the central plot corresponds to traditional story-line development. Instead of arranging the contending parties into, say, groups of homesteaders and ranchers, Ray establishes the power struggle between the gambling house owner, Vienna, who represents real estate investment (the coming of the railroad will make her wealthy), and the town's conservatives, Emma (part-owner of a bank) and McIvers (a local rancher and tycoon). By moving away from the typical conflicts and the ordinary genre characterizations, Ray redirects our attention to the psychological reactions of each character—to the nuances of their encounters—rather than allowing us to watch the typical formulaic reactions that Western characters reveal within the mythic pattern (the underlying archetypal narrative of the determined defender of truth opposing the tyranny of an ignorant and selfish community). Yet Ray does not abandon the myth either. Its materials structure the film and create a plausible basis for the very different situations in the story.

41

There are two sides to Johnny Guitar's character. He is the conventional hero who acts to prevent injustices, but he is also the passive observer, who remains aloof from a stagecoach robbery and a bank robbery, and, while preparing to rescue his girl from a lynch mob, does nothing to prevent the lynching of another man. Still, although he may leave his guns for a long time in his saddle bag, beneath his disguise as a troubadour we easily discover the former gunfighter, behaving much in the Gary Cooper tradition: fearless, provocatively ironic in his sparse conversation, and ready to do what is necessary to protect those he cares about.

But this is one Western in which our interest is not directed solely to the hero's escapades, but also to the neurotic tensions that motivate the characters and their hostilities. The plot clearly sustains a series of obsessions that drive the characters into conflict. The most interesting of the characters is Emma, whose overt hatred and repressed love for the Dancing Kid force her into a kind of perpetual frenzy. From her first appearance, when she

42

rouses the citizenry to take vengeance on the Kid and his three
mining cronies because she believes, incorrectly, that they have
killed her brother during a robbery, Emma's ranting demagog-
uery wins general support from the town's male population and
the leading male authority figure, McIvers, who has economic
reasons for allying himself with these yahoos. It turns out, however, that the main object of Emma's hostility is Vienna, a far
more attractive woman, whom the Dancing Kid loves and whom
Emma envies and despises. Emma tells Vienna that she plans
someday to kill her, and Vienna acknowledges that ultimately
they will confront each other in a fight for survival.

Less psychologically disoriented, but just as unusual, Vienna
is an ex-saloon girl quite ready to speak of her undoubtedly innumerable lovers, though Johnny refuses to allow her to confess
anything. "Lie to me," he tells her, when she attempts to talk of
the five years since they were lovers, and in lying she seems to
convince herself of his belief (that she waited five years for him).
If Johnny's obsession is to resume their past love as if the inter-
vening five years had never occurred, Vienna's obsession has to
do with creating an independent position of power and wealth,
based on five years of putting together her property investment
and now defending it against McIvers's capitalistic designs to con-

trol the whole territory. Later, when it appears likely that Emma will make a good case for Vienna's conspiring in the robbery of Emma's bank, Vienna refuses to flee with Johnny and abandon her own gambling house. She has already proven her status as "hero" (rather than "heroine"—but she is considered mannish by others only because she has the Westerner's virtues of bravery and competence, not because there is any question about her sexual identity). Early in the film, she draws her gun on Emma, McIvers, and a whole crowd of men who threaten her in the gambling house. When Emma points out that Vienna couldn't kill all of them, Vienna sardonically notes that she could at least kill a couple—and she succeeds in subduing the whole crowd.

Thus, while Johnny shares the hero role with Vienna, it is no wonder that his rivalry with the Kid and his ongoing feud with Bart, one of the Kid's henchmen, are less central and less interesting than Vienna's conflict with Emma. When Emma gains the upper hand, her lynch mob followers take Vienna off to be hanged while Emma, gloating at her enemy's hopelessness, sets about burning down the gambling house. Emma's insanity makes her no less cunning than Vienna, though Emma is oblivious to her public image as a neurotic woman, while Vienna is absolutely aware of her role and dresses for it (in a black shirt and pants when playing the part of a gunfighter, a white dress when in the role of a lone, defenseless woman). After Johnny rescues her from the lynching, Vienna is forced into the inevitable one-to-one shootout by the obsessed Emma. The violent ending—several deaths including Emma's—convinces the townspeople that they have no business trying to sort out the ambiguities of other people's motives. They let Johnny and Vienna pass by them; no one is going to press charges, and in any case, both are innocent of the crimes of which they previously had been accused. The film ends with a normalization of the way of life; and so, for all its psychological orientation, *Johnny Guitar* remains within the genre's tradition of the reestablishment of tranquility and justice through the purging of vengeance and passion.

43

THE SEARCHERS
(1956)

Director	Cinematographer	Script
JOHN FORD	WINTON C. HOCH	FRANK S. NUGENT
Producers	Technicolor	Based on the novel by
MERIAN C. COOPER	VistaVision	Alan Le May
A.C.V. WHITNEY		
For Warner Brothers		

PRINCIPAL CHARACTERS

JOHN WAYNE	WARD BOND	JOHN QUALEN
Ethan Edwards	Capt. Rev.	Lars Jorgensen
JEFFREY HUNTER	Samuel Clayton	OLIVE CAREY
Martin Pawley	NATALIE WOOD	Mrs. Jorgensen
VERA MILES	Debbie Edwards	HENRY BRANDON
Laurie Jorgensen		Chief Scar

Length: 119 minutes

44

The theme of the perennial outsider is more impressively embodied in *The Searchers* than anywhere else in the genre. Ford has referred to the story of Ethan Edwards as "the tragedy of a loner."* Actually, it is even more the tragedy of a conservative world view—an approach to life that prohibits the necessary value compromises that would permit a man of noble character to find some lasting relationships, rather than to drift through the world without direction. Ford elaborates on Ethan's probable background, which is supported by the attitudes Ethan displays when he visits his brother's family at the beginning of the film:

> He's the man who came back from the Civil War, probably went over into Mexico, became a bandit, probably fought for Juarez or Maximilian. . . . He was just a plain loner—could never really be a part of the family.†

But Ethan is a loner because, prior to the film's opening, he has already lost everything. He still wears the uniform cloak of the losing side in the Civil War, and when asked by a friend why he did not show up for the surrender, he answers, "I don't believe in surrenders." He does, however, believe in the code of the family. His greatest loss is Martha, the woman who married his brother, but whom Ethan still loves. Although she apparently loves him

---

*Peter Bogdanovich, *John Ford* (Berkeley: University of California Press, 1968), p. 92.

†Ibid., pp. 92–93.

too, nothing can be spoken between them. He remains a man without a country or a love. Above all, he is a misfit of heroic proportions, having all the traits and skills of an epic hero but existing in a world in which he really has nothing to do.

The film's initial disaster, therefore, affords him an opportunity to structure his life by becoming an avenger. His brother's family is massacred by Indians—only Ethan's niece Debbie survives, ultimately to be raised as an Indian squaw. Ethan dedicates himself completely to the task of vengeance and travels widely in the West, tracking the Indians responsible for Martha's rape and murder and the deaths of the other family members. At first, his mission is to reclaim Debbie, but before he finds her, his warped and outmoded values and his neurotic attitude toward Indians make him determined to kill Debbie for what she has become by living among the Comanches. The search develops into an obsession very quickly—not so much because of the massacre's evil and Ethan's own conservative code (by which he seems to interpret Indian aggression as a cultural invasion), but because his existence would be totally empty without some cause that required him to stake his life and test his abilities. He sees a chance of defining himself by this cause, although he probably does not foresee that he will take five years to catch up with the

Indian named Scar, who keeps a willing Debbie as one of his squaws.

Ethan pursues his search accompanied by Martin, a young half-breed who had been living with the murdered family. Martin's normal reactions thus provide a contrast to the more forceful older man, who is gradually losing his perspective on reality. Ford depicts the conflicts and tensions of the search against the magnificent natural backdrop of Monument Valley, and the quality of the cinematography makes *The Searchers* the most beautiful of all color Westerns. Monument Valley seems much less populated and even more massive in this film than in *Stagecoach,* for it serves as more than background here. It reflects the permanence of certain Western values that are distorted in Ethan, but it also stands for values that are no longer operable for Ethan's time. Human warmth and love are notably absent from much of the film; Ethan's devotion to his task is the only positive feeling that is shown with any consistency. The film begins with a warm family sequence, but almost all the action after that is based on emotional suppression or violence. Ethan's single-minded concentration on revenge readily produces his insanity; this pushes Ethan almost to carry out his intention to murder his niece.

Although in most Westerns that employ it the revenge motif is depicted as lawful and commendable, Ford here reverts to the Greek attitude of twenty-five hundred years ago, when the motif was apparently not only a literary theme but a social issue. The futility of endless seeking for revenge is the whole point of Ford's drawing out of the search over a period of years. When Scar and Ethan finally confront each other, Ethan learns that the Indian has acted in the past as a marauding avenger for the killing of his own two sons. The relationship of the two men's values and attitudes was pointed out by McBride and Wilmington: "Certainly Scar and Ethan are the only characters who fully understand each other, because their motives are so similar."* But to stop the cycle of revenge by simply abandoning the search would be esthetically confusing and would hardly make sense within the genre. Ford shares with the Greek playwright Aeschylus the artistic sensibility that requires some final, purgative revenge that will give rise to a new understanding, and thereby eliminate the need for further violence. After Martin has killed Scar, Ethan performs the ritual insanity of scalping his enemy, but the meaninglessness of this gesture seems to restore Ethan's perspective on reality.

Ultimately, Ethan's contact with Debbie forces him to accept the truth that she must live with Comanche tradition, for she

46

*McBride and Wilmington, "Prisoner of the Desert," p. 212.

herself has accepted that fact of her life. Earlier in the film, we witness a strange sequence that introduces a group of white women who, having been abducted and forced to live among the Indians, are now insane. This event apparently stands as the alternative that Debbie has been forced to confront (though perhaps not consciously, since she was, at the time, a child able to adjust to a totally new life even among the people who had massacred her family). At the climactic moment, while we are still unsure of whether Ethan can again attain the emotional level necessary to kill Debbie, he picks her up off the ground, pulls her close, and says, "Let's go home, Debbie." He has finally overcome the bitterness he felt in acknowledging that Debbie would always represent for him conflicting attitudes of love (as his only surviving family, the daughter of the woman he should have married) and hate (she has, in retrospect, sanctioned her own violation by accepting the murderers of her family and learning to consider the Comanches her own people).

The film ends, in a reversal of the opening image, with Ethan riding off alone, unable to form part of the new community with his niece or with Martin, who is to marry. Ethan commits himself **47** to a lifetime of wandering, yet he is not the same person he was earlier in the film. The outcome has not increased his immense cynicism; instead, he leaves with some insight into the way others must live in this world, which is not yet inviting enough for him to join. But his losses are now part of his past—not part of his present, as they were at the beginning of the film. There is no sign that he will ever be domesticated into society, but neither does he seem to carry away with him his old hostility toward the civilized world.

COMANCHE STATION
(1960)

Director-Producer	Cinematographer	Script
BUDD BOETTICHER	CHARLES LAWTON, JR.	BURT KENNEDY
For Columbia Pictures	Eastman Color	
	Cinemascope	

PRINCIPAL CHARACTERS

RANDOLPH SCOTT	CLAUDE AKINS	SKIP HOMEIER
Jefferson Cody	Ben Lane	Frank
NANCY GATES		RICHARD RUST
Mrs. Lowe		Dobie

Length: 73 minutes

The artistry of a Boetticher Western so intensifies our perception of the moral issues that we expect to see a simplistic resolution of the conflict between good and bad that has been formulated previously in virtually abstract terms. Yet even though Boetticher is the most classical of Western filmmakers because of his rapid, clear, and profound development of the struggle between hero and villain, he introduces a pervasive element of ambiguity into relationships that often leads not to a concluding sense of satisfaction, but to a feeling of sorrow that the struggles could not resolve themselves without violence. In the climactic moment of *Comanche Station,* played against the rocky landscape traditional for ultimate showdowns, the villain Ben is trapped by the hero Cody, who aims a gun at Ben and orders him to drop his rifle. The situation is hopeless for Ben, but instead of complying with the order he discusses the alternatives. He explains that, since he has carried his villainy this far, he might as well take the outside chance and wheel around to shoot at Cody rather than surrender. Having reached this conclusion, Ben acts on his decision and, as he anticipated, is killed by Cody. It is difficult for an audience not to admire the courage and perhaps even the code of this interesting Boetticher badman.

Comanche Station is about codes of conduct, but instead of an analysis or even a comparison of such codes, the film presents studies of characters whose integrity is founded on the consistent pattern of response they display in a variety of dangerous situations. Everyone in the film is therefore unusually rational in discussing motivations or in analyzing each other. Frank and Dobie, two young riders who have joined Ben in his enterprises (nefarious, if not criminal—but never precisely explained), have yet to fully adopt codes of their own. Their assumption of their

48

49

dubious way of life, however, commits them—as they recognize—to violence and probably early death. They might be persuaded to change their code, for they discuss the possibilities, but until they do so they are both willing to go along with Ben's plan to murder Cody and Mrs. Lowe—apparently only because it is the logical outcome of their present commitments as Ben's cohorts.

The other villains are the Comanches, peripheral characters, who are on a rampage—but in retaliation for similar actions by derelict white men and thus logically motivated. The film begins with Cody riding into a Comanche encampment to ransom an abducted white woman, Mrs. Lowe. Cody gives the Indians a Winchester and some dry goods and then rides off with Mrs. Lowe, but there is no particular reason why the Indians do not simply kill him and keep the woman captive. Evidently the Comanches, too, operate according to a certain code of fair dealing.

Knowing that Ben Lane intends to commit murder in order to claim the bounty of five thousand dollars that Mr. Lowe has placed on the return of his wife (or her remains, if she has been killed), we have to judge Ben as the fairest of villains in regard to his dealings with Cody. About one-third of the way through the film, Ben tells Frank and Dobie of his plan to murder Cody and Mrs. Lowe. Later he also informs Cody, who is a very old enemy. (Cody and Ben had served in the army together, and Cody had been responsible for Ben's court-martial.) Yet Ben makes no attempt to shoot Cody in the back. Instead he rides along with Cody and Mrs. Lowe as their escort into Lordsburg. Neither Cody nor Ben shows any outward signs of fear as they ride together, though of course they anticipate the eventual hostile action that each other's clear intentions will provoke. Their surface attitudes are highly civilized, but at heart they hate what each other stands for. Nevertheless, although both men sense the potential for an act of treachery, they stay within reach of each other for most of the film because they know the extent of each other's code. In one sequence, when the small group is endangered by a Comanche party, Cody rushes off to combat the Indians, telling Mrs. Lowe, Ben, and Frank to escape by a different route. But when it seems that Cody will be killed in his mission, Ben rides to his defense and saves his life!

50

Living according to a code of behavior will usually modify one's responses to all events, since the code provides a general model for appropriate conduct under any circumstances. This is one of the oldest narrative premises—one used a good deal in classical Greek literature—and this analogical source for Boetticher's presentation of his characters' behavior may make the film seem stylistically primitive. Certainly, Boetticher defines the hero within a limited range of psychological responses. Jim Kitses's insight into the world view of *Comanche Station* (an absurdist comedy, he notes) is especially perceptive in this regard:

> In his purest expression the core of the Boetticher hero is apparent, the figure existing as a *spirit* rather than a person, a *way* of life rather than a life. An abstraction, the hero represents an unrealizable ideal, an experience and knowledge of the world so complete that the character is finally as impervious as the rocks around him.*

> The Randolph Scott figure is the hero only in a technical sense: it is, of course, the villain who is our true hero.†

Yet it is also true that in all narrative art, a commitment to normal decency is, dramatically, less interesting than a commit-

---

Horizons West, p. 102.
† Ibid., p. 103.

ment to any course of evil. Thus, the genre presents innumerable lonely heroes who refuse to articulate their code because they assume that its correctness is obvious—and Cody is notable among them for his reserve, though he exhibits a laconic wit far superior to the type. Cody's commitment stems from romantic passion pursued beyond reason: his wife, abducted by Indians ten years earlier, is the object of his unrelenting search even though common sense would suggest that she is no longer alive. Since the origin of his way of life is so personal, he will never speak of it—no Western hero would—and no more would Mrs. Lowe, a Western heroine, speak about her husband to defend him from Ben's persistent charge that the man must be a coward not to search for his wife. At the end of the film, we discover that Mr. Lowe is blind, but this striking justification would have seemed irrelevant to Mrs. Lowe at any time in the film; she does not require any external confirmation of her faith.

The hero's psychological development in *Comanche Station* seems static because the dramatic developments do not force him to reconsider his notions. But besides the dramatic narrative, there is also a visual narrative that supports the *cinematic* plausibility of his character. From the first image of Cody, appearing as a small figure in a vast arroyo, to the final image of him riding off into the hills, we observe—exactly as in *Shane*—a link between man and place, between the eternal elements of nature and the enduring qualities of the individual. Surely the casting of Randolph Scott as the isolated, middle-aged hero is exactly correct for the film's thematic values. His square, craggy features look indeed "as impervious as the rocks around him." His mastery of the necessary skills of survival in this environment provides him with the strength and confidence to pursue his mission endlessly. Whether he embodies the spirit of the place or is himself the presiding spirit of the Old West, he personifies the major virtues of the genre's lonely hero.

THE WILD BUNCH
(1969)

Director	Cinematographer	Script
SAM PECKINPAH	LUCIEN BALLARD	SAM PECKINPAH
Producer	Technicolor	WALON GREEN
PHIL FELDMAN	Panavision	Based on a story by
For Warner Brothers		Walon Green and
		Roy N. Sickner

PRINCIPAL CHARACTERS

WILLIAM HOLDEN	EDMOND O'BRIEN	BEN JOHNSON
Pike Bishop	Sykes	Tector Gorch
ERNEST BORGNINE	WARREN OATES	EMILIO FERNANDEZ
Dutch Engstrom	Lyle Gorch	Mapache
ROBERT RYAN	JAIME SANCHEZ	
Deke Thornton	Angel	
	Length: 145 minutes	

52   In one sense, Peckinpah's film stands as a lament for the Old West and its departed heroic values, as represented by the doomed gang of badmen. But the violence and futility of this gang's existence in opposition to an equally violent and even more treacherous civilization marks a theme relevant to contemporary society: we all participate in the moral disarray of our world, and the reestablishment of order seems possible only in the mutual destruction of conflicting elements. It is clear in *The Wild Bunch* that if the gang has only one shared virtue—mutual respect and a degree of comradeship—then that is one virtue more than the representatives of "civilized" society appear to have.

Although the category of the sympathetic badman is the oldest in the Western genre, nowhere else do the bleakness and the sense of loss seem so totally fixed from the start. The idyllic respite the Bunch enjoys in a Mexican village, where the family of one of the gang members, Angel, lives, is only temporary. The villagers themselves are jeopardized by the hordes of followers of Mapache, the bandit general, and will eventually engage in some retaliatory form of guerilla warfare. In this film, no true peace exists anywhere for outsiders and losers. After the robbery the gang pulls at the beginning of the film, which results in the death of several members in an ambush, the survivors discover that their spoils consist only of worthless metal washers—a setup planned by the railroad's bounty hunters. The irony of wasted effort symbolizes the whole career of the Bunch—as acknowledged by the oldest member, Sykes, who tells them, "You boys

ain't gettin' any younger." And the sorrowful remark by Pike Bishop, their middle-aged leader, sums up their sense of meaninglessness: "I wanted to make one good score and back off"—to which his friend Dutch adds cynically, "Back off to what?"

The film portrays the manner in which this isolated group of courageous and competent men moves toward its destiny in one of the cinema's bloodiest eruptions of violence. Their destination takes them along a route destitute of humanistic values, except primarily for those the Bunch, with their perverted perspective, bring to their dealings with one another. Holding to a code of communal survival, they destroy a wounded member of the gang who cannot continue with them, and later they abandon Sykes, but these events are understood parts of the necessary ritual of escape that gangs must go through.

Much more to the point of the generic "good badmen" are two characteristics demonstrated in dramatic fashion: skill at their trade and eventual willingness to risk everything for another human being. Their skills are not to be doubted, though indeed they are hunted and outnumbered throughout the film; and so what we admire in their predicaments is their tenacious refusal to hide or remain cornered. From their first enterprise, when they are ambushed by the railroad's bounty hunters, we know they are not lucky, but we have also seen that they have been outsmarted only because one of their ex-members, Thornton, has been coerced into leading the team of mercenaries hired to track them down. By training and sympathies, Thornton is one of the Bunch, a match for his former good friend Pike. Both men are victims of their unfortunate careers who must now live out their opposed roles. Yet Thornton, even with his ability to anticipate the Bunch's moves, never succeeds in trapping them. His function in the film is to underscore the superior skills of the gang and, by contrast with the bounty hunters, to reveal the essential character superiority of his former comrades. At the end, he walks away from the dead bodies of the Bunch and the vulturelike activities of his followers, testifying thereby to the moral superiority of his kind.

The skills of the Bunch are most clearly seen in their counter-moves against the wily Mapache, the Mexican bandit leader. The Bunch agrees to rob a munitions train for him, an operation they carry out with considerable skill, though once again the job has been anticipated by Thornton. Mapache, completely dissolute and corrupt (the culmination of fifty years of Hollywood stereotyping of Mexicans), attempts—as expected—to take the ammunition from the Bunch without paying them. But Pike outmaneuvers Mapache by wiring the ammunition to explosives, threatening to blow himself up along with the goods he has for sale. Thus, outwitted in treachery, Mapache bides his time, in effect setting the stage for the Bunch's finest moment and their immediately subsequent destruction.

When that moment arrives, the code of the Bunch is put to the test, and they reveal in a forceful way their essential generic link to other doomed heroes of the West: their willingness to stake their lives on a hopeless cause. The cause presents itself when Mapache seizes Angel, after the youth has slain his former girl friend, who had left him to go with Mapache. The Bunch, now reduced to four men, decides to attempt a rescue—against all reasonable odds—because it just seems to be something they must do. Peckinpah stages the climactic sequence with great technical verve, handling the extraordinary violence in a plausible way and aligning our sympathies entirely with the small group as they bring havoc to the bloodthirsty followers of Mapache. The battle is touched off when Mapache, amid his drunken swarm of followers, is asked to release Angel but in contemptuous cynicism cuts the young man's throat, and is killed in turn by the Bunch. A long pause follows, as the vicious and dissipated troops of Mapache stop their carousing to stare in disbelief at the Bunch. Then the Bunch instigates the colossal shootout, which they must realize can end only in their own deaths. The sheer number of Mapache's men that the Bunch massacres is overwhelming. The sequence is reminiscent of Indian attacks on settlers, in which the numerically superior forces seem strangely willing to suffer any number of casualties to defeat an insignificant band of enemies. As with Custer in his various last stands in Hollywood, the Wild Bunch unflinchingly fires away at their opponents, finally succumbing to the endless waves of men mechanically attacking them.

The spirit of the heroic West figuratively dies with the Bunch. The bounty hunters who find the bodies are themselves killed, isolating Thornton as a witness to the mutual failure of the pursued and the pursuers. Everyone in the film has been tainted by violence—including the children who appear from time to time as participants, most memorably in the film's opening images, where they are shown torturing a scorpion. In the final gunfight a child shoots Pike in the back. In Peckinpah's view, cruelty and slaughter have pervaded all facets of society, and an inevitable confrontation with violence or its consequences awaits us all.

55

BUTCH CASSIDY AND THE SUNDANCE KID
(1969)

Director	Cinematographer	Script
GEORGE ROY HILL	CONRAD HALL	WILLIAM GOLDMAN
Producer	Deluxe Color	
JOHN FOREMAN	Panavision	
For Twentieth-Century Fox		

PRINCIPAL CHARACTERS

PAUL NEWMAN	STROTHER MARTIN	GEORGE FURTH
Butch Cassidy	Percy Garris	Woodcock
ROBERT REDFORD	HENRY JONES	CLORIS LEACHMAN
The Sundance Kid	Bike Salesman	Agnes
KATHERINE ROSS	JEFF COREY	TED CASSIDY
Etta Place	Sheriff Bledsoe	Harvey Logan
	Length: 110 minutes	

In spite of its stylistic brilliance and persistent comic mode, *Butch Cassidy and the Sundance Kid* presents a rather grim tale of two doomed outlaws unable to avoid the consequences of their careers, whose very success makes them prime objects of society's relentless vindictiveness. Although extremely skilled robbers, Butch and Sundance perform throughout as genial, witty, picaresque heroes. They avoid harming anyone until the last part of the film when, attempting to retire from their life of crime by working as payroll guards, they are ironically forced to kill six robbers in a battle for survival. With honest work like this available to them, the two loyal, inseparable friends return to crime and are gunned down in a nondescript Bolivian town by an overwhelming force of police and infantry.

The frustrating futility of the two outlaws' lives is evidenced by their inability to accumulate money or to make any ultimate escape. Butch and Sundance would like to get out of their rut, were it possible, by arranging an amnesty that would allow them to pay off their debt to society by fighting in the Spanish-American War, but they are too notorious for the authorities to make any such arrangements. Fated to play out the roles they have created for themselves, but superior to their own legend because of their deep-rooted sense of comic irony, they are the most likable and pitiable of Western outlaws.

56

Hill contributes to our understanding of the outlaw subgenre by concentrating on the nature of the outlaws' escape and deglamorizing the cunning antics they use to avoid their pursuers. Butch and Sundance remain heroic because they battle against heavy odds and exhibit much courage in their perilous flight, but they have very little close contact with the men who are trailing them. In fact, Hill's main innovation in the film is the manner in which he handles the group of six men hired by Harriman of the Union Pacific Railroad to kill Butch Cassidy and the Sundance Kid. These men appear suddenly on horseback from a private train arriving just as Cassidy's Hole in the Wall Gang has pulled off a comical train robbery, in which too much dynamite was used on the safe. While the gang members are scouring the area to retrieve the bills that the explosion has scattered, Harriman's men descend. The pursuit starts with the members of the hopeless gang galloping off in different directions—but to no avail for Butch and Sundance as all six pursuers follow them.

In the long chase sequences that occupy the middle of the film, Butch and Sundance travel across wide sweeps of beautiful Western terrain, always only a mile or two ahead of their untiring, unyielding pursuers. Hill photographs the chase from a great distance so that the six agents of the railroad are seen from the heroes' point of view as little more than tiny figures on the horizon—but always there. "Who are those guys?" is the repeated question the two outlaws ask each other. Hill seems intent on making the six men symbolic representations more than hired bounty hunters: they never rest, they never hurry, and they never

57

come close enough to appear merely human. As a modern personification of the ancient Greek Furies, they take on a meaning
similar to that which the Furies apparently stood for in classical
Greek culture—mechanisms of the mind that bring psychological
distraction to the criminal, driving him to desperation because
they are always there. Using every stratagem they can think of,
Butch and Sundance can do no better than find the most temporary of reprieves over a period of days. Several times they are
certain that they have succeeded in getting away, only to realize
almost immediately that their certainty is wishful thinking. The
one escape that momentarily thwarts the pursuit occurs when
Butch and Sundance, trapped at the edge of a tremendous cliff,
make a desperate dive into the river far below. Throughout the
chase they never fire at their pursuers. Nevertheless, these six
riders are indeed human. They are obsessively motivated by the
promise of bounty, having been hired by Harriman at great
expense as agents of his personal vendetta. Butch notes that he
and Sundance never stole as much as it is costing the railroad to
send these men after them.

Since they can neither simply retire and lead peaceful lives nor reasonably expect to bargain for amnesty, they decide to look for an easier life of crime in Bolivia. Taking Sundance's girl Etta with them, they travel first to New York to board a ship to South America. Through some ingenious use of still photography, Hill presents a series of shots of the three enjoying a brief vacation in New York. This is probably the only Western where the outlaws take time off to bathe at Coney Island and go on the amusement rides.

Once they arrive in Bolivia, Butch and Sundance discover that the life of crime will not be as easy as they had anticipated. For one thing, the country is essentially impoverished, and for another, they have trouble operating because they are unfamiliar with the language. Etta has little success trying to teach them Spanish, so she writes out the robbery instructions on a slip of paper—"Hands up," "Get against the wall," and so on—but when Butch and Sundance attempt the robbery they fumble the translations.

Eventually they begin to gain a reputation for bank robberies in Bolivia, but must then take on the same burden that hampered them in the States—their options grow limited as their faces become familiar. One day they see a man resembling the leader of the six pursuers who supposedly had lost the trail back in the United States. The sight of this man makes Butch and Sundance so fearful of being hounded again that they decide to retire from bank robbing and find honest jobs. But the two partners are fated to fail in this attempt, too. Their past finally closes in on them in a dingy small town, where they are accidentally recognized and set up for the final ambush by Bolivian soldiers and police (although the enemy is, for once, Bolivian, the audience knows that these officials are the same stereotyped Mexicans of many a lesser film). The film ends with a poignant freeze frame, as the cornered Butch and Sundance make a desperate dash for their horses but run, unwittingly, right into the cross fire of the hundred armed men who have surrounded them. A film about friendship and futility, *Butch Cassidy and the Sundance Kid* is saddening rather than tragic, but the disparity between the genial camaraderie of the heroes and the violent outcome of their careers offers another provocative insight into the genre's portrayal of outsiders and losers.

58

2

SINGING AND DANCING: THE SOUND OF METAPHOR

THE METAPHORICAL MODE

It is one of those ultimate moments of loss, a romance having come to nothing, and all that remains is for the lovers to say some parting words that will not inflict more pain or turn bitter the memory of their recent past. Lucky, the dancer, his luck now completely run out, must say farewell to Penny in a semidarkened ballroom, symbolic of the earlier, triumphant courtship dances that have led only to this breakup. Penny too moves on the fringes of despair, certain that Lucky has trifled with her and that the feelings she presumes he has for another woman are stronger than the feelings he has expressed in the musical performances he had dedicated to her.

So it is with her confidence shaken, yet with a pride that always enables her to retain her individuality and dignity in the face of Lucky's sometimes overly assertive display of his talents, that Penny probes for the reason why he might have rejected her for someone else. And the question she asks him—given their intuitive manner of communicating with each other—is exactly right: "Does she dance very beautifully . . . the girl you're in love with?" Now because the question is so appropriate, Lucky determines to answer recklessly but truthfully, "Yes, very," since he intends his answer to mean Penny—though it was not his conscious intention even a minute before to revive his own hopes or to obtrude upon her new plans to marry someone else. Yet if he had expected her to miss his ironic remark he was mistaken. Penny's instinct immediately detects the direction of the answer, and she corrects him by clarifying the question in terms of Lucky's fiancée—"the girl you're going to marry." "Oh, I don't know," he replies, his answer indicating at once that his previous response had been a confession of his love for Penny, just as her restatement of the question indicated her understanding of his declaration.

Now they stand facing each other, at an impasse, for the decisions both have made prior to this sequence seem unaltera-

60

ble: they are still to part, to marry others, but now their lives have been embittered by this too-late mutual understanding. Infusing the atmosphere of the ballroom is a sense of failure and frustration, but the environment itself is a continuous invitation to dance, and thus the visual world about them remains open to the possibility of their reconciliation. They are "dressed" for dancing, though immobilized by their impending destinies. Their verbalized attitudes as the sequence develops continue to suggest an inevitable separation, but the accompanying musical background begins to insinuate an artistically truer alternative.

If the situation seems fraught with the paradoxes of their lives, the song that Lucky sings to Penny is paradox itself, carried to a metaphysical extreme. He sings it from the bottom of the stairway on which she stands, about to leave him forever, not only to arrest her for another moment but to articulate the nature and depth of what her loss will mean to him. The camera peers down at him from her point of view as he stands, virtually hopeless, vowing never to dance again. The lyric of his song, "Never Gonna Dance," is astonishing for the context. It is filled with wild comic projections of what he intends to do—essentially give up dancing and spend all his time loving Penny from afar.

Even in the most ordinary film, in a song with the simplest lyrics, the act of singing always takes us beyond the mere literal meaning of the words. The verbal presentation is really heard in terms of intentions, undertones, and attitudes. Often the cinematic environment establishes the mood and broadens the implications of the singer's rendition of the song. With the metaphorical mode of "Never Gonna Dance," Lucky is making a plea for pity and at the same time satirizing himself for the ridiculously futile position in which he finds himself. Having danced with Penny, and being unwilling ever to dance with anyone else, he is left anticipating a future in which he will, as he says, "see myself on my toes, / Dancing to radios / For Major Edward Bowes" (as a contestant on the Amateur Hour).

The comedy precludes the possibility of bathos, for Lucky the master dancer is also a master ironist, and the song is partially a means of self-protection. By playing the clown to express his intention of resigning from the world of the dance and ridding himself of the characteristic trappings of his trade (his shoes, his hat, his clothes, his rhythm: "To Groucho Marx I'll give my cravat, / To Harpo goes my shiny silk hat"), he wishes to disguise the gravity—but not the fact—of his loss of Penny ("For all I really want is you"). But the frustration of the moment cannot be completely covered by the fanciful images, since the repeated metaphor of the song emphasizes the debilitating effect of this parting. Playing on her name, Lucky sings, "Though I'm left without a

61

penny, / The wolf was discreet; / He left me my feet, and so / I put them down on anything but the la belle, / La perfectly swell romance. / Never gonna dance, never gonna dance." This is not simply a refusal to continue to perform in the mode of his art, but a denial of his essential means of expression.

Bereft of illusions, confronting the irreconcilable gap between his intention and inspiration, Fred Astaire in the role of Lucky Garnett sustains this tragic awareness through the dance that immediately and paradoxically follows upon the song, its concluding words ("Never gonna dance, never gonna dance, / Only gonna love you, never gonna dance"*) reverberating visually in the first steps he takes away from Penny (played by Ginger Rogers). She shares with him this moment of realization. It is an unequaled cinematic achievement in which the tragic sense permeating the sequence is projected through the movements of the two dancers, while the accompanying music summarizes the history of their relationship. Several thematic strands of the film are reflected in the music. The solemn chord signifying the "never" of the closing line of Lucky's song is linked to the "never" of an entirely unrelated melodic line from an earlier song ("The Way You Look Tonight"), which Lucky had sung to Penny when their relationship had first reached a level of greater understanding; the lyric of that earlier song contains the phrase "never, never change." The juxtaposition of this melodic line with its antithesis, "never gonna dance"—both essentially articles of faith that will not stand the test of time or reality—points to the limitations in comprehending all human relationships, and to the fragility of one person's position in regard to another. Commitment founders upon unlucky circumstances. The association of melodic lines from two different emotional contexts produces an ambiguity that informs the perceptions of the two dancers and transforms a poignant situation into a moment of tragic awareness. In this sequence from *Swing Time*, Astaire and Rogers, acknowledging their mutual loss, dance for a moment side by side without touching, then dance together, and finally—delicately balancing hope against the reality of their lives—to the accompaniment of musical crescendoes, they perform a series of fantastic swirling movements that lead to the ultimate image of separation: ascending the staircase, she sweeps beyond camera range, leaving him alone and desolate.

Musical films, of course, seldom achieve such effects, but all musicals draw more or less on certain strengths inherent in the

62

---

*"Never Gonna Dance" by Jerome Kern and Dorothy Fields, from the musical production *Swing Time*, copyright © 1936 by T. B. Harms Company; copyright renewed; used by permission.

genre that permit them to move back and forth between a realistic presentation and a metaphorical musical presentation. Within a metaphorical presentation, a song or dance becomes a symbolic revelation of an entire plot situation, or a disclosure of a character's inner feelings and deepest intentions. Aware of this double mode of presentation, audiences expect musical films to convey meaning in brief moments of song and dance, which, like Shakespearean soliloquies, are justified by convention and are supposed to be inconsistent with the realistic presentation that carries the story line forward. Even the most inane lyrics may be an effective vehicle of thematic meaning in a musical number because in this nonrealistic presentational mode meaning seldom, if ever, directly depends on the logic of sentences or even the imagistic range of the lyrics. What counts is "delivery" (if, for example, the singer is talented) or setting (if the song is impersonal, sung by a chorus or a group of people). In regard to delivery, naturally, many factors are involved, and there is no convincing way of describing why in popular music one singer seems better than another or why in films, for instance, Astaire is preeminent in making the lyrics relate profoundly to widely varying emotional situations or states of mind, even when singing about such inconsequential subjects as dressing for a formal dinner, as in the song "Top Hat." The musical number stands as a metaphor for the emotional life taking place in the film. As a cinematic event, it communicates through nonrational resources that viewers grasp intuitively and that augment their responses to what they have actually heard and seen.

63

THE PROCEDURES OF METAPHOR

Given the difficulty of assessing a genre that communicates in so indirect a manner, critics have tended to avoid cinematic analysis of the musical patterns. The musical as a genre is a form conducive to entertainment, certainly, and one that is often badly managed, but its foremost examples are cinematic classics that need never be excused by their admirers as light comedy or escapism. Its most striking characteristic is its tendency to encompass multiple levels of meaning in its musical passages (though not, however, in its nonmusical passages). Because audiences receive more information than the sum of the verbal and visual specifications in such sequences, they are sometimes deeply affected on an emotional level and yet have difficulty articulating a reasonable analysis of their feelings.

The incorporation of two distinctive arts, singing and dancing, should not, certainly, lead to a narrowing of cinematic expressiveness—theoretically, it should increase the possibilities. No doubt an inferior musical sequence will obtrude on the development of a film's plot, and the jumbling of art forms will then be less expressive than the nonmusical portions of the same film. What so often happens in the musical film is that instrumental performances are introduced without adequate visual imagery to support the interruption of the story, or without thematic relevance to the action. Hollywood, always impressed by "Culture," has made innumerable efforts to bring some of the world's finest classical and jazz musicians to the screen, but almost never have the instrumental performances been as cinematically satisfying as the song or dance numbers. It seems that multilevel communication is not practical in the screen versions of pure musical presentations.

If the outstanding generic characteristic of the musical is its capacity to communicate different levels of meaning simultaneously, this may be so because the musical event derives its esthetic appeal from its relationship to the classical standards for art and beauty—rhythm, harmony, proportion, and clarity. The tendency of classical art is to universalize from particulars. In a musical film, a particular song or dance frequently reflects the general condition—emotional, spiritual, or intellectual—of the participants. If, in addition, the visual circumstances bear on the general situation at hand, the musical sequence will likely communicate to us both the abstract and the particular elements of the dramatic situation, even if some apparent conflict exists between these different levels.

64

For instance, in the sequence from George Stevens's *Swing Time* (1936) discussed at the outset of this chapter, the virtually indescribable complexity of feelings aroused by the Astaire-Rogers dance of parting stems from the ambiguities established by combining the comically peculiar lyrics with the solemn dissolution of the lovers' relationship. When Penny and Lucky finally dance, the grace and harmony of their movements present us with a perfect instance of unity: symbolically, it is clear that they belong to each other—that universally appreciated esthetic standards, recreated through their performances, argue that they should remain together. This is, of course, only a visual implication of the scene before us; at the same time, we are cognizant of the problems that separate them. But the disruption of that universal harmony required by the logic of the plot—when Penny leaves Lucky alone at the end of the dance—immediately counteracts the literal meaning we have been absorbing and creates a great sense of pathos, though not of irresolution. In fact, separation is thematically right at the final moment when Penny swirls off camera, but on the visual level the image is one of frustrating regret.

Another significant premise of the musical film is that the chief musical performers are essentially noble or admirable characters. The heavies do not often sing or dance, or when they do they exhibit talents somewhat out of keeping with the environment of the film (for instance, an operatic voice incompatible with the popular style of a particular musical comedy). The reasons for this are philosophical more than psychological: the capacity to go all out, to sing or dance with that internal dedication typical of musical stars, is evidence of a kind of love of life—a commitment to draw from what is basically a very private reservoir of feelings in order to please and perhaps elevate the world the performers live in. At the very least it is a sign of zest and openness. Villains are apt to conceal their motives or hide their deceitful ambitions rather than sing about them. Such characters can pretend to be other than they are, but the important musical moments call for a level of sincerity beyond that attainable by the mere pretenders. Gene Kelly, trapped in the awkward situation of an adult on roller skates on a busy street at night in *It's Always Fair Weather* (directed by Kelly and Stanley Donen, 1955), nevertheless can skate, dance, and sing "I Like Myself" (while eluding gangsters), whereas a villain in such a position could only apologize or escape guiltily.

The heroes of musicals, the performers, may act deviously in complicated situations, but since they are by nature good people, they will eventually get in touch with their better selves and their natural characteristics will emerge. In *It's Always Fair Weather*, Kelly plays a man who has failed to live up to his expectations, partly from bad luck and partly from weakness. When we first see him, getting out of the army, with his youthful hopes, we recognize his potential for success. But when we meet him next, years later, cynical and working on the edges of society as a boxer's manager, we wonder less about the reasons for his decline than about the possible circumstances that will arise to allow him to regain his confidence and live according to his true self. The song done on roller skates, "I Like Myself," anticipates this development in the plot, which, if not necessarily a foregone conclusion, is certainly a reasonable expectation within the world of the musical film.

The premonition of the happy ending that we usually expect in a musical comedy (not all musicals, though, are comedies) is psychologically correct, and not just a simple matter of wish fulfillment: it is based on our knowledge that the life of the musical film passes before us on multiple levels. The temporary surface complexity of an essentially simple problem (Will the heroine and hero solve their difficulties? Will the young singer find success on stage?) seldom deludes us into worrying about the

65

final outcome. Beneath the surface level, the thematic structure of the musical develops inevitably toward emotional unification. The essential good nature of the principal performers will be conveyed to those with whom they are trying to communicate— their lovers or their audience. If the musical is not done well, the inner development might not be clear, and in such a case the happy ending may seem to be just tagged on. But it is tagged on only in the sense that it is not a satisfactory conclusion to the surface predicament, which is simply rushed to a forced happy ending. In a good musical, the ending is the logical conclusion to the surface story as well as to the performers' inner responses to that story, which may be quite another matter. When the musical performances have conveyed clearly those inner feelings and aspirations, the happy ending is merely the outer reconciliation of opposing superficial complexities. The hero and heroine agree to marry because they—somewhat later than the audience—have intuitively grasped the solution to the problem from their quickened perceptions of the musical events.

66

CATEGORIES OF THE GENRE

The various categories of the musical are not especially crucial to our understanding of this cinematic form. It is worthwhile, of course, to note the effects of music in the noncomic musical, but that is a matter of individual cases.* Of all the categories, the one of primary importance is the courtship-romance. Typified by the Astaire-Rogers musicals of the 1930s, this category achieved its last major expression in Donen's *Funny Face* (1957), in which Astaire (then fifty-eight years old) again spectacularly demonstrated the exhilarating dance-courtship process that he almost single-handedly had made one of the patterns of the genre. Of course, in many musicals courtship-romance appears as more of a motif than a structuring process, but in any case its frequent reappearance may make it useful as a categorizing factor.

Other distinguishable categories include the musical biography (examples are Mervyn LeRoy's *Gypsy* [1962], Michael Curtiz's *Yankee Doodle Dandy* [1942], Anthony Mann's *The Glenn Miller Story* [1954], William Wyler's *Funny Lady* [1975]), the show business plot (Lloyd Bacon's *Forty-Second Street* [1933], Charles Walters's *Summer Stock* [1950], George Sidney's *Kiss Me Kate* [1953]), the fantasy-romance (Vincente Minnelli's *Cabin in the Sky* [1943], *Brigadoon* [1954], and *On a Clear Day You Can See Forever* [1969], Joshua Logan's *Camelot* [1967],

*See, for example, the discussion of *Cabaret*, pp. 106–10.

Francis Ford Coppola's *Finian's Rainbow* [1968]), children's fantasy (Donen's *The Little Prince* [1975], Robert Stevenson's *Mary Poppins* [1964]), and parody (George Roy Hill's *Thoroughly Modern Millie* [1967], Ken Russell's *The Boy Friend* [1971]). Many of the most famous musicals do not necessarily fall into any of the key categories—for example, Robert Wise and Jerome Robbins's *West Side Story* (1961), Bob Fosse's *Sweet Charity* (1968), Joseph Mankiewicz's *Guys and Dolls* (1955), Howard Hawks's *Gentlemen Prefer Blondes* (1953), Donen's *The Pajama Game* (1957), and Minnelli's *An American in Paris* (1951).

Apparently, the plot patterns that developed in musicals were not intended to be the truly distinguishing marks of the genre. The studios felt, with some logic, that the public's perception of the genre had more to do with the stars than with the plot. The Gold Digger films of the 1930s are perhaps the best-known examples of that outlook, but it seems very likely that studios thought of all their repeated teamings of musical stars as constituting a kind of genre, and a degree of ongoing characterization does appear in, for instance, the Mickey Rooney-Judy Garland films, the Kelly-Garland films, and the Kelly-Sinatra films. Studios were frequently intent on imitating a successful product in any genre, of course, and the musical lent itself to imitation more readily than most forms since it was not especially important to repeat the plot of a previous success in order to maintain the public's awareness of the genre's formulaic qualities. The effort at duplication consisted mainly of designing production numbers that would allow certain stars to perform in a way equivalent to that of their last successful film—from a Sonja Henie musical skating routine to a duet by Jeanette MacDonald and Nelson Eddy.

67

The studio's perpetuation of star performances extended the minor categories of the musical. A typical example can be seen from a comparison of the MGM casts in *Broadway Melody of 1936* (released in 1935) and *Born to Dance* (1936), which were both vehicles for Eleanor Powell's dancing and which included some of the same supporting cast members: Una Merkel, Sid Silvers, Frances Langford, Buddy Ebsen. Both films were directed by Roy Del Ruth and written by Jack McGowan and Sid Silvers and had dances choreographed by Dave Gould. The only interesting difference between the two films was the choice of the leading man, another instance of the studio's concept of genre through casting. Robert Taylor in the first film is replaced by James Stewart in the second, indicating the studio's feeling that part of this particular subgenre's pattern required a nonmusical male lead.

In considering the categories of the musical, viewers are sometimes surprised to note that most films are primarily realistic in the way they present the plot. Obviously, the musical numbers are usually not realistic, but the narrative material preceding and following such numbers tends to remain recognizable and ordinary both in environments and characterizations. Much stereotyping is apparent, yet this aspect of stylization does not counteract the typical surface realism of most musicals. The majority of these films are located in contemporary situations that stake a claim on credibility, though no such claim could be made for the production numbers. Even when the settings of a musical are not contemporary, they tend to be plausible historical recreations such as those in Gene Kelly's *Hello, Dolly* (1969), Minnelli's *Meet Me in St. Louis* (1944), and Donen's *Seven Brides for Seven Brothers* (1954). Less common are the mythic settings of *Camelot* and *A Connecticut Yankee in King Arthur's Court* (directed by Tay Garnett, 1949). On the other hand, no limitations on the legendary or the fanciful are prescribed for the musical numbers, and extravagance is typically commended by critics and general audiences. Thus, aside from the category of fantasy-romance, it is generally true that the plot of the musical is realistic.

68

FILMMAKERS

One of the obvious facts about the genre becomes clear when, examining a list of its greatest examples, one discovers a notable absence of most, though not all, of the greatest filmmakers. We simply do not associate the top examples of this genre with, for instance, Fritz Lang, Jean Renoir, or Alfred Hitchcock—to mention three who actually did make musicals (but as Hitchcock said of his 1933 English film *Waltzes from Vienna,* "This was my lowest ebb."*). A surprising number of musicals that are memorable at least in part (and some that are quite good throughout) were directed by studio men with no distinctive reputation or commanding style noticeable elsewhere than in the particular musicals they made: Lloyd Bacon *(Wonder Bar* [1934], *Gold Diggers of 1937);* Charles Walters *(Easter Parade* [1948], *Lili* [1953], *High Society* [1956]); George Sidney *(Anchors Aweigh* [1944], *Annie Get Your Gun* [1949], *Showboat* [1951], *Pal Joey* [1957]); Mark Sandrich *(The Gay Divorcee* [1934], *Shall We Dance:* [1937]); Walter Lang *(Moon Over Miami* [1941], *Call Me Madam* [1953], *The King and I* [1956]); and many others such as Norman Taurog, Frank Tuttle, Robert Stevenson, William Seiter,

---

*Peter Bogdanovich, *The Cinema of Alfred Hitchcock* (New York: Museum of Modern Art, 1963), p. 16.

Charles Vidor, and Joshua Logan. Some of the more important directors who have worked in the genre have made only one or two musicals: Howard Hawks, Anthony Mann, Otto Preminger, Fred Zinnemann, and William Wyler. Rouben Mamoulian, Michael Curtiz, and George Cukor have made several good musicals, but of all filmmakers of importance, only two are decidedly associated with the genre and have made their reputation in it: Stanley Donen and Vincente Minnelli. Considering the extensive number of musicals produced by the American film industry, we might very well assume that one probable cause for the musical's not having attracted the continued commitment of major filmmakers is that the films in this genre, more than other films, depend on the collaborative efforts of various artists not entirely under the control of the director—or less under the director's control than in other kinds of collaborative productions.

The collaborators are in most instances collectively more important than the directors themselves, even in determining the unifying style of the film. Indeed, if the choreographic numbers in a film are designed by Busby Berkeley or Bob Fosse, it is often true that their contribution, rather than the director's, is the major creative force behind the film. In any case, the composer and the lyricist are obviously crucial to the success of any musical. Frequently the musical director is primarily responsible for the impact of the production numbers, and it should also be noted that the American film industry, rather early in the sound era, began to excel in the scoring of its films. Seldom have those responsible for the score become household names, but the overall level of technical competence is quite high.

69

The musical is probably the one genre where the performers often actually deserve much of the credit they otherwise habitually receive from the public for the success of all films. Actors in nonmusical films cannot, by themselves, determine very much of the quality of the work they appear in; usually even their own performances are limited by the quality of the director's handling of the cinematic milieu, the photographer's and the editor's skills, and the requirements of the script. But with musical performers, the essential quality of communication depends primarily on their own talents. Whereas great directors can often make artistic use of minor talents or other nontalents in dramatic roles, they can do relatively little to simulate excellence in a song or dance number performed by an incompetent. In those cases where minimally talented performers do a more than adequate job (Ruby Keeler in a Busby Berkeley production, for instance), it is usually the result of an ensemble presentation or a dramatic setting that absorbs the performer into the choreographic environment.

There have been instances where performers not noted for their musical skills have produced excellent results (even without the dubbing in of someone else's voice that is done in certain Hollywood films). Witness the efforts of Marlon Brando singing in *Guys and Dolls.* What of course counts in musical numbers on screen is the performer's ability to project great feeling and awareness about the meaning of what he or she is doing—and mere technical brilliance will seldom suffice (for instance, Mario Lanza never truly transferred to film the overwhelming qualities he possessed as a singer on stage).

The American cinema both created its own musical stars and borrowed them from other media where they had previously attained widespread recognition. This was the case with Al Jolson, whose charismatic singing easily overcame occasional awkward moments of acting before the camera. Fred Astaire, who for many years prior to his film debut had acted on Broadway (most of that time as part of a famous dance team with his sister Adele), went on to star in some films based (remotely) on his Broadway successes. Barbra Streisand, a recording star, had, like Jolson, so huge a following that her initial film role was virtually a guaranteed success. Other stars have had simultaneous careers in film and on records, most notably Bing Crosby in the 1930s and Frank Sinatra in the 1940s. The cinema, however, is undoubtedly responsible for the fame of the majority of its great musical performers: Gene Kelly, Judy Garland, Shirley Temple, Ginger Rogers, Donald O'Connor, Betty Grable, and dozens of others. In addition, there were a few major performers more frequently associated with general comedy than with musicals, but they were indeed outstanding musical artists: Mae West, Danny Kaye, and the Marx Brothers, particularly Groucho.

70

THE THEORY OF INTEGRATION

There is virtually no pattern or methodology employed in the criticism of musical films. Writers on the subject always attempt to hedge on an uneasy ambiguity, recognizing that, obviously, the criteria applied to film drama or comedy cannot be totally relevant to musicals, and that therefore such films must be judged by other standards. But no such standards exist—except that critics award approval or disapproval to the musical or choreographic aspects of the work regardless of their views on its other cinematic qualities. The problem of evaluating musicals—aside from judgments about the artistry of a particular musical number—remains unresolved in contemporary criticism.

Perhaps the largest basis on which critics attempt to build a workable analytical methodology is the distinction between films that integrate the musical numbers and the dramatic intervals into a consistent story line, and films that make little or no attempt at such integration. All the critics who have used this distinction as a theoretical basis seem to agree that the former approach to creating a musical is either more sophisticated or more esthetically pleasing than the latter, in which the plot and characterization periodically come to a halt while the stars perform according to their special musical talents. This theoretical premise, however, is so shaky as a basis for serious criticism that writers on the topic make numerous exceptions—for instance, production numbers in a Busby Berkeley film have often been praised by critics, even though no pretense of dramatic relevance is offered to motivate Berkeley's musical "happenings."

Although for the purposes of criticism there is some value in the distinction between the integrated music-drama film and its opposite musical type, there is no evident reason for generalizing about the inherent superiority of either style. In the Astaire-Rogers films, which because of the variety and impact of their musical numbers serve as the models for the genre, there are integrated dances that advance the meaning of the dramatic action ("Night and Day" in Sandrich's *The Gay Divorcee*), on-stage production numbers that have nothing at all to do with the plot ("Top Hat" in *Top Hat*, also directed by Sandrich, 1935), and production spectacles that exist primarily for themselves but are also crucial to the characterization and plot ("The Continental" in *The Gay Divorcee*).

This is not to dismiss the implicit criticism in the assumption that musicals containing glorious song and dance portions unrelated to the story line are faulty works of art. Unity, harmony, and cohesiveness have been artistic ideals since the time of the ancient Greek musical theater of the sixth century B.C. (the Greek tragic drama was sung or chanted). For the movie musical to depart radically from obviously enduring esthetic principles that have guided all other narrative arts would indeed be a challenge to our critical sensibility—if not our common sense. Yet it seems to me plausible to regard even the overtly "unintegrated" musical film as a unified narrative, as long as the musical numbers are powerful enough to provide an ongoing sense of unity and leave the audience conscious of what the dramatic action is really all about. The typical, seemingly unintegrated Busby Berkeley film of the 1930s, which on the surface is about the difficulties encountered by a producer or a group of chorus girls, is actually about the *process* of putting on a show. The accumulation of the five or six musical numbers becomes the achievement

71

of that process, the real unifying plot thread of films such as Bacon's *Footlight Parade* (1933) and *Dames* (directed by Ray Enright, 1934).

The problem, which is sometimes all too apparent, is that the dialogue intervals between numbers are frequently tedious or insipid, even in Busby Berkeley films, and film scholars who want to sit through these films several times surely must find such dialogue slow going. In musicals created by somewhat less talented men than Berkeley, it must be recognized that the unintegrated musical often cannot draw its disparate elements together with any convincing sense of unity. But it remains unproven that a lack of integration in itself precludes artistic success. There is no rule that requires dull dramatic interludes in such films, though quite likely the design of mediocre musicals imposes at least one added burden on the people who shape them: they must explain why there is so much dancing and singing. The filmmakers' usual answer is to make the story about the lives of people who are professionally engaged in show business.

72   The simplicity of story line that results from this structural injunction is largely responsible for the hierarchical values assigned by critics, whereby the unintegrated musical with a show business plot is valued least. After all, simplicity is not one of the commanding virtues of twentieth-century art. The entire genre has always lacked artistic status because its formats appear to eliminate the complexity associated with major films by acknowledged master directors. People are in the habit of reading the history of all art forms as a progression from simplicity to complexity, a false notion that seems to have achieved immortality over the centuries, and one that is particularly inappropriate to the cinema in light of the brevity of its history.

Historically, the general line of development within the musical genre is clouded by the influence of an obviously dual tradition. Starting with the first popular sound film, an Al Jolson vehicle, *The Jazz Singer* (1927, directed by Alan Crosland), there is evidence of both integration and unintegration. Since the plot of this film concerns a young man going into show business, the songs naturally have a certain structural justification. At the same time, the peculiar technical presentation of the film— essentially silent with insert titles, but the singing sequences are of course done with sound—definitely separates the musical numbers from the rest of the film—even from the few lines of sound dialogue. Indeed, the public immediately became aware of the fact that the film was made to give Jolson the chance to sing "My Mammy," and the very usable plot hardly mattered at all. (How interesting, then, to note that twenty years later, in 1946, much of the same plot could be incorporated into the biography of Jolson's life, *The Jolson Story*, directed by Alfred E. Green; but in that film the plot is thoroughly integrated with the singing.)

From *The Jazz Singer* into the thirties, the musical develops both opposing tendencies of the genre, to integrate and to separate. There is no convincing way to demonstrate that the artistic development of the musical was accompanied by an increasing commitment to the integration of music into the plot. Some historical accounts try to do so in terms of the first two great "proponents" of the two structural styles, Astaire and Berkeley, but these accounts usually bend historical facts by claiming that Berkeley's unintegrated musicals preceded Astaire's integrated films, when many of the films appeared at the same time and each style influenced its opposite. Among the outstanding American musical films prior to Astaire's and Berkeley's are Ernst Lubitsch's *The Love Parade* (1929) and Rouben Mamoulian's *Love Me Tonight* (1932), both with Maurice Chevalier and Jeanette MacDonald, in which some of the songs not only advance the plot but actually change its location (in the latter, the Rodgers and Hart score occasionally serves as recitative, that is, as a substitute for dialogue). Therefore, the theory that the unintegrated musical developed into the integrated musical or progressed in complexity to meet the increasing sophistication of the audience is unfounded in fact.

The discernible trend in the 1940s toward the integrated musical can in part be attributed to increased interest in relating the environment to the thematic movement of the film. The three classic musicals of this decade—Minnelli's *Meet Me in St. Louis* (1944) and *The Pirate* (1948) and Donen and Kelly's *On The Town* (1949)—are very much concerned with extending the symbolic sense of their locations into the musical expression of the films' themes. *Meet Me in St. Louis*, a nostalgic tribute to the midwestern American city, concerns the value of a family's roots in St. Louis. The father changes his mind about moving away when he notes the unhappiness such an upheaval would create. He observes that his young daughter is distraught at the idea; when her older sister (played by Judy Garland) sings "Have Yourself a Merry Little Christmas," the child rushes outside to knock down her snowmen. *The Pirate*'s theme relies heavily on the romantic Caribbean town that the heroine (again played by Judy Garland) desperately wishes to leave. And *On the Town*, one of the most influential of all films in the genre, celebrates New York as three exuberant sailors (Kelly, Sinatra, and Jules Munshin) on one-day passes frantically try to absorb the excitement of the entire city. The emphasis on place in these three films and several others of the period makes it plausible and indeed necessary

73

for the musical numbers to arise spontaneously from the characters' response to where they are at the moment—rather than the numbers that arise from the stage rehearsals that musical characters are so frequently working on in films of the 1930s. With musical numbers often keyed to these locations (such as "The Trolley Song" in *Meet Me in St. Louis* and "New York, New York" in *On the Town*), the 1940s films most often feature the star performers in "improvisational" routines, and exclude the chorus-line production style typical of numbers that are aimed at observers not participating in the plot. Therefore, the apparent integration of song and plot in the genre as it developed in the 1940s had much to do with the fact that in those films the main performers, responding to the situations at hand, sing to each other rather than to an audience in a theater or to a rehearsal director. When the three sailors and their girlfriends in *On the Town* meet atop the Empire State Building to begin their one night of shore leave, their tremendous enthusiasm to seize the moment seems naturally to burst into the song "On the Town" as they set out on their adventure.

74

THEMATIC INTEGRATION:
A STAR IS BORN AND *AN AMERICAN IN PARIS*

Instead of theorizing about the artistic viability of the unintegrated musical, we can best come to terms with thematic integration by examining two memorable examples of musical numbers that, at least on the surface, do not relate directly to the nonmusical aspects of the stories in their films. The questions raised by the appearance of such numbers in a film are whether the musical number itself or the dialogue material constitutes an interlude (a falling-off of the film's artistry), and whether at certain times one supplies the other with some esthetic reinforcement or relationship, even in a film that overtly offers the public a flimsy plot for the sake of the musical experience.

All unintegrated musical numbers in narrative films that contain any kind of plot at all have some tangential connection with that plot, usually in the sense that the film's musical stars are also in show business and part of the film contains sequences of their work—that is, their singing and dancing. At arbitrary points in the film the performers go "on stage" or "before the camera." The dramatic movement of the plot comes to a temporary rest and the musical number takes over. Yet since musical films always advertise themselves in regard to their musical sequences, the creative idea behind the film must lie in its musical conception.

This is why it is essential to see a type of integration operative in all musicals—even those that offer merely the most casual linkage of dramatic action and musical performance. All successful musicals employ a form of thematic integration of the musical and nonmusical sequences, and this is the crucial quality of the genre—whether or not an additional level of integration in regard to plot or characterization is also apparent.

Judy Garland's "Born in a Trunk" number from *A Star Is Born* (1954) provides a memorable example of a level of integration that underlies the surface nonintegration. On the surface, this long number occurs during a sneak preview of the first movie made by Vicki Lester (Garland) on her road to stardom. As such, the number is a sequence from a film within a film. Had the director of *A Star Is Born,* George Cukor, intended merely to convey to us the fact that this preview screening will reveal to the public and the Hollywood press the star quality of Vicki Lester, the studio's new discovery, he might have shown us merely a few seconds of Vicki's performance. But in fact Cukor is simply looking for an excuse to showcase Judy Garland's talents, not to advance the plot of the film. Yet we as viewers may know all this without the least concern for the lengthy interruption of the plot (and the plot of this film happens to be extremely interesting in its own right, and was the basis of an entirely successful nonmusical of some seventeen years earlier). Moreover, though we see nothing else of the preview than the "Born in a Trunk" number, we realize that no such number could ever be part of the plot of Vicki's sneak-preview film, since it is the biography of a singer "born in a trunk in the Prince's Theater in Pocatello, Idaho." The biography itself is show business hokum, not at all resembling the story of Vicki Lester's rise to fame, which is a key part of *A Star Is Born.*

Yet with all these considerations against it, this number not only stands on its merits as a musical routine but also reflects some of the underlying motifs in the film's dramatic action. The number depicts the story of a girl growing up in vaudeville, becoming part of her parents' act, going out on her own, facing the rejection of agents, and finally attracting the attention of a producer who makes her the star in a show. The details of the number help to synthesize two crucial themes of *A Star Is Born* — talent and luck. Vicki's career (we do not see her as a child and do not know what her training has been) combines both elements, but our sense of the ambiguous but crucial intermingling of talent and luck is sharpened by this musical number. We first meet Vicki at a benefit performance, where, as a total unknown, she reveals such extraordinary stage presence (especially when the actor Norman Maine stumbles onstage aggressively drunk,

75

apparently intent on destroying his own image and ruining her act) that we can account for it only by assuming that her experience is figuratively the equivalent of being born in a trunk. In any case, her talent is real and inborn, not to be gained merely by hard work, but instinctive. On the other hand, the film has to do with the chance aspects of life, even in regard to someone who has the gift of talent. The film never explains why Vicki's gift was unappreciated before Norman saw her, even though it is so clear to us from the beginning as she performs with him in his drunken state and later that night when he seeks her out and she sings brilliantly (with all the intensity generally associated with Judy Garland) "The Man That Got Away" number. In addition, the film never explains why Norman, who is also talented, deteriorates. It seems that success as a motion picture performer depends greatly on luck; character seems to be the outcome of a person's experiences, not the cause of them. The "Born in a Trunk" number brings together these thematic strains in a separate, unrelated story of its own—but it is precisely in the unintegration of plot and musical number that this musical sequence serves to integrate thematically the various dramatic developments of the whole film.

Sometimes the seemingly unintegrated musical number may actually give structural unity to a script that does not otherwise fully integrate its conception of character into the action of the plot. *An American in Paris* to a large extent overcomes some mishandling of its genre traits in the dialogue because the ideas successfully conveyed within the musical numbers compensate for deficiencies engendered by the script. For much of the film we perceive two conflicting characterizations of the hero Jerry (played by Gene Kelly)—one provided by the dialogue and the other by the musical numbers. As portrayed through the dialogue, Jerry is a man willing to accept sponsorship from Milo, a wealthy woman who is sexually attracted to him, though he has moral qualms about what he is doing and even some doubt about his ability as a painter. He aggressively pursues Lise, a shopgirl he has fallen in love with, while at the same time acting thoroughly insensitive to the older woman. Jerry apparently is not a very attractive character. Yet for the sake of consistency the inner logic of the genre requires him to truly deserve our sympathy as well as the reward he achieves at the end, when Lise deserts her fiancé for him. The musical numbers collectively provide another level of characterization much more favorable than that of the script, and modify the negative traits Jerry exhibits in the story.

The ambiguous nature of the script of *An American in Paris*, with the hero's tendency for self-indulgence and the possibility of his being a pseudo-artist, cannot be easily accommodated by the conventions of the genre. In musicals, hero-villains (like those played by Astaire in Minnelli's earlier *Yolanda and the Thief* [1945] and by Marlon Brando in *Guys and Dolls*) turn out to be essentially good characters at heart, and for an important reason: this effusion of good spirits, enthusiasm, and deep-rooted emotions could not spring from the hearts of those who need to conceal their true selves. Minnelli's instinct for the genre reinforces this generalization in *An American in Paris*. Relatively early in the film, before his entanglements become complex, Jerry sings and dances the George Gershwin song "I Got Rhythm." His performance is directed at the gamins of his Left Bank neighborhood, in what appears to be merely one of several musical numbers introduced for their own sake and readily separable from the rest of the film. However, this number actually serves to prepare us for understanding the real emotional identity of the hero as it is revealed later in the film. Among the children, Jerry is lavish with his time and energy, teaching them not only bits of the English language but a philosophy of the simple life. As   77 they chant, "I got . . ." he completes each line of the lyric: "rhythm"—"music"—"my girl"—and the declarative emphasis of this recitation gives credence to a belief in the potential self-sufficiency of the marvelous performer who can assert these views with so much endearing vitality. Jerry's inner being shows, he "lets loose," and he convinces us of his talents. And in doing so he symbolically transforms the art of his performance into the potential art he must be capable of producing as a painter.

Thus, from this point on, we not only attribute proper motives to Jerry's actions (knowing he is essentially a good man), but we also allow for the inconsistencies of passivity and aggressiveness (knowing he is both true artist and true lover, yearning for achievement in each pursuit by seizing the opportunities that come to hand). Furthermore, since the "I Got Rhythm" number emphatically proclaims his lack of real interest in money and his attraction to simple innocence, we know that the inner logic of the plot—counter to certain hints in the story line—demands that he woo and win the shopgirl, not the wealthy sponsor. (The fact that Lise is also a dancer is of course a conventional determinant of the plot as well.) The visual environment of the dance, a Left Bank street filled with children and Parisian shopkeepers, enhances Jerry's fundamental association with the community and fixes certain qualities of his character so that any future action that seems to be deviously motivated will be dismissed by us as a minor, temporary confusion. Jerry's openness and good nature, so firmly established by this number, subsequently supply an underlying unity to actions and sentiments not entirely assimilated into the later portions of the plot.

A NOTE ON THE MUSICAL THEATER

Although the relationship between the American musical theater and the Hollywood musical film has not been explored in any definitive sense, the common assumption is that the first sound movies generally copied the kind of musical entertainment that had proven successful on stage. There were distinct modifications, of course, and by 1929 original Hollywood musicals began to appear frequently. Even in those cases where stage musicals were turned into the early musical films the changes were often significant, and later films were sometimes total revisions (*Funny Face*, a 1927 stage play in which Astaire appeared, is, except for certain songs, unrelated to the Astaire film *Funny Face* of 1957). The most obvious distinction between film adaptations and original stage shows in the 1930s would be in length: the films were shorter and contained fewer musical numbers. But this distinction diminished in later years.

78

The nature of a stage musical, however, is different from that of a film musical. Even in the absence of any official studio theory on the subject, those who made the earliest film musicals set about their business with no overriding commitment merely to duplicate on film what had succeeded on stage. In fact, stage dramas and comedies in the 1930s were normally brought to the screen with much more adherence to the original than is typical of the same process with musicals. The reason probably lies in the fact that the musical number on film requires a certain overt cinematic presentation; it has to take on a new quality of depth relationship with a camera, with the action usually flowing around the camera rather than taking place in a fixed position in front of it. Musical numbers on stage are presented with fixed or at least well-defined backgrounds and are projected toward an immovable auditorium. On screen, the camera is constantly limiting the visual area, separating parts of the performance from the total environment, emphasizing aspects of the presentation rather than the whole. It thus became apparent very early that both choreography and staging demanded rethinking for the purpose of cinematic form.

In any case, the tradition of the stage musical was in no way binding on the presentational mode of the motion picture musical even from the first attempts. The American musical stage play throughout the 1920s (and, notwithstanding a few brilliant exceptions, such as the Stephen Sondheim musical *Company* [1970], still the predominant style in our day) insisted on the separation of the musical numbers from the continuity of the plot development. And this seems to be true regardless of the thematic relationship between the story line and the musical number—even when the orchestra would carefully lead into the number by playing under the dialogue immediately preceding the song, and often continue during the following change of scene. In almost all types of Broadway musical stage productions, the persistent theatrical style halts the action—with the consent and encouragement of the audience—in order to leap into a "production number" that deliberately and overtly interrupts whatever reality has been created by the story line. The performers address the audience directly in these numbers, which are staged in a fashion designed to emphasize the break between the normal reasonable world of the dramatized story and the exalted emotional world of the musical number.

In the presentational modes of both opera and operetta, the musical sense of the play integrates all narrative elements within the (stylized) reality of the artwork. Gilbert and Sullivan's works are all excellent illustrations of this, and remain viable possible models for contemporary musical narratives. Therefore, it is not out of necessity but through choice that the American musical comedy play developed a unique mode that separates the musical numbers' special reality from whatever other reality has been achieved in the rest of the play. Musical theater rejects integration. In contrast, musical film is readily adaptable to either integration or separation.

The choice made by filmmakers usually depends on the quality of the original "book" (the nonmusical portion of the script), as well as the possible cinematic devices they might use for the musical numbers. It is usually possible, however, for filmmakers to avoid the impression of a musical number's theatrical origins when adapting a stage musical, even when they choose an unintegrated style. The major change from theater to film requires the replacement of the audience by the camera; the performers in the musical number no longer need to perform directly for the audience (though frequently they do, as in a Berkeley number). Instead, they may perform for other participants in the story— Fred Astaire sings to Ginger Rogers in the privacy of an empty ballroom in *Swing Time*—not in the presence of an assumed audience. The realism of the moments preceding and following such a musical "interruption" is not affected but rather is on just about the same stylized level of realism as that interruption, since the performers' behavior has not been influenced—as in a stage play—by the presence of observers. For the stage to emulate the cinema, it would have to turn from its great strength— the sense of a *public* performance—to a presentational mode of privacy, thereby losing many of the staging values cherished by audiences and of great esthetic merit in their own right.

GOLD DIGGERS OF 1933
(1933)

Director	Cinematographer	Script
MERVYN LEROY	SOL POLITO	ERWIN GELSEY
Producer	Songs	JAMES SEYMOUR
DARRYL F. ZANUCK	HARRY WARREN	Based on the play *The Gold Diggers* by Avery Hopwood
For Warner Brothers	AL DUBIN	
	Choreographer	
	BUSBY BERKELEY	

Songs: "The Gold Diggers' Song (We're in the Money)," "I've Got To Sing a Torch Song," "Pettin' in the Park," "The Shadow Waltz," "Remember My Forgotten Man"

PRINCIPAL CHARACTERS

DICK POWELL	RUBY KEELER	JOAN BLONDELL
Brad Roberts	Polly Parker	Carol
(Robert Treat Bradford)	WARREN WILLIAM	NED SPARKS
GUY KIBBEE	J. Lawrence Bradford	Barney Hopkins
Thaniel H. Peabody		GINGER ROGERS
ALINE MAC MAHON		Fay Fortune
Trixie Lorraine		

Length: 96 minutes

In spite of the general impression that the 1930s Busby Berkeley musicals were all designed to distract Americans in the era of the Great Depression, in *Gold Diggers of 1933* money looms as an obsession, poverty as an ever-present threat. Since all the Berkeley films tend to merge in our memories into a series of spectacular musical productions, we are pleasantly surprised on rediscovering in a few of them certain tough-minded attitudes, perhaps there sometimes only as a defense against the troubles of the era that created them, but still capable of providing insights into the realities of the time. *Gold Diggers of 1933* differs markedly in tone from the later Gold Diggers and other Berkeley films, though the recurring plot lines are indeed hard to distinguish from one film to another.

The film's preoccupation with money is sounded in the opening sequence of *Gold Diggers of 1933*. Ginger Rogers, whose role is relatively minor in the rest of the film, is seen dressed in a costume of simulated large gold coins, as are the other chorus girls, singing the ironic song of the decade, "We're in the money . . . We've got a lot of what it takes to get along."* The ironic and the ludicrous go side by side, for the girls who are rehearsing a stage show are literally dressed in money, while the lyrics remain blatantly preposterous for that era. But since the lyrics essentially signify nonsense, the effect is strikingly captured by having Ginger Rogers sing the song again in "pig Latin"—an unintelligible rendering of an implausible idea. The production number is quickly followed by a closing of the show for nonpayment of debts. The chorus girls are thrown out of work and are forced to confront directly the overwhelming problem of the time.

The typical genre solution to the girls' problem—and a common enough real-life solution of the period—is to put on another show, gainfully employing them all. Although the girls are innocent victims, some of them adopt the hardened, aggressive mannerisms of the era (especially in the roles played by Joan Blondell and Aline MacMahon; the role of Ginger Rogers is even more cynical as far as scheming self-interest is concerned). But at least the sweet, simple character of one girl, Polly (Ruby Keeler's typical role in the 1930s), remains unaffected by the tribulations of hard times. All the girls are "gold diggers" because it is necessary to be so in order to survive. The implications of not being "in the money," suggested indirectly in the opening song, are entirely clear to the chorus girls once their show has closed. In this film the battle for survival in show business is complicated by the opportunity to strike real gold—that is, to marry well, to marry out of one's social class and thereby permanently free oneself from the continuing struggle of Depression-era existence. Through a series of disguises and deceptions, the three most deserving chorines eventually pair off with two millionaire brothers and their family lawyer, all presumably happily matched. The immorality of these deceptions is justified partially by the conditions of the time, but mainly by the equally devious conduct of one of the millionaire brothers, who originally had planned to deceive the girls and use them for his own scheme.

Gold Diggers of 1933 is memorable principally for three grand-scale Berkeley production numbers, two of them—"The Shadow Waltz" and "Pettin' in the Park"—typical of the gigantic

---

*"We're in the Money" copyright © 1932 by Warner Bros. Inc.; copyright renewed; all rights reserved; used by permission.

82

imaginative displays he is famous for. The beautiful, glamorous girls collectively form visual patterns that are at once startling and funny; for instance, at one point dozens of girls, each playing her own luminescent violin in the dark, form the shape of a huge violin. The sexual motifs that often appear in Berkeley production numbers are equally inventive, visually astounding, and yes, perhaps vulgar. But Berkeley's achievement never leaves us feeling that such effects are merely cheap exploitation, for first of all, undeniable scenic art informs all his work, and secondly, even the sexual presentations are not provocative but radiate a remarkable degree of innocence. And in many cases his numbers seem to be conscious self-parodies; surely they are funny and are meant to be.

In a much more serious vein, Mervyn LeRoy concludes the film with a Berkeley-staged number that might seem too somber for the rest of the film, though the plot does lead up to it; the new show was supposed to deal with the problems of the average working man in the Depression. This "Remember My Forgotten Man" number ends the film with a patriotic display to remind us of men who fought in World War I and are now unemployed, unshaven figures on an immense breadline. Joan Blondell as a streetwalker sings: "Remember my forgotten man; / You put a rifle in his hand, / You sent him far away, / You shouted 'Hip

Hooray!' / But look at him today."* The film has moved from the flippant opening of "We're in the Money" to a bitter reminder of reality, and yet because the subject of the whole film relates both musical numbers, audiences do not feel any disruption in the unity of presentation. The concluding humanitarian plea counters the satirical or ironical handling of the depression theme in the opening sequence. Far from leading us to escape the social realities of the day, *Gold Diggers of 1933* allows us to confront the issue on a moving imaginative level.

TOP HAT
(1935)

Director	Cinematographers	Script
MARK SANDRICH	DAVID ABEL	DWIGHT TAYLOR
Producer	VEF	ALLEN SCOTT
PANDRO S. BERMAN	Songs	Based on a story by Dwight Taylor
For RKO	IRVING BERLIN	
	Choreographer	
	HERMES PAN	

Songs: "No Strings," "Isn't It a Lovely Day," "Top Hat, White Tie and Tails," "Cheek to Cheek," "The Piccolino"

PRINCIPAL CHARACTERS

FRED ASTAIRE	GINGER ROGERS	EDWARD EVERETT HORTON
Jerry Travers	Dale Tremont	Horace Hardwick
ERIK RHODES	ERIC BLORE	HELEN BRODERICK
Alberto Beddini	Bates	Madge Hardwick

Length: 101 minutes

To many viewers *Top Hat* is the best musical of the 1930s, and even of all time; it is certainly the most popular of the Astaire-Rogers films. For those who prefer to think that musicals ought to be about nothing, *Top Hat,* with its hero in formal clothes and its highly stylized Venetian sets, seems archetypal in the era of Depression America and fascist Italy: pure escape into the marvelous abstractions of singing and dancing. Yet, though its sub-

*"Remember My Forgotten Man" copyright © 1933 by Warner Bros. Inc.; copyright renewed; all rights reserved; used by permission.

ject is romance, *Top Hat* is not really romantic fluff. There is no doubt that the overwhelming reality of 1935 was the Depression, and movies were providing audiences with suggestions for attitudes that would help cope with it. But unless we insist rather rigidly that only those films dealing with economic reality could provide significant attitudes, then the 1930s musicals can also be viewed as very much part of the imaginative life of the American people during the Depression era.

Although *Top Hat* totally ignores economic reality and even the reality of place, the Astaire characterization, Jerry Travers, reflects an interesting type of the time: the outsider, aggressive and rebellious, existing within the establishment by means of his talents. The film opens with Jerry sitting in a wealthy men's club inhabited by older, stodgy men, who react with extreme annoyance when he folds a newspaper. As he leaves this sacrosanct temple of wealth and idleness, he tap-dances noisily in front of them, ruining their nervous systems for the day. Decorum seldom concerns the hero; his pursuit of Dale (Ginger Rogers) at one point has him disguised as a hansom cab driver, and while he virtually imprisons her in his cab he taps out a message to her from atop the driver's seat. Before they met he had awakened her by dancing in the hotel room directly above hers. He persists in this style of courtship to the point where he gets slapped a couple of times, but his victory is assured by the nature of the genre — which of course emphasizes worthiness of character in terms of singing and dancing.

The film imitates, but exceeds in quality, the earlier, excellent Astaire-Rogers film, *The Gay Divorcee*, though the earlier film has the better plot and its major dance duet, "Night and Day," is a classic of narrative iconography in dance format, surpassing its more famous equivalent in *Top Hat*, "Cheek to Cheek." But all the numbers in *Top Hat* are quality achievements, with Astaire in such complete control that he seems to make even the somewhat witless "No Strings" sound as good as the brilliant "Cheek to Cheek." "The Piccolino," a comical reminder of a previous Astaire-Rogers production spectacle ("The Continental," in *The Gay Divorcee*) is best remembered for its lyrics. The two numbers most effectively staged, "Lovely Day" and "Top Hat," are triumphs of psychological expressiveness, and they extended the range of meanings that musicals could convey. In one of these numbers, in a park, the assertive hero has forced his presence on the heroine, but before she can rid herself of him a thunderstorm comes up. They take refuge in a covered bandstand, and he sings "Isn't It a Lovely Day (To Be Caught in the Rain)?" The second line of this song is, "You were going on your way, now you'll have to remain," and though it is entirely in keeping with his psychol-

84

85

ogy of pursuit, he seems only to be rubbing salt in a wound. Nevertheless, within the psychological framework of the genre, musical performance communicates the essentially good nature of the performer. Dale listens to Jerry sing and is affected in such a way that her response becomes less and less hostile. The ensuing dance—during which thunder frightens Dale momentarily into Jerry's arms—has been explained by Arlene Croce:

Is there anywhere in movies more wonderful thunder and lightning? Rain numbers are always fun, but what could match that *second* clap of thunder that shifts the rhythm into double time, or the moment when we see the bandstand through the rain and the whirling pair alone on their private stage? Basically, this duet is a challenge dance (he does a step, she copies it, he does another, she tops it, and so on) . . . the point isn't tap-dancing, it's romance. And in "Lovely Day" every step has the dewiness of fresh, young emotion. Those spurting little phrases that end in a mutual freeze . . . as if to say "try and catch me," and that ecstatic embrace when they pivot together in a wide circle all around the stage, whipping into a froth—if this isn't perfect dancing, it is the perfect joy that dancing like this aims for and a shining moment in the history of the musical film.*

The other remarkable number from the film is the title song, which Irving Berlin tailored just for Astaire. The song has only the slightest narrative connection with the plot, in that before going on stage to perform it in a show Astaire does receive an invitation to a party, and in the ultimate logic of the genre's illogic, he of course seems to improvise the words: "I just got an invitation through the mails; / Your presence requested this evening, it's formal, / A top hat, a white tie and tails."† And dressed that way, Astaire dances in front of a chorus of twenty men similarly dressed. The effect of this massive masculine tap dance may be more startling today than it was forty years ago, but it is hard to imagine that Astaire intended it to be anything less than a magnificent mixture of drama and comedy. The lighting and certain dance movements suggest something sinister about the arrangements—as if these men were either rivals or enemies of Astaire, who remains several feet in front of them—yet the implication of antagonism is kept deliberately unclear on this point because Astaire is building to a rather astounding climax. He takes his cane and, aiming it as if it were a machine gun, begins methodically shooting down the now stationary chorus. It is an ominous mass rubout, shocking, unprepared for, grotesque—and an exhilaratingly comic way of dispersing a threat. The psychological moment, as striking as it is, does not really seem open to explication. In its incongruity and wit, its grim implications and the lyrics' celebration of joyous expectations, it stands as a symbol for the highest attainment of one aspect of the genre—the expression of meaning beyond the articulation of dialogue. It is pure cinematic mime.

86

---

*The Fred Astaire and Ginger Rogers Book (New York: Dutton, 1972), pp. 60–62.
†Above excerpt from "Top Hat, White Tie and Tails" by Irving Berlin, © copyright 1935 by Irving Berlin, © copyright renewed 1962 by Irving Berlin; reprinted by permission of the Irving Berlin Music Corporation and of Irving Berlin (England) Music (Chappell and Co. Ltd.).

SWING TIME

(1936)

Director	Cinematographer	Script
GEORGE STEVENS	DAVID ABEL	HOWARD LINDSAY
Producer	Songs	ALLAN SCOTT
PANDRO S. BERMAN	JEROME KERN	Based on a story
For RKO	DOROTHY FIELDS	by Erwin Gelsey
	Choreographer	
	HERMES PAN	

Songs: "Pick Yourself Up," "The Way You Look Tonight," "Waltz in Swing Time," "A Fine Romance," "Bojangles of Harlem," "Never Gonna Dance"

PRINCIPAL CHARACTERS

FRED ASTAIRE	GINGER ROGERS	VICTOR MOORE
John ("Lucky") Garnett	Penny Carol	Dr. Cardetti ("Pop")
HELEN BRODERICK	ERIC BLORE	GEORGES METAXA
Mabel Anderson	Mr. Gordon	Ricardo Romero
BETTY FURNESS		
Margaret Watson		

Length: 105 minutes

87

Swing Time provides Astaire with several excellent opportunities to play the role of ironist, which is integral to his best performances (such as in *Top Hat*). The film itself sustains an ironic mode throughout, but particularly in the "Never Gonna Dance" number discussed at the beginning of this chapter (pp. 61–62). Four other numbers similarly express the ironies built into the texture of the film. The title of the great ballroom dance, "Waltz in Swing Time," in itself seems a paradox, but does not, of course, create the slightest paradoxical sense while we watch Rogers and Astaire dance it. For "The Way You Look Tonight" Astaire accompanies himself on the piano while Ginger Rogers shampoos her hair in another room; the song celebrates her loveliness at that particular moment, though Astaire doesn't see her as he sings "Never never change, / Keep that breathless charm." Captivated by the music, she enters the room with shampoo in her hair as he concludes singing a vow of his love based on the line "Just the way you look tonight."* The irony, however, is partially reversed because even a somewhat disheveled Ginger Rogers represents the ideal of Hollywood beauty.

*"The Way You Look Tonight" by Jerome Kern and Dorothy Fields, from the musical production *Swing Time,* copyright © 1936 by T. B. Harms Company; copyright renewed; used by permission.

88

The irony is complicated by the situation in "A Fine Romance": Astaire is making a last stand to extricate himself from
this affair and fulfill his commitment to the girl he left back
home. After Rogers announces to him that she feels cold from
sitting in the snow-filled park—an overt invitation for him to put
his arm around her—he answers, "Well, flap your arms; that will
restore circulation." He refuses other romantic advances, which
angers her, and she sings to him: "A fine romance, with no
kisses . . . We should be like a couple of hot tomatoes, / But you're
as cold as yesterday's mashed potatoes." The irony here is carried
both by the witty Dorothy Fields lyric and by the fact that we
know that Astaire would like very much to follow up Rogers's
advances. Within a couple of minutes she discovers that he is
engaged, but he does not know she knows this, and he changes
his mind, determining to declare his love for her. Suddenly,
within the same setting, he finds her now as aloof as he had
pretended to be moments before. It is his turn to sing to her: "A
fine romance, with no clinches, / A fine romance, with no
pinches. . . ."[*] And with the irony left unresolved in this sequence, their mutual mistrust and disillusionment lead up to the
"Never Gonna Dance" number, in which the comic tone of the
earlier song is replaced by one of sad absurdity.

[*]"A Fine Romance" by Jerome Kern and Dorothy Fields, from the musical production *Swing Time*, copyright © 1936 by T. B. Harms Company; copyright
renewed; used by permission.

The film's first number, "Pick Yourself Up," provides the most overt dramatic irony in any Astaire film, for it takes place in a dance studio with Astaire pretending to be an incompetent novice. He seeks dance lessons only as a means of getting acquainted with the dance instructor, Rogers. The setup is perfect and is played out with exact timing so that almost at the very moment when it seems too late for Astaire to reveal his "true self," he does so and saves the instructor's job. But first he flubs the elementary lesson, confusing his right foot with his left and falling down. As she becomes exasperated and starts to give up on him, he sings, begging her for patience: "Please teacher, teach me something . . . / My two feet haven't met yet, / But I'll be teacher's pet yet," and his apparent humility and eagerness to learn convince her to try again. She then sings to him a lyric that ever since has been associated with Astaire, though he actually is the one being sung to, not the singer: "Nothing's impossible I have found, / For when my chin is on the ground / I pick myself up, dust myself off, / Start all over again."* But even after this indomitable credo, Astaire falls again, and this time she does give up. Her employer, hearing her chase away a customer, fires her on the spot. But Astaire insists that the employer actually see what she has "taught" him. He exhibits an intricate tap step, grabs his instructor, and together they dance around the studio in a most polished and engaging manner. The psychological expectation that this sequence creates in the film audience is immense: it is actually an exercise in mass audience manipulation, throwing upon us the tension of Astaire's restrained energy. The dancing is not just our physical release from this tension but also our reward for participating in Astaire's play-acting at ineptitude.

89

The other production number in the film, "Bojangles of Harlem," is the only one unrelated to the advancement of the story. A chorus sings the remarkable lyrics—second only to those of "Never Gonna Dance" for striking imagery (but unfortunately not quite intelligible on the soundtrack)—while Astaire reclines on the rooftops of Harlem, behind two enormous legs. The number is done in blackface, the only time Astaire performed that way, in order to further his imitation of the dance style of Bill "Bojangles" Robinson, who no doubt was an influence on Astaire. This imitation is one of Astaire's great performances: he manages to capture the essence of another great dancer, a fantastic impression of Bojangles' style—and yet remain entirely Astaire. From a modern standpoint, we might object to the use of

*"Pick Yourself Up" by Jerome Kern and Dorothy Fields, from the musical production *Swing Time*, copyright © 1936 by T. B. Harms Company; copyright renewed; used by permission.

blackface, but Arlene Croce offers this defense of Astaire's performance:

> Astaire isn't simply beyond good and evil, he's beyond good and better. The we-don't-do-these-things-anymore people should be told that we didn't do them then either, but *beyond* that, if they cared remotely for the art of dancing, they might recognize the deep dignity of homage that is in the piece—not the homage of one white to one black man, but of one great artist to another. And it is homage, not impersonation.*

THE PIRATE
(1948)

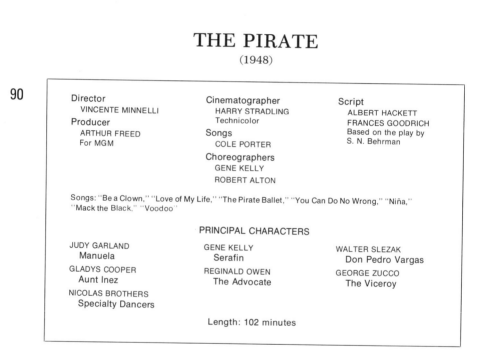

Director	Cinematographer	Script
VINCENTE MINNELLI	HARRY STRADLING	ALBERT HACKETT
Producer	Technicolor	FRANCES GOODRICH
ARTHUR FREED	Songs	Based on the play by
For MGM	COLE PORTER	S. N. Behrman
	Choreographers	
	GENE KELLY	
	ROBERT ALTON	

Songs: "Be a Clown," "Love of My Life," "The Pirate Ballet," "You Can Do No Wrong," "Niña," "Mack the Black," "Voodoo"

PRINCIPAL CHARACTERS

JUDY GARLAND	GENE KELLY	WALTER SLEZAK
Manuela	Serafin	Don Pedro Vargas
GLADYS COOPER	REGINALD OWEN	GEORGE ZUCCO
Aunt Inez	The Advocate	The Viceroy
NICOLAS BROTHERS		
Specialty Dancers		

Length: 102 minutes

In the same year as *The Pirate,* Gene Kelly starred in what was essentially a musical without music, *The Three Musketeers,* directed by George Sidney. It was a film in which the few songs were incidental, almost unnoticeable, and Kelly instead of dancing performed various feats of physical prowess in the style of Douglas Fairbanks. In *The Pirate,* the same adroit and impres-

* *The Fred Astaire and Ginger Rogers Book,* p. 107.

sive Fairbanksian activities are performed by Kelly with engaging verve, but in this film he also sings and dances. Like Fairbanks, Kelly had the ability to convey the inner life of his characterization simply by the manner in which he swung through the air or attacked an opponent—choreographed movements communicating an equivalency to the dancer's vitality and forcefulness. On a mythic level, his characterization in *The Pirate* transforms Prince Charming into Zorro. Yet because he performs some swashbuckling feats in this film, reliance on dance as a primary means of communication is dimished. The dancing is nevertheless superb, but some of it—including the film's best production number, "Niña"—is ancillary to the film's themes, and for this unusual reason *The Pirate* loses certain strengths typical of the genre's other classics. However, once we see that Kelly's swaggering, swinging portrayal of a pirate serves as an extension of the film's choreography, we discover that the film's meaning resides in the art of acting, the power to create a role and to assume an identity.

The plot concerns a young girl, Manuela, living in a small Caribbean town, who reads about the escapades of the pirate Macoco and readily envisions an adventurous existence with him, a self-contrived infatuation for a legendary figure who supposedly is far away and will never be encountered. Manuela's character should not be underestimated. By no means a romantic innocent or stereotyped daydreamer escaping from the dullness of her environment, she is on the contrary a clear-sighted realist, disappointed by her condition (she is well bred, but she must depend on her relatives for support), who goes so far as to accept the marriage proposal of the rich but unattractive mayor of the town. She yearns for new experiences and is saddened when her future husband announces to her that instead of taking her traveling, he will keep her home and tell her about Paris. She knows very well what she is doing. Capable of a realistic appraisal of her possibilities, she offers no romantic rebellion. Even when the experienced traveling player Serafin meets her, declares his own affection in Cyrano fashion, and proposes to her a world of adventure and love, she turns him down—unlike a heroine of a romance. Gene Kelly's persistence, charm, air of mystery, good looks, and wit are refused by this intelligent though inexperienced woman in favor of going through with marriage to Walter Slezak!

Spotting Manuela in the audience while his troupe is performing, Serafin hypnotizes her and learns of her infatuation with the pirate, which she reveals publicly in the song "Mack the Black." Hypnotized, Manuela sings and dances with great energy in a style completely out of keeping with her ladylike, upper-class

92

background. Awakening to this public display, she feels humiliated and flees from Serafin, who meets up with her later and
again tries unsuccessfully to talk her out of marrying the mayor.
When the enraged mayor comes to wreak vengeance on the actor,
Serafin recognizes him as Macoco, now retired on his plundered
wealth and leading a new life far from his criminal past. Oddly
enough, the irony of a girl on the verge of marrying for the sake of
convenience the same man who in his secret identity is actually
the symbol of her dream life is for the most part played down in
the film.

In fact, somewhat counter to the implications of the plot, *The
Pirate* is not at its center a musical romance, nor does it empha-

size the romantic irony inherent in its dramatic situations. The film really concerns—and it is a rather unusual subject—the nature of the acting profession itself. Both a satire on and a celebration of acting, *The Pirate* revolves around the problem of how to enforce upon reality (which is seen as drab and uneventful) the colorful romantic illusions of the stage. Acting is the noblest of work, for it enables the performer to control his existence. But to abandon one's role, to perform poorly, is disastrous. Macoco survives as long as he sustains his artificial characterization as the bourgeois mayor, but he must constantly battle his impulse to revert to his true identity as the imperious, ruthless pirate. In contrast, when the traveling trouper Serafin discovers Macoco in his new identity, he quickly becomes the manipulator of events because, as the professional performer, Serafin can loom as more menacing to all observers than the real villain. The skilled actor knows how to make an imaginative projection of the part he wishes to play. Assuming the role of Macoco, who remains silent under the threat of exposure and subsequent hanging, Serafin hopes to fire the love of Manuela and proceeds to terrify the town with his antics. As Serafin prances about in the streets, Manuela watches from a window, and is indeed impressed enough by his posturing in front of a donkey to concoct, in a daydream, the magnificent ballet sequence in which Serafin, transformed into the desperado Macoco, performs a scintillating dance on his ship.

93

Manuela also excels at acting, as we witness in her hypnotized performance of "Mack the Black." As Serafin begins to overplay his role as the notorious Macoco, the entire citizenry calls upon Manuela to sacrifice herself to his demands. Manuela fakes the proper maiden's reluctance, but sees to it that no substitute offers herself instead. Then, when she discovers Serafin's ruse, she takes her revenge first by pretending innocently to berate Serafin's acting ability. Acting, which in this film takes precedence over love, means everything to the wounded Serafin, who is caught completely off guard and ignores his role as the pirate as he attempts to defend himself as an actor: "I have a review by the *Trinidad Clarion* . . . comparing me with David Garrick." The ham in him emerges, and for the only time in the film he seems to be truly suffering.

The real Macoco, having gained an advantage from Serafin's success in publicly imitating a pirate, calls in the army and has the actor arrested and condemned to hang. Thus, the last part of the film develops into a contest of acting techniques—who will appear most convincing to the public gathered for the hanging? It is a three-way challenge between Macoco, Serafin, and Manuela, the latter two working together to overcome the performance of the real pirate, who has the benefit of all the circumstantial evidence. And the arena for this contest becomes, fittingly, a stage, when Serafin, gaining his last request from the army commandant, transforms the town square into an area for his "final appearance" with his troupe. With the excitable Macoco in an extremely tense condition, Serafin's one hope is to draw out of him a public confession, and he almost succeeds in getting the mayor under hypnosis. But it is Manuela, suddenly discovering who the mayor really is, who effects the public revelation. Pretending to be hypnotized once more, she descends from the gallery to the stage and sings to Serafin "Love of My Life," a song calculated to draw out the mayor. The song itself is an overwhelmingly emotional pronouncement of her love for the pirate about to be hanged. The mayor finally cracks under the pressure and in a rage declares his true identity (pointing out, with much justification, that Serafin could never command the respect of a pirate crew, and that after all, Serafin's pirate portrayal is merely an extension of a stereotyped swashbuckling role that exists only in the theater). Macoco destroys his opportunity to rid himself forever of his true identity because he is an amateur performer, one who confuses acting with reality and so loses his grip on the part he creates for himself.

94

The film ends with a sequence indicating that after a lapse of time Manuela has joined Serafin's troupe. She and Serafin perform a riotous comic number, "Be a Clown," in appropriate dress. The number sums up some thematic motifs of the film: the clown is the archetypal actor, and "all the world loves a clown."

SINGIN' IN THE RAIN
(1952)

Directors	Cinematographer	Script
GENE KELLY	HAROLD ROSSON	ADOLPH GREEN
STANLEY DONEN	Technicolor	BETTY COMDEN
Producer	Songs	
ARTHUR FREED	ARTHUR FREED	
For MGM	NACIO HERB BROWN	
	Choreographer	
	GENE KELLY	

Songs: "Would You," "Singin' in the Rain," "All I Do Is Dream of You," "I've Got a Feeling You're Fooling," "Wedding of the Painted Doll," "Should I?" "Make 'Em Laugh," "You Were Meant for Me," "You Are My Lucky Star," "Fit as a Fiddle and Ready for Love," "Good Morning," "Beautiful Girl," "Broadway Melody," "Broadway Rhythm"

PRINCIPAL CHARACTERS

GENE KELLY	DONALD O'CONNOR	DEBBIE REYNOLDS
Don Lockwood	Cosmo Brown	Kathy Selden
JEAN HAGEN	DOUGLAS FOWLEY	MILLARD MITCHELL
Lina Lamont	Roscoe Dexter	R. F. Simpson
RITA MORENO	MADGE BLAKE	KING DONOVAN
Zelda Zanders	Dora Bailey	Rod
CYD CHARISSE		
Dancer		

Length: 103 minutes

95

One of the most genial of musicals, this film has all the substance that one would expect of a work that credits as its source only the song used as its title. But if the film avoids any moments of profundity, its surface nevertheless glitters continuously, and the fluff of its subject matter remains peculiarly suitable to a film about Hollywood. It is a cordial satire on the nature of movie illusions, particularly in regard to the industry's problems in converting to sound in the late 1920s. The entire film deals with the difficulty of discerning reality in the midst of so much illusion, though the development of this theme is so closely allied to obvious weaknesses in various characters that it never produces the least sense of ambiguity. We, the audience, are always able to discern the truth, and eventually everyone involved in the film is too.

The reality-illusion motif is played for gags throughout. The film begins with Don Lockwood and Lina Lamont, two glamorous silent screen stars, being interviewed at the premiere of their latest film. Gene Kelly plays the role of Don with all his usual charm and enthusiasm and conveys a tremendous sense of Don's versatility and showmanship. Jean Hagen's excellent portrayal of

Lina, the main satiric object of the film, makes this character exactly the opposite: a vacuous beauty, petty, self-serving, without any talent. In this first sequence in front of the movie theater she remains silent while Don relates to the radio reporters a fake, publicity-styled narrative of his rise to stardom. During this narrative, however, brief scenes are intercut showing the truth about his early career. The image he concocts verbally for the public is one of a dignified professional history, while the visual intercuts reveal the truth of his anything-but-dignified vaudeville background, hoofing with his lifetime friend Cosmo in an amusing burlesque act and singing "Fit as a Fiddle and Ready for Love." Yet despite the studio-designed biographical distortions, the illusion of Don Lockwood's biography is not at all damaging to anyone; underneath his present glamor, he really is talented.

Lina Lamont, on the other hand, is a fraud. Arrogant and vain about her imagined talents, she seeks an opportunity to speak to her public, which she assumes will continue to love her even with her peculiar voice (she is not, of course, aware that her squeaky voice is comical and that her elocution is vulgar). Under certain conditions her illusions, which are self-delusions, might create sympathy for her, but her possessiveness about her co-star Don, her assumption that she "owns" him, and her mistreatment of the ingenue Kathy, whom Don falls in love with, mark her as the "heavy" of the plot. It is, very likely, inevitable from the start of the film that she will be finally exposed and her undeservedly successful career brought to an end.

Throughout the film, the contrast is maintained between Lina and the good characters—the three who have genuine musical talents, Don, Kathy, and Cosmo. *Singin' in the Rain,* more clearly than most musicals—but definitely sharing with them this genre trait—associates musical talent with moral character. These three are, therefore, in their nonmusical existences within the films, more confident, more willing to speak with sincerity, than others who have no talent. Because they are characters with the capacity for an intensive emotional experience in music, they are inwardly happy. Their musical performances are the effervescence of their personalities.

Probably the two most memorable instances of this are Cosmo's madcap, acrobatic dance to cheer up Don, "Make 'Em Laugh," and Don's zany performance of the title number in a drenching rain, to the bewilderment of a policeman and other passers-by. Swinging around a lamppost or splashing in puddles, Gene Kelly overwhelmingly demonstrates Don's inner joy about his love for Kathy. In a cinematic environment where the good people are also those with all the talent, it is just a matter of time before the untalented Lina is upstaged and loses her place to the new star, Kathy.

From the start, the real villain is pretentiousness, or simply pretense. The match between Don and Kathy gets off to a shaky start because both are not yet in touch with themselves. Don, after the introductory sequence, meets Kathy while escaping from his overexuberant fans, who want to tear his clothes apart for mementoes. Don and Kathy argue over the respectability of different types of performing arts, and she claims, snobbishly, that as a legitimate stage actress her profession is nobler than his. That same night Don discovers, to Kathy's devastating embarrassment, that she is only a chorus girl in a burlesque-type routine. This of course ends their mutual posturing. Later they find compatibility in their real talents as singers and dancers (though Debbie Reynolds's achievement in the latter category does not stand up too well in comparison with those of O'Connor and Kelly, and in the big "Broadway Ballet" number, Cyd Charisse, with no other part in the film, is summoned to dance with Kelly).

The film's satire aims broadly at the Hollywood method of creating cinematic illusion on the basis of very little substance in reality. As the sound film threatens the economic viability of their silent film, Lina and Don must convert their film to sound. Lina cannot speak, let alone sing, and Kathy becomes her screen voice, though the public is not to be told. Don too needs to take elocution lessons, but with his natural abilities the sound film poses no problem for him. This point is dramatically reinforced in a sequence where Don and Cosmo confound the elocution professor with a tour de force rendition of an exercise: "Moses supposes his toes-es are roses, but Moses supposes erroneously." At the same time, the studio itself practically breaks down in its attempt to master the medium of sound: microphones are misplaced, wires are tripped over, and synchronization fails pathetically during a sneak preview. Yet the satire manifests itself in a positive fashion. We do not think less of Hollywood for revealing a few of its tricks, because the film itself suggests that under the illusion lie the real talents of the star performers. After all, this genre is premised on the idea of real musical talent bursting through whatever temporary restrictions are placed on those who have the genius of song and dance.

98

THE BAND WAGON
(1953)

Director	Cinematographer	Script
VINCENTE MINNELLI	HARRY JACKSON	BETTY COMDEN
Producer	Technicolor	ADOLPH GREEN
ARTHUR FREED	Songs	
For MGM	ARTHUR SCHWARTZ	
	HOWARD DIETZ	
	Choreographer	
	MICHAEL KIDD	

Songs: "By Myself," "A Shine on Your Shoes," "Dancing in the Dark," "I Love Louisa," "That's Entertainment," "I Guess I'll Have To Change My Plan," "Triplets," "New Sun in the Sky," "High and Low," "Louisiana Hayride," "Beggar's Waltz," "You and the Night and the Music," "Something To Remember You By," "Girl Hunt Ballet"

PRINCIPAL CHARACTERS

FRED ASTAIRE	CYD CHARISSE	JACK BUCHANAN
Tony Hunter	Gabrielle Gerard	Jeffrey Cordova
OSCAR LEVANT	NANETTE FABRAY	JAMES MITCHELL
Lester Marton	Lily Marton	Paul Byrd

Length: 112 minutes

This is one of the few American films structured in terms of a theme, and an unusual theme at that: the need to reconcile the two abstract notions of art and entertainment, which are presumed to conflict during part of the film and are finally shown to be essential to each other by the end. As an esthetic concept, entertainment pure and simple is shown to be insufficient—its satisfactions do not last and the public can tire of it. On the other hand, art—"high art," such as that which self-consciously intends to be uplifting—will just not reach the public if it is not entertaining.

The first idea, entertainment, is embodied in the role of Tony Hunter, a movie star in decline who has lost most of his fans. At the very beginning of the film his characteristic top hat and cane are up for auction but fail to get a bid even at fifty cents. Arriving in New York, presumably to make a comeback on the Broadway stage, he finds at the railroad station a friendly group of reporters, who immediately abandon him when the star they have actually come to greet gets off the train. He then proceeds to walk, not dance, out of the station, singing "I'll go my way by myself," a remarkably affecting ballad capturing the spirit of isolation, failure, and encroaching middle age. A short time later, Tony dances to "A Shine on Your Shoes" in a Times Square penny arcade, in what is perhaps the most memorable routine in the film. Enlivened by the atmosphere of New York (which, as he notes, is decadent), Tony animates the arcade with his singing and dancing. The entertainment unites all sorts of people passing through and also involves a large shoeshine man who dances a tap solo and a mysterious contraption that seemingly does nothing until magically given life by Tony—when it turns into a magnificent calliope.

After this beginning, the remainder of the film achieves several brilliant moments, but there is some falling off as the other thematic aspect is established. A new style in musical comedy is dreamed up by the personification of high art, Jeffrey Cordova, a writer-producer-director-actor filled with ideas about elevating the musical genre to the level of the "classics." The comedy writers Lester and Lily Marton have created a simple entertainment, to be called *The Band Wagon*, to star Tony Hunter, but Cordova turns it into a modernized musical version of the Faust legend and insists on co-starring Gabrielle (Gaby) Girard, a ballerina, as Hunter's dance partner. The concept of a musical Faust is overpowering to Tony, and though he is skeptical about the project at first, he is won over by the writers and the director. They sing to him the theme song of the film, "That's Entertainment," and he joins in. In that song, the justification for all the performing arts, from *Oedipus Rex* "where the boy kills his father and causes a lot of bother" to "the clown with his pants falling down," is the exhilaration given to audiences while they are being entertained. But the reason for this stems from a famous rhetorical passage in Shakespeare, paraphrased in the song as: "the world is a stage, the stage is a world of entertainment." That's not quite what Shakespeare meant by "All the world's a stage," but the film borrows the concept for its own purposes, and from this point on attempts to depict the joining of quality art and widely appealing entertainment.

The merger of culture and popular art, another way of stating the thematic alternatives, creates the plot difficulties. The ballerina represents the higher claims of culture. Gaby at first projects a disdainful attitude toward Tony who represents popular art. She is cold as well as nasty, and in their initial meeting they argue. But culture and popular art only appear to be in opposition. As the two performers begin to work together, Gaby finds that she need not compromise her standards by dancing with Tony, and he discovers no difficulty in dancing with her, though he at first anticipated that he would be incompetent doing so. The culmination of this realization occurs in a beautifully photographed dance at night in Central Park. The two, while wondering if they really can dance together, stroll across a crowded dance floor, watching the nonprofessional couples enjoying the summer entertainment. We expect them to dance right there, and it is a fine touch of Minnelli's that he prolongs this expectation by allowing the two dancers to pass through the scene without joining in. Only when they are isolated from the other dancers do they begin a few trial steps to the music emanating from the background of the dance floor; these trial steps are done individually, as if the two were practicing alone. When they finally begin their dance together (with Gaby's white dress set off spectacularly, for a color film, against the surrounding darkness), they successfully reconcile one of the problematical threads of the plot by demonstrating that proponents of culture and of popular art can work in unison.

The film at this point has not yet demonstrated the premise that art and entertainment can mesh completely in the musical form, which is the burden of the main plot and is visualized in the production of the show. Under the domination of Cordova's acting and directing, the show becomes further and further removed from the plausible range of popular art by the increasing pretentiousness of its staging and its themes. First he places the values of art well above those of entertainment (the tyranny of the highbrow), and then he begins to enlarge his own role at the expense of Tony and Gaby's parts (the tyranny of the ham). Predictably, the show is a failure, its reception presented visually by a drawing of an egg hatched during the New Haven opening night.

100

101

To salvage the show, Tony takes over the production, which is willingly relinquished by the defeated and repentant Cordova. Since Tony has already shown in personal terms that he now incorporates both high and popular art, he is the most fitting representative of "combined culture" to guide the show to its needed rebirth. This time there is no opposition; this is symbolized by the excellent but simply staged new production numbers in which the two men perform, "I Guess I'll Have To Change My Plan" and "Triplets" (where they are joined by Lily Marton in the comic highlight of the film).

The climax of the film in terms of both plot and theme is the "Girl Hunt Ballet," a stunningly apt joining of ballet and jazz dancing by Tony and Gaby. This number manages to convert into true visual and dramatic art its unlikely source material: the era's symbol of vulgar popular art, the private detective novels of Mickey Spillane. The parody of Spillane is carried out by Tony's straightforward voice-over commentary, speaking Minnelli's burlesque of the writer's prose. The dancing itself easily blends stylized melodrama, serious romantic encounters, and ludicrous plotting without ever violating the tone or the consistency of approach.

The film concludes in an unusual way, with the now-successful cast of the show assembled on stage to express their appreciation to Tony for setting them on the right track. Cordova and the

Martons again sing "That's Entertainment," but as Tony joins them the reprise is directed to the movie audience. The screen becomes in the last image a stage itself because "the stage is a world." Finally, dressed in formal evening attire, the stars of the film sing of the ultimate compatibility of culture and popular art, merged in the ongoing association of performers and audience. Success lies in the mutual participation of the entertainment experience: the stage as a microcosm of the world lives supremely in the performers' capacity to impart that entertainment and the audience's to receive it.

FUNNY GIRL
(1968)

Director	Cinematographer	Script
WILLIAM WYLER	HARRY STRADLING	ISOBEL LENNART
Producer	Technicolor	Based on the musical
RAY STARK	Panavision	play by Isobel Lennart
For Columbia	Original Songs	
	JULE STYNE	
	BOB MERRILL	
	Choreographer	
	HERBERT ROSS	

Original Songs: "I'm the Greatest Star," "If a Girl Isn't Pretty," "Roller Skate Rag," "His Love Makes Me Beautiful," "People," "You Are Woman, I Am Man," "Don't Rain on My Parade," "Funny Girl," "A Temporary Arrangement." Other Songs: "Second Hand Rose," "My Man," "Swan Burlesque," "I'd Rather Be Blue," "Sadie, Sadie"

PRINCIPAL CHARACTERS

BARBRA STREISAND	OMAR SHARIF	KAY MEDFORD
Fanny Brice	Nick Arnstein	Rose Brice
WALTER PIDGEON	MAE QUESTEL	LEE ALLEN
Florenz Ziegfeld	Mrs. Strakosh	Eddie Ryan
ANNE FRANCIS	GERALD MOHR	
Georgia James	Branca	

Length: 151 minutes

Film biographies of real-life stars do not often produce notable dramatic musicals, since the careers depicted seem comprised of one success after another. Most of the best of these films such as *The Jolson Story* provide mere narrative linkage between a great many musical numbers. To create drama in such films, the Hollywood formula stressed either the "early hardships" or the romantic life of the star, but aside from *Funny Girl* and a few others the drama of musical biographies seldom seems convincing. Wyler handles his material to emphasize the inherent drama by counterpointing Fanny Brice's accomplishments as a performer with her failures in her private life with Nick Arnstein, the colorful gambler she loved and lost. Throughout, an ambiguity enriches the film's texture through the revolving motifs of the private anxieties and the public successes of a great entertainer.

In the tradition of the best musicals, the production numbers carry much of the film's meaning, both in terms of theme and character, beginning with her mother's defense of Fanny's appearance: "Though she looks a bit off-balance, she possesses golden talents."* When, as a young unknown failing to get a chorus job, Fanny prolongs her audition by singing "I'm the Greatest Star," we learn about the kind of artist's self-image she possesses, and we know that her persistence insures the eventual recognition of her talent. The comic numbers, such as "Sadie, Sadie, Married Lady" and "Second-Hand Rose," reveal her humorous ironic style, modifying the romanticism that at other times dominates her nature. The pathos generated by "My Man" magically captures the romantic, almost tragic, side of the singer's biography. The alternating ironic and idealistic sensibilities create an ambiguity in Fanny's psychological makeup and produce the thematic depth of this film.

103

A most striking example of Fanny's complex personality is captured in the title. Fanny is a funny girl by choice, a gifted comedienne by nature and training, having decided early in life that her plainness could be used to her own advantage if she alluded to it with such geniality that it became a virtue—humanizing, if not quite equaling, the beauty of her talents. Fanny is a brilliant performer, but beneath her brashness is a sensitive, insecure young woman—an incurable romantic who craves that superior kind of lover capable of appreciating inner beauty. Her need is to conquer the world, to prove her ability, and to overcome what she considers her physical handicap of plainness. "I'm a bagel on a plate full of onion rolls," she says, but in Fanny's milieu the remark is no joke when we think about it: the bagel is ultimately more beautiful than the roll.

To be misjudged while aspiring to external beauty, however, is a disturbing possibility to Fanny, who at one point argues with the great producer Ziegfeld against appearing in one of his musical "glorifications" of the American girl, "His Love Makes Me Beautiful." She loses the argument, but fearing that audiences

will laugh at her, she upstages everyone by appearing in the number costumed as a pregnant bride. As long as she controls the comedy and deliberately creates the laughter, she can sustain her public role of the beautiful performer superior to the ordinary standards of acceptability, based on such trivial things as physical beauty. "I ought to fire you, but I love talent," Ziegfeld says to her, accepting her role and thus succumbing to the control of the performing artist, the creator of a stage personality that is itself a work of art.

Nick Arnstein symbolizes something else, the possession of which means more to Fanny than any other sign of public adoration. As the Prince Charming who actually perceives her inner beauty and falls in love with her, Nick becomes for her both beloved object and testimony to her real worth. There is no question about their mutual love, but Fanny needs Nick for the reassurance of her validity as a person, while he only loves rather than needs her. Although we do not fully comprehend Nick, we understand quickly enough his two main functions in the film. He is, first of all, the incredibly attractive mystery man who descends into Fanny's world and brings her to that cultured and refined world to which he seems inexplicably to belong. He does not pursue Fanny, and his seduction of her in a private dining room is pictured in her mind as a kind of meeting with destiny. She pursues him, literally, in the spectacularly staged number "Don't Rain on My Parade," and he is irresistibly seduced into marriage.

Having initiated Fanny into her idealized world, Nick is no longer able to sustain his own romantic life style. His other function in the film, as Fanny's husband, is to rebel against her engulfing spirit. He exists as an aristocrat without funds, with no legitimate profession and no possibility of permanent employment (even an executive position would destroy the basis of his romantic, mysterious nature and make him, for Fanny, less than he is). Thus, he lives as a continual sojourner, gaining and losing "stakes," fluctuating between having a good deal of money and being broke. "That's how I live," he explains honestly to Fanny. Fanny's desire to "bankroll" him is futile—she cannot domesticate him and still keep him as her romantic ideal. His pride and wanderlust preclude accepting anything from her; he would rather associate with shady characters to maintain his independence. When Nick naively gets involved in a confidence scheme, he feels humiliated, refuses to fight in court, and pleads guilty. Sentenced and shorn of his dignity, he insists that Fanny divorce him, but her love remains undiminished by Nick's attitude. The film ends with the most simply staged and most affecting of Fanny's songs, "My Man," in which she renews her vow of eternal love for Nick, who has abandoned her, for whatever he is, he's her man.

105

The ending very clearly establishes Fanny's realization of her predicament and its hopelessness. It led to an unfortunate sequel, *Funny Lady,* but it is not in itself an indecisive conclusion. Her private grief is submerged in her public performance of "My Man," in a sense integrating her ironic and idealistic modes, but our response is probably directed to the main characters' sad awareness of their incompatible love. However, our perception of the film as a whole is not limited by the regrets projected from the irreconcilable position at the end. Basically, the film encompasses a theme that deals with the ambiguities of achievement and happiness—as seen from the perspective of public success. Wyler presents most of the film as a flashback in the mind of Fanny, a great star standing in an empty theater a few hours before showtime and another personal triumph. "Ziegfeld is waiting for *me,*" she says at the beginning of the film, as a comment on her status, but having achieved wisdom as well as fame, Fanny reflects on both the glory of life and the vanity of ambition.

CABARET

(1972)

Director	Cinematographer	Script
BOB FOSSE	GEOFFREY UNSWORTH	JAY PRESSON ALLEN
Producer	Technicolor	Based on the musical play
CY FEUER	Songs	"Cabaret" by Joe Masteroff,
For Allied Artists	JOHN KANDER	the play "I Am a Camera" by
and ABC Pictures	FRED EBB	John Van Druten, and the book
	Choreographer	*Goodbye to Berlin* by
	BOB FOSSE	Christopher Isherwood

Songs: "Wilkommen," "Mein Herr," "Two Ladies," "Maybe This Time I'll Be Lucky," "Money, Money, Money," "Heiraten," "If You Could See Her Through My Eyes," "Tomorrow Belongs to Me," "Cabaret"

PRINCIPAL CHARACTERS

LIZA MINNELLI	JOEL GREY	HELMUT GRIEM
Sally Bowles	Master of Ceremonies	Maximilian von Heune
MICHAEL YORK	FRITZ WEPPER	MARISA BERENSON
Brian Roberts	Fritz Wendel	Natalia Landauer
		ELISABETH NEUMANN-VIERTEL
		Fraulein Schneider

Length: 123 minutes

106

Cabaret moves the movie musical very directly into the stage tradition of Bertolt Brecht, wherein the songs provide a running commentary on the action of the plot. At this time it is not clear how influential this film will prove to be, since film may be inherently resistant to the Brechtian form, which always incorporates a framing device. That device in *Cabaret* is supplied in the person of the Master of Ceremonies at the Kit Kat Klub, whose reappearances afford us an ironic slant on the drama that unfolds in the rest of the film. *Cabaret*'s success with its framing device may prove to be unique, since the technique of staging musical numbers in the cabaret that employs the heroine of the film is perfectly suited to the atmospheric demands of the script. In 1931 Berlin (which is just about the era of Brecht's development of his theatrical techniques in that city), the decadence and the instability of society are readily mirrored in a nightclub devoted to satisfying the decadent instincts of a pleasure-seeking public intent on escaping from the problems of the real world.

Each musical number relates with some immediacy to the situation of the moment in the lives of the main characters, unsettled young men and women in a spiritually bankrupt society. The central idea reflects one of the traditional problems of moral philosophy, *carpe diem*, living for the day in a world too complicated to be truly endurable. Hitler's iconography looms in

the background, an effective motif forty years later when we know what Nazism meant for Germany. But the film contrasts that alternative of fascism only with the useless life style of the bohemian Sally Bowles. Sally carries on recklessly, dreaming of becoming a movie star, but ends where we find her at the beginning, as a performer in the Kit Kat Klub, having gone through three lovers and an abortion along the way. The introductory song and the final number welcome the audience of the club (as well as the film audience) to the transitory entertainments of a grotesquely unreal world. The presentation offers its own moral justification that life must be regarded as a cabaret (that is, an opportunity for entertainment). Since these numbers enclose the series of Sally's adventures, which consist of various forms of unsatisfactory pursuit along with the whole series of degrading activities that capsulize the rise of the Nazi party, the film projects a cynical, virtually bitter view of the world. The strident musical presentation of a nihilistic philosphy fascinates us without being depressing, because the era covered remains historically closed and never quite menacing enough to threaten the structure of contemporary society.

For all the seriousness of the plot, *Cabaret*'s style disengages our sympathies from the characters, for they too are associated with the make-believe world that the Master of Ceremonies urges on the club's clientele. Each major incident leads us back to the cabaret's incessant burlesque of *all* matters, even the rise of the fascists. The Master of Ceremonies presides over the vulgarization of all values as the supreme cynic who ridicules politics, love, sex, and the possibility of any real relationships between people. It is self-parody that finally establishes parody as the only value in a nihilistic society.

The assault on values appears from the very beginning as the Master of Ceremonies bids welcome to the customers of the cabaret, noting that in the club "life is beautiful." Since he appears with white clown makeup emphasizing a continually lecherous grin, yellow teeth, and aging skin, he himself represents the decadent artificiality that stylizes all the productions in the Kit Kat Klub. But even elsewhere in the cabaret beauty cannot be found. The chorus line is made up to resemble worn-out whores; the few who might under ordinary circumstances appear somewhat attractive are powdered so as to reflect the garish coloring of the stage lights. All the women are deliberately mannered to stress sexual invitation at the same time that they satirize the whole notion of sexuality. Indeed, the best-looking one in the cabaret is the Master of Ceremonies himself when he appears in a later number dressed as a woman, bare-legged and wearing a wig. The hope for beauty and pleasure trumpeted from the start by the Master of Ceremonies is meant to appear overtly insincere. The opening is intercut with the arrival in Berlin of Brian, a Cambridge student working on his dissertation, who for a few brief periods in the film suggests a naive innocence and enthusiasm before he succumbs to the lure of Sally's bohemian life style. Through the intercutting, Brian is seemingly ushered into the film with the opening welcome of the Master of Ceremonies, and though we may at the time be uncertain about Brian's fate, the heavy ironic tone even then suggests that he will eventually become part of the cabaret, at least spiritually.

If the possibility of beauty is disposed of in the opening number, the possibility of sincerity goes next, as Sally in imitation of Marlene Dietrich performs "Mein Herr" with a chorus of girls similarly displayed Dietrich-style on chairs, performing salacious calisthenics. Subtlety and good taste are demolished next as the Master of Ceremonies stages a wrestling match between two large women in a greased ring, moving around behind them and spraying them, to the howling approval of the audience. He puts a spot of grease under his nose and for a second does a Hitler mime. The ridicule of Hitler is a motif throughout, which Fosse carefully designs to seem less and less funny as the film progresses. Later during a ridiculous Bavarian-type dance at the Kit Kat Klub, we witness intercut shots of Nazis beating someone up.

108

As the film begins to explore the more leisurely dissipations of a valueless society, the garish production numbers undermine even the pretensions of pleasure. Brian confesses problems about his sexual identity to Sally, who tries to seduce him. Eventually they do have an affair that seems to coincide with a growing love for each other. Then the epicurean Baron arrives on the scene, meeting Sally by chance. He offers to give her a ride, and as she glances at his limousine, Fosse cuts abruptly to Sally and the Master of Ceremonies doing a duet at the cabaret, "Money." But even money, which "makes the world go round," loses real significance as it is crassly expounded in the song. To the poor people in the film—Sally, Brian, and their friend Fritz (who is attracted to a rich Jewish girl at this dangerous point in German history)—the attraction of money is only one more source of dissipation and does not run deep. Fritz reveals that he too is a Jew, and marries the girl, not for money but for love. At the Kit Kat Klub the Master of Ceremonies, no sentimentalist, sings of his affection to a performer who is in an ape costume ("If You Could See Her Through My Eyes") and ends up blasting all sentiment with his cynical plea for the customers' tolerance of his ape lover: "She doesn't look Jewish at all." Sally and Brian are attracted to the Baron more for physical reasons than for his wealth—and both have sexual affairs with him, surprising each other with mutual confessions during an argument. The Baron then leaves both of them, but only after the *menage à trois* has been ridiculed in the "Two for One" number at the cabaret.

109

The two most effective numbers are given political references by their audiences. In a peaceful outdoor restaurant, the Baron and Brian watch a handsome blonde boy sing what at first appears to be a song of youth and hope, "Tomorrow Belongs to Me," but as the camera slowly tilts down we discover that the boy is a member of the Hitler Youth, and the charm instantly transforms itself into a grim threat as all the many children and most of the adults in the restaurant join in, while the boy raises his hand in a Nazi salute. The film ends with Sally performing the final number, "Cabaret," immediately after parting with Brian. They both realize, after her impulsive decision to have an abortion, that they could not succeed together indefinitely. The sadness, the emptiness, the futility of her experiences are reflected in the lines "Life is a cabaret, old chum, / Come to the cabaret." The irony of the alternative—"What good is sitting alone in your room? / Come, hear the music play"*—suggests that neither turning away nor participating in the pleasures of escape

*"Cabaret" by John Kander and Fred Ebb, copyright © 1966 by The New York Times Music Corporation (Sunbeam Music Division), New York, New York; all rights reserved; used by permission.

really works. Then the Master of Ceremonies makes his final appearence, as in the film's opening, repeating his claim that "here life is beautiful." Fosse gives us another glimpse of the grotesque, beefy, all-female band, but not to reinforce a satiric point—that would be excessive in this context; the real point is that the blatant lies about beauty piously pronounced by the Master of Ceremonies are primarily an attack on the grossness of the customers' lives. The film ends with shots of the audience at the Kit Kat Klub, changed very much from the beginning, for the spectators are mainly Nazis and their sympathizers. The middle-class pleasure-seekers of the cabaret have been transformed into the fascists of the new era. The old innocent decadence has given way to a far more insidious evil, though one that retains the Master of Ceremonies within the symbolic framework of the old style. His cynicism may prove a mode of survival, but the value of survival in such a place in such an era is itself doubtful.

3

THE NIGHTMARE WORLD

FEARS AND HORRORS

Despite its honorable origins in the German expressionist cinema, despite its artistic triumphs and its popular successes, the horror genre richly deserves its abject status among critics and audiences, and even among many of its own followers who half-ashamedly confess to an addiction for it. It seems to me incontrovertible that the horror genre in the American cinema has been primarily exploitative, artless, frequently without taste or restraint or sense, and generally unworthy of serious attention. And yet the horror genre, ultimately, is a major genre because major artists of our time have worked seriously in it and produced notable films that range beyond the depiction of the horrific event to probe the nightmare world hidden in all of us. The conjuring up of monsters of the mind and the objectifying of them in the cinema is a symbolic form of exorcism, which very likely the general public intuitively grasped from the genre long before William Friedkin's *The Exorcist* (1973) popularized the subject. In an era that intellectually gives little credence to devils, witches, and monsters, but lives continuously with massive violence, perversion, and nihilism, the horror film provides us with a protected access to a nightmare world otherwise shunted outside of civilization by the twentieth-century forces of sophistication, science, and sociology.

The cinema of horror concretizes this nightmare world—our abstract fears of destruction and death. The midnight visits of vampires, the laboratory-induced reincarnations, the skull deformities, the murders in the fog—these visual images of the genre may be the symbols of our fears rather than the psychological source of them, but terror without a body is terror deprived of a means of menacing us. Nevertheless, it is lamentable that along with the whole modern movement toward cinematic explicitness in all genres, the horror genre should in recent years have lost much of its suggestive power. The giant shark rising from the ocean in Steven Spielberg's *Jaws* (1975) is merely a familiar creature of the sea, and the havoc it creates confined to the physical world and subject to the laws of nature; it will not leave the beach with us. In contrast, Carl Dreyer's Danish film *Vampyr* (1932), a tour de force of implicit horror, seems only a remote ancestor of the blood-lust films of the seventies. However, the genre is still open to creative talents who can give form to the explicit materials demanded by producers for financial success, and still suggest the unlimited terrors lurking in the recesses of our nightmare world.

If the depiction of archetypal fears is one aspect of the genre, the process whereby these fears become dramatic incidents in a film reveals at least two other genre traits: the degree of unpreparedness on the part of the endangered victim, and the vitality or strength of the source of horror. The source is never, for instance, merely a human murderer. It may turn out to be so later in the film, but when it strikes, it is either supernaturally empowered (psychotics always have great energy in the cinema and usually the strength of several men), or simply a supernatural creature, a Frankenstein monster, a zombie, an immortal force likely to return for another killing (or worse, a film sequel). As for the characteristic of unpreparedness, Hitchcock himself has elaborated on the distinction between the kind of suddenness typical of ordinary films and his own brand of suspense, which plays on the gradual development of the potential horror in a situation—known to the audience, but beyond the film character's awareness. And certainly Hitchcock is right in the psychological sense, as well as in the esthetic sense: murder in a dark alley which he has often discounted, is less effective than murder in a crowded, well-lit U.N. Building. But even so, we will always have ordinary films with us, and if filmmakers cannot pull off the Master's style of suspense, mere shock will be used instead. Often the duration of an incident designed to shock is prolonged foolishly past the point where the audience fully expects it; for example, the never-exhausted use of the situation of the innocent young woman exploring the darkened, murder-filled house (which originated in the eighteenth-century gothic novel in England and was so overused even then that Jane Austen, in the 1790s, wrote one of her early novels parodying it). In such sequences our common sense tells us of the immediate danger of which the woman seems entirely unaware.

It is worth reflecting on the motif of exploration in the house of horrors. There are two types of exploration in such situations; one is the relatively logical procedure involved when the searcher does not know that some horror is lurking in the house. In this aspect of the search motif, the levels of irony reinforce the ele-

113

ment of terror in the sequence. A second type of exploration far more common in the genre occurs when the character actually is aware of great danger, even when the threat is ambiguous. This intrusion into the haunted house by a fearful yet determined figure, often a defenseless woman, almost always establishes an identity between the searcher and the audience; we may not know exactly what evil will befall the searcher, but we sympathize with him or her at each turn of the perilous corridors and at the opening of each squeaking door (in many low budget horror films, one can of oil would convert all the eccentric mansions into normal houses).

Yet if we sympathize with the irrational pursuit of the nightmare—when a telephone call to the police station or waiting until daylight would diffuse the inherent terror of the place—what does this say about our own involvement in the situation? It does not seem to be some insatiable curiosity, for that could be satisfied by the characters' examining the threatening situation.

It seems that as frightened as we are of the dark horrors ahead of the searcher, we must force ourselves to explore them, to continue on toward that confrontation with whatever ultimate form the nightmare can take. But it perhaps goes even further than that. The final horror is extremely limited in its possibilities. And do we not know in advance what the worst of these possibilities are? An unusually brutal man, halfman, or full monster with a knife, either lunging at our back or jumping from the shadows at our face. There are some other alternatives, ghosts of indescribable forms, but essentially, for the horror to be as unbearable as we hope it is when we purchase our tickets, it has to represent death—the death of the searcher, and indeed the death of our surrogate self. Perhaps the ultimate irrationality of this typical moment of horror in the nightmare film represents our own subconscious desire to confront our inevitable dread: to meet death before we really die. Or looked at another way, such moments of horror are cathartic, symbolic suicides, speaking directly to our hidden wish to attempt everything and to survive unaltered, to get murdered without being murdered.

114

THE CINEMA OF REASON AND NIGHTMARE

The nightmare world, with which we all have a personal and very private acquaintance, derives from the suppressed fears within every individual and differs for each of us, at least in its details. Some very clever illustrators and makeup artists design movie monsters that are effective in capturing some universal idea of horror but of course strike us as original all the same. A monster readily visualized by everyone is probably not very monstrous, though there do seem to be a few images derived from certain real "monstrosities" that have permeated the unconsciousness of the human race (prehistoric animals and huge spiders, rats, bats, roaches, and so on). Nevertheless, the depiction of the horrific represents a major challenge to filmmakers, for by its nature the cinema objectifies and externalizes abstract concepts so that they take on a visual embodiment. If the horror film is to succeed, some care must be taken that the essence of whatever is supposed to be the horrible object remains suggestively terrifying. A monster once seen becomes rather quickly assimilable into the environment of the film and correspondingly less intimidating. Its mere physical appearance will not do for long.

This is the basic reason for the lack of success of so many films that concern the threat of some outside force such as a monster or a creature from another planet. Once the force is visualized, we feel that it then can be handled and destroyed sooner or later, and during the process the threat loses its initial impact. Science fiction films differ from true horror films, though they both frequently employ monsters, in that the implicit danger in the former is supposed to originate in the outer world and to be dealt with accordingly, whereas the dangers in the world of the horror film are symbols of our nightmares, projections of our inner reality—even though the necessity of the cinematic form requires, in most cases, some overtly corporeal menace. The horror film aims at psychological effects, the science fiction film at logical possibilities. Many aspects of both genres overlap, certainly, since the minor examples of both aim for sensational depictions of terror with little regard for the sense of good science fiction or the sensibility of the real horror film.*

When worked out properly, the science fiction film is premised on people's ability to handle things that intrude into their comfortable physical reality. For example, in the Howard Hawks-Christian Nyby science fiction film *The Thing* (1951), the strange vegetable monster is destroyed by electrocution (that is, it is fried), and even though the film ends with a warning that earth may be repeatedly invaded by other monsters or civilizations, we can hardly worry about that possibility as long as we have electricity. But in the nightmare world, dreams recur; fears sometimes take on new shapes but seldom disappear entirely (if they did, so would the practice of psychiatry). The stake is inevitably thrust into Dracula's heart—over and over again. Dracula returns, not merely for crass commercial reasons, but because he has become rooted in the psychology of modern moviegoing soci-

115

*For an example, see the discussion of *Invasion of the Body Snatchers,* pp. 136–38.

ety. The monsters that spring from our own psyche are either the zombies we constantly recreate or symbolic archetypal figures of evil. At the end of a science fiction film, order is restored—the spaceship crew or earth itself is saved, permanently. When we awaken from the nightmare world, we have only a temporary reprieve; another dream may follow on the next night. In that case, all that has happened has been an evaporation of a monster, which simply returns to its spiritual or disembodied form, to be picked up by our brainwaves and re-embodied sometime in another film.

The nightmare genre is thus not entirely suited to rational explanations, since its primary thrust is toward the exploration of emotional states—horror and the more or less irrational reponse to it. If the source of the horror were itself entirely rational (for instance, an escaped lion on a city street), an irrational response to it would reveal no more than outrage or cowardice, but rational plot patterns run counter to the basics of the genre. It is necessary, in those horror films where at least a rational explanation is offered, to postpone that logical moment until all the usual effects of the genre have been achieved. But it is not at all necessary— though it usually does happen—that the source of the horror be logically categorized by the end of the film. The critical dumfoundedness that greeted Hitchcock's *The Birds* (1963) resulted from the filmmaker's failure to provide any ultimate explanation of the bird attacks. Had Hitchcock been working in the realm of science fiction, some explanation would have been needed to finish the film, but such a requirement is irrelevant to the horror genre, even if it could have been supplied. Hitchcock reveals no interest in how the situation came about; what matters is the depiction of the rebellion of birds, a usually pleasant aspect of nature. Surely this is not a sensible theme for us to ponder in the way that we might ponder the possibilities of an invasion of flying saucers. We might be invaded by inhabitants of another planet— that is within the realm of scientific possibility; but to speculate about disruptions of nature is to engage in nightmares with an unlimited scope of possibilities beyond the laws of science and the evidence of our senses. *The Birds* is a masterpiece of another type, a probing into the response of various people to a reversal of the natural order. It is beyond the issue of plausibility.

THE TERROR OF THE PLAUSIBLE: AN ASPECT OF SCIENCE FICTION FILMS

The tone of horror is sometimes a quality of science fiction, but as a genre the horror film seeks to recreate the imaginative life of nightmare. Science fiction, on the other hand, firmly establishes a believable base for both its horror and its fantasy elements. It spends a great deal of time insisting on the plausible—sometimes, in fact, asserting the plausible beyond the limits of scientific reasonableness in the sense that almost all bad science fiction films propose a menace that the advocates of plausibility continue to deny long after the presentation of good circumstantial evidence.

Science fiction may be a lesser genre than others discussed in this book, not because of any inherent limitation in its cinematic patterns—but because it has attracted only a handful of major filmmakers who have worked once or twice in the genre: Kubrick, Truffaut, Frankenheimer, Losey, Siegel, Godard, Woody Allen, and a few others. Its close ties to good literary sources and its occasional thematic seriousness have not helped the genre avoid the exploitation of its most outlandish visual possibilities, its creatures from other worlds, its atomic-born monsters, and its endless flashing panels aboard its tinny spaceships. In no real way has the cinematic genre achieved the craftsmanship of its equivalent literary type. Nevertheless, it has produced a few artistic films, and one English film, Stanley Kubrick's *2001: A Space Odyssey* (1968), has achieved critical esteem. The genre remains open to future artistic efforts that conceivably might further develop its potential. We should here take note of some of the genre's attributes as they bear on the realm of the nightmare world.

117

The science fiction film is persistently antiscience, that is, antiprogressive, and therein lies one of the genre's frequent dilemmas. Relatively few of its films can sustain an antiscientific bias throughout and also exhibit artistic control. That control of course is lacking in most run-of-the-mill science fiction films, which start out with an antiscientific theme but become enamored of the mechanical and technological aspects of theme implanted in the decor and produce contradictory impressions. Yet the genre's antiscientism, when well done, is as good as anything found in science fiction literature—for example, the cleanly functional but unesthetic and uninviting space ships of *2001* or the inoperable weapons and malfunctioning flying machines of Woody Allen's *Sleeper* (1973). The horror film, too, propounds a doctrine of antiscientism, but for different reasons; the "mad scientist" goes "too far" beyond the limits of what God intended man to know or create, but the emphasis falls on the scientist's lustful ambition, his Faustlike spirit. The antiscientism in the science fiction film has to do with degenerate tendencies in society such as the exploitation of nature, the desire to replace humans with robots or computers (a strong anticybernetics attitude is apparent), and the playing around with instruments of death such as radiation or poisonous chemicals.

Although aiming for effects distinct from those of the horror genre, science fiction sometimes contains elements of nightmare films in the sense that certain scientific possibilities, or simply rational projections dwelt on at length, produce terrors akin to those associated with irrational fears. The modern world provides sufficient opportunities for science to loom before us, with all its implacable methodology and its irrefutable logic, as a source of nightmare. Since the horror of the plausible seems restricted in comparison with what the uncontrolled, unscientific mind can conjure up, most science fiction films fall short of achieving the true effects of horror films, but a few succeed, usually by their relentless pursuit of their own logical premises. These are films of awakening—the horror coming with our gradual understanding of what kind of terror lurks just beyond the seemingly innocuous mechanism or event set in motion by some external, explicable source.

Science fiction extends the realm of nightmare in two directions. Certain films begin with recognizable or acceptable premises of scientific technology, and then incorporate into their development unlooked-for consequences that provoke a type of intellectual terror; the element of fear arises from the knowledge that the technology contains within itself the seeds of disastrous possibilities no expert could foresee, and that therefore no preparations have been made to control the technology. The real world affords the genre enough examples to give substance to the potential threat of science: for instance, the tragic misapplication of the drug thalidomide produced a worldwide nightmare unmatched in its horrifying suggestiveness, I believe, by any science fiction film. Contemporary civilization, indeed, provides the basis for most of the disasters in science fiction films, as it does in the literature of science fiction. If civilization insists on developing weapons of mass destruction, it is logical to expect their use and the inevitable success of the overkill theories of military intelligence; thus, it may be assumed that it is only a matter of time until some error or some ineptitude releases the doomsday machinery of Kubrick's *Dr. Strangelove* (see pages 289–91); or starting from a point after the machinery has gone into effect, as in Stanley Kramer's *On the Beach* (1959), it is logical to imagine the futile, desperate attempts of men to find a way out—to undo the events no longer subject to man's benevolent or malevolent interference.

The other significant way in which science fiction encroaches on the nightmare genre is in the confrontation with a hostile force different in kind from that ordinarily found in real life and suggesting superiority either in its pervasiveness (as in Don Siegel's *Invasion of the Body Snatchers* [1956]) or in its physical power (as in Fred Wilcox's *Forbidden Planet* [1956]). This type of menace may be easily distinguished from the typical science fiction invasion film in which, for instance, a spaceship arrives to take over the earth, or some slovenly beast arises from a lagoon in search of human prey. In such typical films, our scientific and military establishment can be counted on to protect us, but while we are being treated to an adventure in scientific warfare, we are not endangered by the same sort of terrors found in the nightmare world. However, in science fiction films such as the two mentioned above, the opposition poses a threat that is intellectually terrifying, and in these instances the horror indeed partakes of the nightmare world.

IRRATIONAL TERRORS

Often the irrationality that permeates the horror film is excessive given the circumstances and the alternatives. A woman held in the palm of King Kong most certainly may be permitted screams of hysteria, but in the minor aspects of the genre hysteria too becomes standardized as a stock response to something not quite abnormal enough. Murder in the cinema may be the common indication of the abnormal world, yet most murder films are not of the nightmare genre. Often portrayed as a most logical act (committed for money or power), murder on screen is relevant to the horror genre only when there is something unusual about the killer. He must be some sort of psychopath, sadist, or mass killer in order to take on the trappings of a figure of horror. The mass murderer produces an irrational response on the part of those who learn about him, in real life as well as in movies, and therefore one of the popular categories of the horror film deals with a more-or-less human source of repeated killings such as Jack the Ripper. If, however, a sensible pattern exists to the killings—that is, if the killer has logical reasons for what he does—then the film is not part of the horror genre, for its rationality removes it from the nightmare world.

There are, of course, certain rational threats that work on us in irrational ways, and if the emphasis within a film falls on the psychological conditions of the threat, then such a film belongs to the nightmare genre. In the world we live in, crime is constant and widespread, permeating the city and the country, threatening political rallies, police stations, embassies, and churches. Motives for the most atrocious crimes may nowadays be proffered in rational rhetoric, and criminal threats made so blatantly public that preventive measures are frequently taken. Yet such threats may also become elements of psychological warfare, in which the

119

potential horrors are designed to look like symbols of a powerful cause. Guerilla warfare in the 1970s is an attempt to spread horror in the normal world to achieve political or social ends.

Because of the commonness of contemporary real-life horror of this logical sort, we require narrative art to concentrate more on the nature of the threat than on the effects of the action. Otherwise, the depiction of what ought properly to be considered horrible to a civilized audience becomes another exercise in ruthless but comprehensible violence. The irrationality of contemporary rational violence has led to at least one fairly significant horror category, films about the invasion of a house. This category may sometimes belong to the crime genre, as in John Huston's *Key Largo* (1948) or Archie Mayo's *The Petrified Forest* (1936). But if the invaders are essentially psychopathic, regardless of whether they have their own logical reasons for entering the house, they represent those creatures from the nightmare world who will pursue us irrationally into the most private corners of our mind. The horror genre encompasses various types of invasions of one's ultimate refuge for safety and privacy, the home, as in Richard Fleischer's *The Boston Strangler* (1968), and *The Birds*.

The threat to the house is closely related to the common horror motif of the specifically intended, and carefully planned, threat from an inexorable, apparently insane force. This is particularly true when the threat is aimed at children, as in Charles Laughton's film, *Night of the Hunter* (1955) and J. Lee Thompson's *Cape Fear* (1961). The specifically aimed threat differs from the more generalized threat of, for instance, the mad killer who stalks the streets of London and kills passing strangers, either at random or in some pattern meaningful to himself alone. The designated peril is much subtler. It poses a direct challenge to the victim's ability to defend himself—or often to defend a loved one or a child. This kind of horror may at first appear to be part of some other genre, since the planned assault and its counterattack are on the surface quite rational responses to a set problem, as in Robert Mulligan's *The Stalking Moon* (1968) and Terence Young's *Wait Until Dark* (1967); the former matches two rather equally able men in a Western setting, and the latter overbalances the odds by presenting a couple of criminals, one virtually insane, against a blind woman trapped in her apartment. The reason such films belong to the genre of horror is a matter of the way in which the surface strategies of attack and survival become at last intense contests of irrational violence and hatred.

These films eventually become sieges of terror when the victims or sympathetic characters are decisively trapped in a situation of such desperate nature that they are forced to strike back

120

with equal violence. There is something gruesomely provocative about turning the victims into the enraged attackers. They become the ones who eventually win, not because their position is morally right to begin with (though it must be morally right to gain our sympathy in the first place), but because through cunning and perhaps luck they manipulate the situation to their advantage. The blind woman in *Wait Until Dark* manages to cut off the electricity, and the audience is made shockingly aware of the possibility that in pitch-blackness, the blind person may actually become more terrifying and dangerous than the would-be killer.

This insight into the potentiality of the desperate victim suddenly reversing the conditions and becoming the master of violence did not originate in Sam Peckinpah's *Straw Dogs* (1972) as several commentators seemed to think, but appears in much milder forms throughout this invasion category. Peckinpah's film, generally criticized for its excesses of violence, works on this truth—which may be true in real life too, since it is a motif found in films that do not condone violence, as *Straw Dogs* certainly seems to do. The horror of being invaded, in Peckinpah's view, is that it evokes within us our latent hatred for those who assault our possessions and our privacy. Peckinpah's main character, a mild mathematician, is harassed throughout the film; he awakens to the value of violence as revenge when his wife is raped while he, due to a trick, is out of the house. In order to regain his sense of manhood, he then incites a group of violence-prone village thugs to invade his home. In the course of defending his home, the mathematician's ingenuity shows itself in the various protective means he uses to gain the advantage over his enemies and to kill them off one by one in horrible ways, the most remarkable employing a large steel animal trap. Through it all, the hero seems to exult in the mayhem he is creating among his stupid, vicious enemies. The film, though evidently justifying his violence, makes it visually clear that his viciousness equals theirs and that violence in a just cause is virtuous, manly, and a real possibility for all of us.

This last point is especially hard to accept on the basis of a film that many viewers found repulsive and dehumanizing. Nevertheless, even if Peckinpah is wrong about general human psychology in the crisis of a violent attack, the frequent use of the motif suggests that it probes a universal truth about latent violence. If we are not essentially violent, it may still be true that we fear the potentiality of turning violent when pressed to extremes. The identical problem is handled with considerable intelligence in *Cape Fear,* where the psychopath's determination to take revenge on the family of the idealistic lawyer he blames for his

121

past imprisonment takes a subtle form: the psychopath's invasion of the lawyer's house is intended as the final stage in a psychological war, whereby the lawyer—in responding to his family's plight and abandoning his ideals of civilized behavior—will recognize that all people are essentially brutal. It does not work because the lawyer, in foiling the plot, manages to restrain his hatred and anger and does not kill his enemy. Certainly, the fear that normally nonviolent people may have about having to resort to violence is not based in any strong desire to avoid injuring a person who will otherwise surely injure them. Rather, it probably stems from a fear of testing their own capacity to engage totally in a prolonged outburst of violence. With *Straw Dogs*, the alarmingly affirmative audience response to the hero's brutality (noted by a number of critics) reflects the vicarious experience of seeing someone letting go under tremendous pressure. But to let go totally—to participate in unrestrained violence—means unleashing the animal nature within us and yielding (perhaps permanently) all human values and the mind's governance over instinctive senses. To be civilized requires curbing whatever violence we feel in numerous small daily attacks on our sensibility, usually by local merchants, colleagues, or neighbors. But perhaps it remains a function of the horror genre to project the possibilities of a situation so terrible that we would want to strike back with overwhelming force, not just to stop but to demolish what we consider an evil entity. This desire would be, of course, insanity. The glorification of an insane impulse is hardly a credit to art. But the recognition of that impulse in the unreality of a horror film may be a way of restraining it in the reality of civilization.

ROMANTIC ISOLATION

Eventually the zombies of the mind can be battered down, and if not permanently laid to rest, at least buried in crypts that might remain sealed for decades to come. But there are other fears engendered by the horror genre that do not readily subside because they are by nature nothing more than an extension or alteration of the hero. This type of horror film usually gains its peculiar effectiveness by making the hero into a monster and eventually leading us to relate to the monstrous condition, which points toward the hero's inevitable doom. This type of film relies almost equally on our underlying pity as well as on our usual fears.

The werewolf is perhaps the best representative of this ambivalent placing of the beast within the body of the hero, though the actual American appearances of the character have not been notably successful (such as Stuart Walker's *The Werewolf of London* [1935], George Wagner's *The Wolf Man* [1941], Eric Kenton's *House of Frankenstein* [1944]). The werewolf, a good man who turns periodically into a creature of violence, cannot prevent himself from killing when, under the influence of the full moon, he becomes a huge deadly wolf. Considered from a psychological perspective, the werewolf is just the archetypal schizophrenic man, with uncontrollable impulses toward evil. We share with him these impulses, but watching him on screen we undergo a purgative experience as he acts out for us the process of inevitable doom awaiting the person who loses control, who destroys in a moment of madness or passion. He is a cousin to Dr. Jekyll, the difference typically being that the doctor (that is, the mad scientist) willingly brings about his own downfall by his overweening scientific pride or curiosity. Turning into Mr. Hyde, he becomes temporarily a mad monster, his lucidity restored for shorter and shorter lengths of time when he can revert to his normal self. The Jekyll-Hyde category of the horror genre is rich in attempts to devise new insights into this simple Robert Louis Stevenson story of the split personality within all of us, and it has attracted filmmakers from Jean Renoir to Jerry Lewis.

123

Werewolves and Hydes are also related to a larger group of horror films that deal with the obsessed maniac, but in most cases the maniac is so depraved we cannot identify with him. Psychotic killers can hardly be expected to pass as acceptable members of society even when their need to kill has been temporarily satisfied. For this reason, the werewolf turned back into his normal self, the urbane Count Dracula (in the daytime) and Dr. Jekyll, are far more frightening figures of the nightmare world than their more realistic kin, the diabolical murderer. Although the monster may have chemical or physiological causes for his murders, we can often interpret his motives as a kind of temporary insanity, though not in the legal sense. On the surface he murders because as a monster he has to, but on another level— not really a disguised level either—he kills because he finds it gratifying. We in the audience never yield to the equivalent temptation, yet we note how often the first murder committed on screen is against a somewhat unsympathetic character. Viewers are thus led toward plausible identification with the monster, even though as the crimes increase all pretense toward moral sympathy on a rational plane disappears. We remain horrified, but we persist in feeling sympathetic toward the monster as he succumbs to his terrifying worse self.

In a relatively few but memorable instances, the nightmare genre has been able to achieve a sense of the pathetic as strong or stronger than a sense of the terrifying. It might seem that the combination of pathos and horror would not work, but we should remember that the genre as we know it today derives from a branch of nineteenth-century literary romanticism that was much more at home with pathos than with horror. The theme of the savage or misfit or monster in romantic literature is not easily duplicated in film today because the physical appearance of the movie monster would probably need to be toned down to generate sympathy, thereby becoming more human and less horrible. Nevertheless, the existence of some classic portrayals of pathetic monsters indicates that the nightmare world is much broader and more complex than it appears in the majority of its films which present a horror lurking somewhere "out there." Watching Dr. Frankenstein's laboratory-created monster, the audience identifies with the pursued creature driven to destruction by a frenzied mob.

James Whale's *Frankenstein* (1931) is usually among the first films that come to mind when this aspect of the genre is discussed, along with his *The Bride of Frankenstein* (1935), Tod Browning's *Dracula* (1930), Ernest Schoedsack and Merian C. Cooper's *King Kong* (1933), and a number of other masterful contributions of the 1930s. *Frankenstein* is one of the most romantic films Hollywood ever turned out, and Whale might well have achieved major status as a filmmaker had he directed films with more normal, respectable surfaces. But below the surface of Whale's expressionistic fantasies, yet there in the most palpable way, are the themes of isolation and the desire to be loved, material that often seems the stuff of films that have greater pretensions to art, though few films of the era had greater claims to cinematic art. Boris Karloff's impersonation of the monster is so filled with humanity that despite the creature's clumsiness and a temper readily provoked to violence, there is no point at which we do not feel for the monster and oppose his persecutors, the townspeople, who in their uncomprehending fear chase and destroy the creature without communicating with him or learning of his gigantic potential for goodness. Though unnamed in the film, the monster has been from that time on named after his creator, Dr. Frankenstein, by the general public. The banal framing story of the overambitious scientist creating a living thing that goes out of control, escapes, and in various ways punishes the scientist for trying to be a god, was less important than the brief biography of the monster. Left to himself, the monster seeks only to establish some human contact—that is, to be loved on the level of his understanding, which is that of a big pet dog. He is, for thematic purposes, less the creation of the laboratory than the "natural man," a large, lumbering animal that fights only when

124

he is cornered or tormented. He cannot speak in the film, though he learns to do so in the sequel, *The Bride of Frankenstein*. In the latter film he finally forms his sole friendship—with a blind hermit—though that too is doomed by interlopers who represent society and civilization. But for most of both films, the monster himself is the most frightened character.

With *Frankenstein* the motif of romantic isolation almost immediately became a dominant influence in the development of the genre—though it had appeared in at least one classic instance as early as 1925 in Rupert Julian's *Phantom of the Opera*. In this film the disfigured madman lives a subterranean existence because of his terrifying face, emerging only because he has fallen in love with a woman he determines to abduct. After *Frankenstein*, numerous films depicted humans or monsters isolated in an alien environment, though the motives for that existence varied with the horror figure's degree of intelligence. In 1933, for example, *King Kong* followed directly the *Frankenstein* pattern of an innocent creature destroyed by a world that will not respond with understanding at a moment of implicit danger. In the same year, Whale turned out another classic of the genre in *The Invisible Man*, which features a scientist who has taken a drug that produces not only his invisibility but a growing insanity that leads him to try to conquer the world. And in Michael Curtiz's *Mystery of the Wax Museum* (1933) we find another sort of archetypal figure of romantic isolation: the artist. In this case, the artist has been driven insane by a fire that ruined his wax statues and made his face hideous. Designing a mask for himself, he is able to exist within society in an outwardly unremarkable way, but nursing a desire for revenge and committing murders; he is a variant on both the *Phantom of the Opera* motif and the Jekyll-Hyde split personality.

125

SOME MINOR CATEGORIES

The artistry of a horror film does not derive in any set way from the source of its horror. The degree of fright projected by a particular sequence can hardly stand as a measure of quality even within a genre that sometimes seems to strive for that effect alone. The effect is too easily produceable and appears in the most worthless of films, for apparently certain locations automatically conjure up the psychological conditions of fear and trembling. Crypts and graveyards, for instance, will do the trick without any need for subtlety, though perhaps adults ought to resent being subjected to the mental anxieties of a child watching such films. The element of mere shock—which is so short-lived that it is avoided in most films—is not the essential ingredient of horror. Shock all too frequently springs merely from surprise, generated equally well by a murderer leaping from a dark alley with knife in hand, and a child jumping from behind a wall and yelling "boo." And indeed many such effects are carried off equally well in nonhorror films; for example, one of the most meaningful moments of shock in the cinema occurs in David Lean's English film *Great Expectations* (1947) when the boy Pip comes across Magwitch in the churchyard (surpassing the effect in Dickens's novel). The horror film, then, cannot be judged on its surprises unless the surprises are integrated into a meaningful pattern of horror.

Similarly, certain categories developed around shocking ideas are essentially meaningless except for their visual effects. Most monster films that project grotesque creations exist merely on the strength of the creature's makeup. For instance, films in which the monster is a skeleton or films in which hideously disfigured characters are considered entities escaped from the nightmare world—these may surely relate to our subconscious fears, but unless the visual image is transformed into some significant examination of the event, it is by no means clear what the simple depiction of a mental abstraction can be used for. Sheer sensationalism, the standby ingredient of the genre, is of course often merely an avoidance of art and thought.

One large and ever-popular category that seems usually irredeemable as far as serious art is concerned deals with insane villains. Insanity, of course, has the great advantage of being beyond necessary explanation. There is no need for a filmmaker to explain a Jack-the-Ripper personality; merely labeling the evil "insane" informs the audience that it is observing just one more manifestation of the awfulness of contemporary life. Thus, a semblance of plausibility is spread over the thinnest level of exploitative violence. It is true that major films have been made from this very subject, but the difference between Hitchcock's handling of *The Lodger* (1926) or *Frenzy* (1972) and the ordinary film about insanity is the shift in emphasis away from the murderer to the effect of the murders on everyone else. (It is for this reason that Hitchcock can be amusing when dealing with such subjects, while minor filmmakers are so often guilty of dubious taste in treating the same subject with more seriousness.) Insanity, for some other films, can be a valid motif if it is studied within the film or if it is subjugated to other elements. As a central structuring device of a horror film, existing as an unexamined source of terror, it can supply only shockingly graphic violence but hardly a satisfying denouement.

The category of prehistoric creatures, except for *King Kong* and a few others, remains relatively minor and forgettable. Two of the prevalent types of such films are the "historical" period pieces (Hal Roach's *One Million B.C.* [1940], Don Chaffey's *One Million Years B.C.* [1967]) and films about the discovery of prehistoric remains (Cooper and Schoedsack's *Mighty Joe Young* [1949], Irwin Allen's *The Lost World* [1960]). More common than either of those are the 1950s films about prehistoric creatures revived by atomic blasts or radiation. Nominally science fiction in that some farfetched scientific possibility brings the creatures to life, these films proceed primarily as horror films. But so close are they to one another in plot and so close collectively to sheer nonsense, that the basic production premise of them all became merely a testing of the uses of special effects photography. How these creatures would go about destroying civilization and how civilization would finally destroy them were the recurring dramatic questions of the cinema of Godzilla.

The atomic monsters and mutants category structures itself around the idea of an overwhelming threat. Certain tacit science fiction premises are operational, since most of these creatures pose a wide-scale menace to society more than to individuals. **127** Where the atomic monsters relate to true horror projections of the nightmare world is in films about catastrophes. It is not so much a matter of who will be caught in the catastrophe as how the event is presented. When it is presented mainly in its logical dimension, the film is science fiction—for example, a superbeast marching on London or Tokyo immediately poses the obvious danger of knocking over buildings and crushing citizens, and this—cinematically the heavy-footed approach to terror that revels in hundreds of fleeing, screaming people—simply extends the logical outcome of the premise that such a creature might exist. But when the terror is gradually revealed for its ultimate potential, as in *The Birds*, it matters less whether it will involve a few or many; its effect lies in the awareness of what it means to the human mind, and this is the traditional method of producing the best effects of the genre. The recent revitalization of the catastrophe film has taken either of two forms: the indiscriminate violence of natural creatures as in *Jaws* or the unpredictable mishap of modern technology as in John Guillermin's *The Towering Inferno* (1974) and Ronald Neame's *The Poseidon Adventure* (1972).

Studying the most impressive works created within the vast number of nightmare categories, I think it fair to generalize that the major films tend to rely more on the suggestive inducement of terror than on the actual presentation of the horrifying. For this reason, connoisseurs of the genre show high regard for the low-budget "B" films of the 1940s, produced by Val Lewton working at RKO and supervising such directors as Mark Robson, Robert Wise, and Jacques Tourneur. Lewton refined the 1930s horror conventions into a continuously suggestive emotional hybrid of fear and expectation. Sometimes, as in *The Curse of the Cat People* (1944), where the source of the terror stems from a child's overactive imagination, hardly anything ever does happen. In films like *I Walked with a Zombie* (1943), *The Seventh Victim* (1943), and *The Body Snatcher* (1945), Lewton carefully derived his effects from a thorough knowledge of how cinematic art operates in its psychological dimension.

Some few films, however, manage to subsist on a continual running depiction of nightmare elements, but as exceptional as they might be, they do not prove a new rule. A prime case is Browning's unique classic of the grotesque, *Freaks* (1932). On a much lower level, many minor horror films tend to combine several elements from better films so that a series of chills and thrills can serve for the sustained buildup we would get from a major filmmaker. These minor horror films—among which are all the horror works of the prolific director-producer Roger Corman, most of the starring vehicles of actors Christopher Lee and Peter Cushing, and every recent Edgar Allan Poe–inspired film, even if not directed by Corman—can be quite entertaining and, in some cases, deliberate camp or self-parody (bad horror and science fiction films move more quickly toward self-parody than the minor works of any other genre). But they induce a kind of passive observation in us; we can finally be glutted by the simple accumulation of visualized terror. Unless we have some peaceful moments to think through the implications, the overall sense of nightmare may be dissipated by the sheer number of bats flying from the belfry with a train of ghouls and zombies lunging at us as we flee across the cemetery under the waning glow of the midnight moon.

KING KONG
(1933)

Directors	Cinematographers	Script
MERIAN C. COOPER	EDWARD LINDEN	JAMES CREELMAN
ERNEST B. SCHOEDSACK	VERNE WALKER	RUTH ROSE
Producer	J. O. TAYLOR	Based on a story
DAVID O. SELZNICK	Chief Technician	by Edgar Wallace and
For RKO	WILLIS H. O'BRIEN	Merian C. Cooper

PRINCIPAL CHARACTERS

FAY WRAY	BRUCE CABOT	ROBERT ARMSTRONG
Ann Redman	John Driscoll	Carl Denham
SAM HARDY	FRANK REICHER	NOBLE JOHNSON
Weston	Captain Englehorn	Native Chief

Length: 100 minutes

Critical appreciation of *King Kong* was hindered for decades by the fact that it is so entirely a genre film, so decidedly within the juvenile range of the horror genre, that it almost defies serious commentary. One can be serious, of course, about anything, including fairy tales, but it was not until *King Kong* had been around for so long that it was a classic to everyone, either in a historical sense or in a stylistic sense, that the film could be mentioned without condescension or laughter.

It is still a child's film, certainly, in that its themes are developed in a richly emotional vein and its effects calculated to be thoroughly intelligible at all times. This is not to say that they are jejune or simplistic; the film embodies many of the subjects that great writers have dealt with and that great filmmakers have taken up in more complex and reputable works. A recent history of the American film neglects to mention *King Kong*, indicative perhaps of a deliberate choice, but possibly merely an oversight. One could not write at length about the achievement of the American cinema and ignore *Casablanca* or *Gone with the Wind*, but a tale about a prehistoric lovelorn beast still does not strike everyone as the potential stuff of adult contemplation.

If *King Kong* had evinced some ambition to be poetic it might have created its own critically respectable following, as did Jean Cocteau's charmingly flimsy French film *Beauty and the Beast* (1946). But the gigantic solidity of *King Kong* took a firm hold on its place in the American realist tradition. What could be more realistic than its plot—once we accept, by our "suspension of disbelief," the premise that if such a monster gorilla existed, it would be exhibited as a commercial venture? And if the gorilla were exhibited in this way, it would be part of a larger entertainment enterprise, not just held as a zoo spectacle. Accepting these premises, as we do with other works of the preposterous such as Homer's *Odyssey* and Shakespeare's *Tempest*, we follow a logical development of events leading toward a tragic solution. The worthiness of the film's theme and the quality of its cinematic presentation have always been less in question than the issue of whether we ought to care about the destiny of a giant ape in the first place. But the answer to such a question is obvious: in fiction, traditionally, animals are surrogates for humans or human qualities; there are really no narrative films or books about animals but only about beasts with human qualities.

King Kong is almost pure cinema, its essence displayed visually with an immediate clarity that transcends the need for any critical articulation. It is surely one of the visual splendors of the cinema, not because of its technical virtuosity (Kong was an eighteen-inch miniature) but because its great images remain forever in our consciousness. Early in the film, as the ship brings the explorers (a group making a travel film) to the unchartered island, the first great image appears: cliffs that rise straight up to an immense height, suggesting an interior vastness beyond them that is unknown yet terrifying. The image works on a psychological level to suggest impenetrable darkness, challenging the instinct within us that must find out what lurks beyond our perception. At the same time, however, we are certain that whatever is there will be dangerous to us. When the heroine is abducted by the natives and left as a sacrifice for Kong, whom we at first only hear approaching, the film captures an image of anticipated terror never excelled on screen and entirely consistent with the development of the film's suspense.

The giant ape himself is not portrayed "realistically"—that is, he does not act like an animal but like a human, in the Frankenstein monster tradition of the savage or uncivilized man. This is also the tradition of the noble savage, the uncivilized and uneducated figure who has somehow received from his Maker an innate sense capable of moral discrimination. Kong does kill people, but those people are not entirely innocent—the primitive tribesmen, who believe in human sacrifice and are therefore beyond the pale of civilization, and the white men, the interlopers from the civilized world, who are trespassers. Later Kong kills New Yorkers, but they too are tainted because of their attitude toward him. All in all, the film is designed to create sympathy for this prehistoric creature who is sought out, captured, and removed from nature to an imprisoning environment (another wide-ranging motif in the genre). Kong has a capacity for love greater than that of most of the human characters in the film, and his feeling for the heroine

130

leads him to adopt knightly traits in her defense—killing creatures from his own world who seem to imperil her and handling her with considerable affection, even in the ultimate memorable sequence atop the Empire State Building. Our sympathy at the end is completely with the monster. His tormentors, the representatives of our human civilization, are primarily bullies who collectively destroy him by an airplane attack he cannot fully comprehend.

These broad images compellingly present the film's romanticism and keep us close to the basic myth patterns: the movement toward the unknown, the conquest of the uncivilized, and the bringing of the uncivilized entity into an alien, hostile city which destroys him. The psychology is simple, but we are nevertheless manipulated by it. To see the giant creature humiliated by lesser beings when chained on stage for exhibition makes us identify with him and oppose the bejeweled spectators, who do not care about the agony this "king of creatures" is feeling. We are uplifted when he breaks loose (to defend his beloved from the threatening flashbulbs), and though we are aware of the destruction he will spread, we side with him and hope that somehow he can manage to survive the weapons of civilization that will be launched against him.

The nobility of the creature close to nature often manifests itself at some crucial point such as the savage's ability to sacrifice itself for another creature. In *Son of Kong* (1933), the sequel to *King Kong*, which though made by the same team appeared so quickly that it suffered by immediate comparison, the huge white ape dies by drowning, while holding in his palm his human friends, who are rescued by boat as the ape disappears from view. Romanticism of this sort seems too hard to accept, and this film has never had much popularity compared to *King Kong*. The Kong of the first film is noble and brave too, but he goes to his death fighting back against the encroachment of the overwhelming forces of technology on the majestic ferocity of nature.

THE BRIDE OF FRANKENSTEIN
(1935)

Director	Cinematographer	Script
JAMES WHALE	JOHN MESCALL	JOHN L. BALDERSTON
Producer		WILLIAM HURLBUT
CARL LAEMMLE, JR.		Based on a novel by
For Universal		Mary Shelley

PRINCIPAL CHARACTERS

BORIS KARLOFF	ERNEST THESIGER	COLIN CLIVE
The Monster	Dr. Praetorius	Henry Frankenstein
ELSA LANCHESTER	O. P. HEGGIE	UNA O'CONNOR
The Bride / Mary Shelley	The Hermit	Minnie
VALERIE HOBSON	DWIGHT FRYE	ANNE DARLING
Elizabeth	Karl	Shepherdess
E. E. CLIVE	TED BILLINGS	DOUGLAS WALTON
Burgomaster	Ludwig	Percy Shelley
		GAVIN GORDON
		Lord Byron

Length: 80 minutes

Now frequently considered the greatest of monster films, *The Bride of Frankenstein* probably surpasses Whale's first version of the story, *Frankenstein*, made four years earlier; but the classic genre qualities of both films are so similar that it is difficult to establish the cinematic superiority of one or the other. Yet there is no question as to why most critics prefer the later film: *The Bride of Frankenstein* for the modern viewer is a black comedy, and

133

though *Frankenstein* has a comic implication too, its style and photography are completely dominated by the horror aspect of Boris Karloff's role as the monster. Karloff, along with Colin Clive (the scientist-creator), returns in this brilliantly contrived sequel, but this film also introduces a new element, a witty mad scientist with subdued signs of effeminacy, Dr. Praetorius. The result is a curious kind of horror film, straining at one extreme toward comedy (not necessarily parody, though) and yet retaining its identification with the tone and movement of a genuine horror film. Indeed, if the film no longer affects many of us as a presentation of the nightmare world, it is probably merely because we have seen it too often and have learned to respond more easily to its humor than we could on first viewing.

The comic portions generally border on the macabre so as not to distort the eerie tone imposed by the filmmaker's essentially expressionistic style. Whale employs in this film the gothic atmosphere of *Frankenstein* in the predominantly dark or fog-shrouded sets, but the presence of Dr. Praetorius brings a new level of vitality to this familiar environment of mad scientist films. Filled with energy and enthusiasm for creating a "world of gods and monsters," Praetorius attempts to inspire a now-reluctant Dr. Frankenstein to return to work in collaboration by exhibiting his own creations—miniature people he has developed from seeds. They parade and entertain us, having the same fascination that the Lilliputians had for Gulliver. The miniatures of Dr. Praetorius, charming as they are, cannot overcome his friend's revul-

sion at the terror caused by his own monster, and Dr. Frankenstein is forced to return to the laboratory after Dr. Praetorius and
the monster kidnap his fiancée. The concept of creating a mate
for the monster, presumably to start a race of monsters, reflects
both the insanity and the humor of Dr. Praetorius, for he seems
self-conscious enough of how the world will view him and also of
the absurdity of the situation. When the mate is manufactured, it
is Praetorius who amusedly calls her the "bride of Frankenstein"
(it seems by this time that the monster and his creator share the
same name, as they already did in the public's mind after the
1931 film).

Karloff's depiction of the monster differs markedly from that
in the first film in its variety of expressive attitudes, from rage
and fear to extreme sensitivity: weeping at hearing music, smoking a cigar, even laughing. He learns to speak from a blind
hermit, who befriends him in a sequence that mixes great pathos
with a profoundly comic idea: two isolated beings, one a created
monster, find friendship and understanding through their incom-
plete understanding of each other. Here the monster has found a
satisfying way of life, where his clumsiness and horrible appearance mean nothing and his natural goodness is allowed to surface. This return to childlike simplicity is humorously portrayed,
though the inevitable intrusion of representatives from the civilized world leads to violence and the death by fire of the hermit.

The Bride of Frankenstein does not alternate comic and horror modes, however, for the mood is consistently pessimistic and
the atmosphere overhung with the usual portents of ultimate
destruction. Yet what really holds together the horrific and the
comic is the sentimental or romantic motif: the monster in search
of an identity. Discovering that he can never find peace and
acceptance unless he finds a companion like him, he finally
destroys himself through the tragic revelation of his essential
loneliness. He becomes, in his moment of tragedy, what used to
be called the "Byronic hero," after the creations of the poet Lord
Byron—who appears along with the author of the novel *Frankenstein,* Mary Shelley, in the film's prologue, which is needed in the
film to explain to the audience how it was possible to have a
sequel about a monster who was killed off four years earlier.

On the way to his tragic discovery, the monster has his consciousness raised in two ways. He witnesses the animosity that
outraged citizens have for him both because he kills people (in
order to escape from his tormentors, in self-defense) and because
he disturbs the balance of respectable society by looking like and
being a monster. In *Frankenstein,* he was driven to his murders
originally by bad treatment, for though he is created with a streak
of violence his primary trait is simplicity. In both films we are

134

made to feel that given a better environment, he would be rendered harmless. However, it is equally clear in both films that the world does not provide that sort of possibility, because the vast majority of ordinary people cannot tolerate the extraordinary—whether the extraordinary be a simpleminded monster or a scientific genius such as Dr. Praetorius or Dr. Frankenstein. The townspeople who corner the monster in *Frankenstein* and imprison him in *The Bride of Frankenstein* are the representative voices of bigotry attempting to impose a uniform standard of mediocrity on society. It is interesting to note how this literary movement of the nineteenth century seems to take on powerful new emphasis in the nightmare film genre of the 1930s. It is doubtful that Americans widely disapproved of science, but the films lend weight to the belief that science can go too far. However, a few films like *The Bride of Frankenstein* seem to counter that view by depicting the opposition to the monster as worse than the monster with all the destruction he has wrought.

The classic sequence of this film, one that draws together the film's comedy, pathos, and horror, is the ending in the great laboratory to end all mad scientists' laboratories, where numerous flashing lights and overhead storms signal the moment of the ultimate experiment: the creation of a new being. On the sidelines an eager monster awaits his last chance for happiness. Whale's eccentric camera angles—down toward the set or up to reveal the huge life-generating machinery, which is raised to the roof to catch the lightning—and rapid, tension-building cutting are perfect for the situation, which is at once terrifying to the audience in its concept and exhilarating to the scientists participating in this godlike activity of creation. When the female monster begins to live—seen by a gigantic close-up of her eyes in her completely bandaged body—a brief moment of triumph occurs. But once she is unbandaged and shown to her mate, we witness one of the great tragic moments of the cinema of romanticism. She takes one look at the Frankenstein monster and screams; he tries to approach her but his ugliness (which is matched by her own grotesqueness) seems to frighten her and his touch repels her. Realizing that this is a conclusive rejection, he says "She hates me," and sets about to destroy the laboratory, but first he frees Dr. Frankenstein and his fiancée, whom he seems to hold innocent. Telling Praetorius, "We belong dead," he pulls the switch that explodes the lab, Praetorius, himself, and his would-be mate in a final gesture of recognition of his inevitable isolation and alienation.

135

INVASION OF THE BODY SNATCHERS

(1956)

Director	Cinematographer	Script
DON SIEGEL	ELLSWORTH FREDERICKS	DANIEL MAINWARING
Producer	Superscope	Based on a story by
WALTER WANGER		Jack Finney
For Allied Artists		

PRINCIPAL CHARACTERS

KEVIN MC CARTHY	DANA WYNTER	CAROLYN JONES
Dr. Miles Binnel	Becky Driscoll	Theodora
KING DONOVAN	LARRY GATES	JEAN WILLES
Jack	Dr. Danny Kauffman	Sally
RALPH DUMKE	VIRGINIA CHRISTINE	TOM FADDEN
Nick	Wilma	Uncle Ira
	WHIT BISSELL	
	Psychiatrist	

Length: 80 minutes

136

Although it draws considerable strength from its affinities with the horror genre, *Invasion of the Body Snatchers* is one of the best-conceived science fiction films because its social content—essential to this type of science fiction—finds an effectively menacing visual counterpart. Its theme derives from the disintegration of communal feeling in contemporary society, particularly the growing alienation among people. The film evolves a highly amusing yet horrifying metaphor for the problem: vegetable-grown humanoids replace the ordinary citizens of a small town one by one, first duplicating their bodies and then taking over their minds—leaving the people with enough awareness of the change to *prefer* their new condition because it frees them from the troubles of human emotions. Don Siegel, consistently one of the best contemporary genre directors, usually presents his themes tautly. The dialogue barely suggests the symbolic scope of his subject (a technique that is perhaps fitting for an intellectual artist almost completely ignored because of the genres he works in). The science fiction genre is most conducive to the analysis of broad social concerns, since it tends to pit human beings against a societal force or a technology that represents a logical extension into the future of a symptomatic problem existing in our present society. Although these concerns cannot easily be turned to cinematic material, in the increasingly horrifying realization of the body substitutions in Siegel's film, we are in each successive instance given greater insight into the kind of world we would inhabit if these pod-grown human replacements were a possible

real life alternative. Indeed at certain points in the film, the dramatic action implies that this alternative symbolizes the mechanical civilization we exist with today.

The film also proceeds in the manner of the horror genre as it follows the doctor-hero and his girlfriend in their growing knowledge of the possibilities of the invasion. First the genre's usual "strange events" occur and ordinary citizens act peculiarly. Then a friend of the doctor discovers a body with the friend's own face, and based on the recurring instances of this type of incident the horror plot is more overtly stressed for much of the film than the science-fiction invasion aspect. The horror consists in the growing isolation of the hero and heroine as they discover the rapid transformation that has occurred to those friends who aided them earlier in their investigation. But the horror element does not entirely dominate even this aspect of the film. The idea of an invasion of an alien species is developed in an objectively logical way, and the emphasis falls more on the science fiction genre problem of how to stop the invaders than on the horror genre problem of how to survive an onslaught of zombies. Yet stopping the invaders seems more a metaphysical than a dramatic issue— for in fact, there are no physical entities invading at all. What we see are the results of an encroachment upon civilization of some mysterious force, but no overt invasion, no hostile infiltration. The source of the problem is not specified, only its perversion of the human spirit and its threatened extension into an all-encompassing catastrophe.

The encroachment of this alien culture and the corresponding isolation of the hero are carried through to the very last sequence. Near the end of the film the girlfriend is conquered by the enemy and becomes one of them, turning on the doctor, who then, left to himself, rushes wildly to the nearest element of civilization—the highway—trying to stop cars and inform the outside world of the danger. In a nightmarish sequence, he almost fails completely and seems himself on the verge of losing his mind, jumping aboard a truck only to discover that its cargo is the giant pods heading toward another city to spread the disaster.

The film utilizes a framing device to present a traditional aspect of the science fiction genre: the attempt to convert general disbelief. The film begins at a hospital where the hero, who appears drunk or insane, has been taken after escaping the town. (We learn eventually that the town is completely controlled by the body snatchers.) A psychiatrist listens to his story, which is the chronological unfolding of the rest of the film, and at the end of it we return to the hospital, where the psychiatrist believes the story and takes action by alerting the government. Presumably the world will be saved, as it conventionally is in science fiction cinema. Still, *Invasion of the Body Snatchers* presents a desolate and grimly pessimistic view of contemporary alienation clothed in the exciting melodramatic action of a vivid film.

138

PSYCHO
(1960)

Director-Producer	Cinematographer	Script
ALFRED HITCHCOCK	JOHN L. RUSSELL	JOSEPH STEFANO
For Paramount	Special Effects	Based on a novel
	CLARENCE CHAMPAGNE	by Robert Bloch

PRINCIPAL CHARACTERS

ANTHONY PERKINS	JANET LEIGH	SIMON OAKLAND
Norman Bates	Marion Crane	Dr. Richmond
JOHN GAVIN	MARTIN BALSAM	VERA MILES
Sam Loomis	Milton Arbogast	Lila Crane
LURENE TUTTLE	JOHN MC INTIRE	
Mrs. Chambers	Sheriff Chambers	
	Length: 109 minutes	

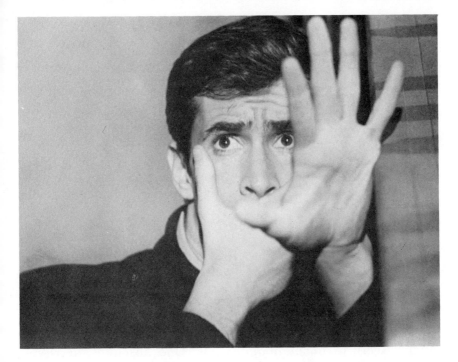

Psycho stands at the apex of the American gothic horror movie. It incorporates several traditional motifs of this genre, integrated on the conceptual level by Hitchcock's artistic sensibility which balances various elements on the verge of black comedy. The tone of horror remains even with repeated viewings, yet the filmmaker's insistence that *Psycho* is a "fun picture" is neither flippant nor foolish once we see how he has conceived the nature of the genre. Without any attempt at parody or even grim humor, Hitchcock has taken the essence of a nightmare vision and structured it around certain ideas that, divorced from the context of such a subject, would indeed be comic. They are the usual Hitchcock sendups of our shared tendency toward misperception. Nevertheless, viewers have no doubt about their own responses to the film and which genre it properly belongs in.

The setting of the film is brilliantly chosen to reinforce visually the sardonic intellectual milieu of the film, and no viewer is likely to appreciate the setting's full symbolic relevance without seeing the film a few times. The Victorian house next to the motel combines the conventional elements of the old house of terror and the modern mundane refuge representing an unsettled society. Not only does the horror haunt the Victorian house, when, for instance, someone attempts to explore it in the ultimate sequence of that traditional Hollywood kind—but the motel too is invaded by the demonic force in the house. Prior to exposing us to the terror that supposedly resides in the house and cannot be contained there, as it usually is in haunted house films, Hitchcock takes care to extend the atmosphere conveyed by the exterior of the house to the visually commonplace motel. This is done by the lighting, by the rainy weather, by the motel owner's stuffed bird collection, and by the hole in the wall, which enables the owner to spy on an occupant in the room adjacent to his office (equivalent to the secret panels of traditional horror houses). It is all rather innocuous on the surface, as Hitchcock intends. The art of horror, in his hands, depends on the arrangement of the ordinary elements of the context, which predisposes the audience to anticipate danger.

The rather pathetic-looking Norman Bates, leading a dull, lonely existence, yet turning out to be a ferocious murderer when he lapses psychotically into the role of his deceased mother (whose decomposed body he preserves in his fruit cellar), is a grisly figure, but amusing in his grotesqueness because the character is not entirely real. Even the murderous old "mother" (that is, Norman speaking as the mother) is able to make a joke about the fruit cellar and about being "fruity" (crazy—it is also used suggestively to mean homosexual). One absolutely terrifying moment occurs when Lila, searching the Bates' cellar, comes across the seated figure of what she and we think is the living Mrs. Bates (we also think we know that Mrs. Bates is a homicidal maniac). But both Lila and the movie audience have assumed erroneously, an instant discovery made as the chair swirls around to reveal the toothless skull of Mrs. Bates's corpse, followed by the sudden mad entrance of Norman in an old-fashioned dress and wig and carrying a raised knife. Yet when within a few seconds Norman, wig askew, is overcome by Sam, the whole event is instantly exposed as a ridiculous, though murderous, charade. The reality of the events completely demystifies the film, leaving the audience feeling somewhat stupid for misreading the signs that only in retrospect seem significant. Of course we have been tricked by Hitchcock, who has done this elsewhere in his career for similar effects—as long ago as *The Lodger* (1926).

Our sense of sobriety prevents us from ever laughing at pitiable Norman, who in a straitjacket has fallen further from normality and "become" entirely his mother. Perhaps it is too much of a sick joke, or would be if it were played for laughs or just for surprise, but *Psycho* has much in it that leads to moral discovery in the Hitchcock cosmos. This is one of the very few films of major artistry in which a deliberate structural reversal occurs that forces the audience itself into the central characterization (the hero's role) in the film. When Marion Crane, who at first seems to be the center of the plot, is murdered long before the middle of the film, and the audience is forced to reevaluate what

140

it thought the story concerned, Norman temporarily emerges as the possible main character. Yet almost immediately after he gets rid of the evidence of the murder and submerges the victim's car containing her body in a swamp, the perspective changes again. His actions do not control the development of the plot but merely serve to limit the actions of those who come seeking the murdered victim. The shifting perspective working upon our intense curiosity invites us to develop the focus of the film from our subjective perception of events. We saw (or thought we saw) the murder, and therefore we know what the searchers cannot discover. Our knowledge is set against their ignorance—particularly in the classic sequence in which the private investigator Arbogast steals into the house to confront what we know will be extreme violence, though he expects merely to dig up some information. Indeed, for all the interesting effects, the film is primarily about how wrong we can be in what we unthinkingly gather from our immediate perceptions.

The eye is the agent of external perception, which is continuously wrong in the film. Hitchcock employs the image of the eye as a symbol of fear, horror, or nonperception throughout the film. In what is now probably the best-known horror sequence in the contemporary cinema, Marion's murder in the shower, the shocking disbelief of what is happening (ours and Marion's) is reflected by an image of the water swirling down the drain of the bathtub, followed by a close-up of the dead Marion's face, emphasizing her eye. What starts out as a simple voyeuristic scene (in which Norman spies on Marion undressing through a hole in the wall), followed by Marion's shower (in which she seems to renew herself and decides to return the money she has stolen), turns into the unforgettable horror of repeated stabbings in unprovoked, relentless violence. The sanctity of this private moment intruded upon by such horror frightened millions of Americans for a long time, but the technique of the film had already developed a pattern of prying or spying throughout. In the first scene, the aimlessly moving camera eye closes in on what almost seems a random hotel room window in a large city, behind which Marion and her lover meet during their lunch hour. Later the reflected glare from a policeman's sunglasses awakens the guilty Marion, asleep in her car after absconding with $40,000; she feels persecuted by the questioning of the policeman, but of course his hidden eyes represent only blankness as his suspicions lead to nothing. The "private eye," confident of finding the correct reason for Marion's disappearance, is killed by a knife aimed first at his face, very close to the eye. And the final shock of the film is the sight of the hollow eyes of Mrs. Bates's body in the cellar. The film ends with another eye image symbolic of nonperception: Nor-

141

man, now permanently identifying himself as his mother, sits motionless in a room, the only movement discernible in his eyes, as he vows not to swat the fly on his hand; he will remain forever unable to perceive his reality.

For Hitchcock, none of us perceives most of reality. More than any other film by Hitchcock, *Psycho* makes this point with thoroughgoing cynicism. We are not redeemed of our misjudgments simply because Norman at last is found to be a maniac. Spared the disaster that overtakes Marion for her misjudgment, we are nevertheless put through the wringer for ours. The solution to the horrible, we finally discover, is the ludicrous. By jumping to conclusions we are left flat on our face.

142

THE BIRDS
(1963)

Director-Producer	Cinematographer	Script
ALFRED HITCHCOCK	ROBERT BURKS	EVAN HUNTER
For Universal	Technicolor	Based on the story
		by Daphne du Maurier

PRINCIPAL CHARACTERS

ROD TAYLOR	TIPPI HEDREN	JESSICA TANDY
Mitch Brenner	Melanie Daniels	Lydia Brenner
SUZANNE PLESHETTE	VERONICA CARTWRIGHT	ETHEL GRIFFIES
Annie Hayworth	Cathy Brenner	Mrs. Bundy
CHARLES MC GRAW	RUTH MC DEVITT	
Sebastian Sholes	Mrs. MacGruder	
	Length: 120 minutes	

Although its effects are clearly within the tradition of the horror genre, *The Birds* has rarely been categorized as a genre film. However, it is unique only in the sense that all classics of film art are different from other works; in the broader sense of sharing characteristics with other films, it partakes of the genre in a rather interesting way. Unlike all other nightmare classics including *Psycho*, *The Birds* perhaps does not derive its basic power from the specifically horrifying situation but from Hitchcock's usual dramatic strategy, the examination of human reaction to imminent peril. Still, it draws on the genre's deep-rooted

neurotic projections: the slow, impenetrable, and unpreventable movement toward catastrophe.

The concept of using birds as the force of this catastrophe might strike us at first as typical of Hitchcock's black comedy, and yet aside from certain flashes, Hitchcock avoids that visual wit of the macabre that typifies his artistry in the majority of his films, even his one previous sound-era horror film, *Psycho*. Birds are indeed innocent creatures of nature inasmuch as they do not normally terrorize, though since the release of the film a couple of actual occurrences of bird massings have created somewhat threatening situations (but no organized attacks on humans). In any case, the element of horror that Hitchcock expands upon is the turning of nature against man in a new way, through its mildest of emissaries, the friendlier species of birds (no eagles or vultures, for instance, are used in the film). It takes quite a while for the overwhelming possibilities to make themselves clear to us visually, though at one point in the film an expert on birds, who at first disbelieves the reports of the birds' deliberate attacks, remarks on the incredible number of birds, the idea of which as a potential force united against mankind is indeed intellectually provocative.

It is, however, only after witnessing the next attack, at the gas station, that it becomes clear on a visual level that the birds represent not just a source of danger but a new form of natural catastrophe. We see the birds deliberately flying against a glass telephone booth in which Melanie Daniels is trapped. Outside, in chaos, the birds attack firemen attempting to put out a fire that has killed one man. Now, while the glass booth would provide no safety against a human being who was determined to injure Melanie inside, it seems at first that the structure might be sufficient to stop a group of wild birds. But then to break in, the birds begin to smash themselves against the glass—and this becomes the ultimate sense of the terror they represent! Suddenly, we realize that they are, after all, a species, with a collective mentality: without hesitation, they will kill themselves to attain the objective of the species, which is at the moment the destruction of human beings. We intuitively understand from this point on that the only possible defense is a more effective shelter against attack.

The film concludes with the issue of a viable defense still unresolved. The final attack seems to end in partial victory for the humans. Mitch Brenner encloses his sister, his mother, and Melanie in his house, boards it up, and except for a few minor casualties succeeds in resisting the birds; he does not, however, feel that he can hold out forever against renewed attacks. In fact, unknown to him, the birds have broken through the attic, and when Melanie goes to investigate a noise up there, she is almost killed by the birds inside. The final image of the film required some remarkable studio work (for as Hitchcock pointed out, he did not have all that many birds available for the film): tremendous numbers of resting birds are seen in a long shot as Mitch's car drives past them during a temporary reprieve from attacks. The sense we are left with is that things will get worse before they improve.

Hitchcock's insight into the true nature of horror allows him to stage his most terrifying episodes in the most comforting of surroundings, a rather snug small town. Implicit in this technique is a criticism of the house-of-horror mentality typical of the genre (and exploited of course in *Psycho*). The first inkling of disaster is a single gull's attack on Melanie as she sits in a motorboat in the middle of a peaceful bay. She has just performed a mild practical joke that appears to be the beginning of a comic courtship film. The first mass attack happens outdoors at a children's birthday party, where relatively little damage occurs except for the pecking of balloons. A later attack on children fleeing from school, again entirely outdoors, leads to an escape in a car, where it becomes questionable as to whether the car—the microcosmic American home—can keep the birds at bay. The car is spared only because the birds mysteriously weary of their attack, and later at the end of the film as the family escapes by car we cannot feel any confidence in their still-jeopardized situation, though the birds just watch as they drive off.

144

Perhaps the classic sequence of the entire genre in regard to the combination of visual wit and terror occurs in this film on the playground outside the schoolhouse. Melanie sits smoking a cigarette with her back to the monkey bars on which sit a couple of crows. We are alert to her general nervous state, but our most literal understanding is that there is no immediate danger. Our intuition tells us something else. Like the cornfield sequence in *North by Northwest* (see p. 287), Hitchcock isolates a character in a visually peaceful setting—to which we ascribe all sorts of potential terrors of which the characters are blissfully unaware. In *The Birds* Hitchcock cuts back and forth between Melanie's nervous smoking and the monkey bars which, each time we see them, contain a few more birds—but not enough to be threatening as a visual image. We then follow the flight of a single bird, the camera as graceful as the bird's approach, but when the bird lands on the monkey bars, the audience and Melanie at the same time are shocked to see that now, instead of a few additional birds, the bars are completely filled and the threat is suddenly immediate. The sequence and the film establish the motif of *suddenness*. There is no resting point; survival depends on perpetual awareness. The real horror of life in a Hitchcock film comes with our awakening to the immediate perils implicit in existence itself.

NIGHT OF THE LIVING DEAD
(1968)

Director-Cinematographer GEORGE A. ROMERO	Producers RUSSELL STREINER KARL HARDMAN For Walter Reade	Script JOHN A. RUSSO

PRINCIPAL CHARACTERS

DUANE JONES Ben	JUDITH O'DEA Barbara	KARL HARDMAN Harry
RUSSELL STREINER Johnny	KEITH WAYNE Tom	KYRA SCHON Karen
MARILYN EASTMAN Helen	JUDITH RIDLEY Judy	
	Length: 90 minutes	

A rather remarkable conglomeration of horror elements, *Night of the Living Dead* gained fame as an underground film that outdid most of the standard industry genre films in sustained tension

and in the persistent development of the nightmare threat. Constructed basically on the themes of the living dead (zombies) and
their hostility toward the living, and the defense of the house, the
film incorporates a great many other familiar aspects of horror
films. These include reminders of motifs from *Psycho* (stuffed
animals, a slashing murder reminiscent of Hitchcock's shower
murder) and *The Birds* (sealing off a house against the attack of a
collective force). The zombies of Romero's film act much the
same as Hitchcock's birds in that their threat is not a matter of
individual strength but of en masse attacks, obsessive and
unyielding. There is also the sense of an enveloping widespread
catastrophe; in the film the zombie phenomenon is reported to be
occurring all over the eastern third of the country. Other nightmare motifs found in this film are the relentless pursuit of a
defenseless woman (starting in a graveyard), the attempt by one
member of a family to murder another (the dead girl, becoming a
zombie, kills her mother, and a brother upon his return from the
dead tries to kill his sister), and cannibalism.

146

Unlike the standardized technique of horror in the cinema
that emphasizes a gradual buildup and audience preparation, in
Night of the Living Dead the source of the terror is introduced
almost immediately. The film begins in a cemetery, a common
enough location for the genre, where a sister and brother are
visiting the grave of their father; a strange-looking man grabs the
sister, and when the brother intervenes a fight ensues leading to
the brother's death and the sister's terrified flight. She escapes to
her car, only to discover that she does not have the ignition key,
as the strange man pounds on the car windows, a horror motif in
itself rarely seen in film up to that time. The sequence introduces
the motif of the vulnerable refuge, and as such prepares us for the
rest of the film, in which the threatened group must deal with
their vulnerability inside the house.

Escaping from the car, the girl Barbara flees to a nearby house
in this sparsely populated area of western Pennsylvania, and
there is joined shortly by Ben, who is also escaping from a group
of the living dead. Eventually, others are discovered hiding in the
cellar, including the Coopers and their dying daughter and a
young man and woman. The body of the woman who owns the
house is discovered upstairs, hideously decomposed. To cope with
the danger of the numerous zombie-like creatures surrounding
the house, Ben sets about singlehandedly preparing to keep them
out. He remarks that the zombies do not have great individual
strength, so the threat they pose is primarily a matter of their
combined efforts. Although the zombies are afraid of fire (another
common motif), the humans can take no great advantage of them

with it, for the zombies do not scatter at the sight of a torch but merely retreat a few steps.

The basic situation consists of planning the best strategy for survival in conditions of continuous panic. Harry's behavior is that of a terrified individual desperate to save his family but less concerned for the survival of the group—not intuitively aware that his survival depends on cooperation. He wants to hide in the cellar, which has only one entrance, though Ben resists that possibility, intending to keep open the option of escaping to the outside. But the group within the house cannot function coherently in the face of the impending disaster. Barbara suffers a breakdown as a result of her fright at the cemetery. Harry contributes nothing to the defensive strategy and continually adds to the atmosphere of panic. He does, however, help in the one futile attempt at an escape by hurling homemade explosives at the zombies while Ben and Tom try to fuel a truck with gasoline from a nearby pump. The effort fails, the young man and his girlfriend are killed when the truck explodes, and Ben is barely able to get back inside the house.

Those within the besieged house continue to lose ground spiritually. Their desperation increases when they discover that the living dead are motivated by the need to eat human flesh. The film graphically depicts the zombies tearing apart the bodies of the burned victims and devouring them. The only thing that mitigates the tone of inevitable destruction at this point is the television reports of the national guard and other groups going about the countryside, searching out the living dead, and shooting and then burning them. In spite of the possibility of rescue, the general sense of pessimism heightens with the pace of events.

147

Ben kills Harry when the latter becomes too much of an obstructionist, practically costing Ben his life by not letting him back in the house. Harry's child turns into a ferocious flesh-eating creature and kills her mother. Barbara recognizes her brother among the zombies and is killed by a group of them. Alone, Ben finally takes refuge in the cellar as the living dead break through his barriers and invade the house. At last they are stopped, unable to get into the cellar. The film ends ironically with the arrival the next morning of the sheriff's party, shooting down at a distance all of the living dead. When Ben emerges from the cellar, he is spotted, taken for one of the creatures, and shot down. The concluding scene is comprised of grainy images of the sheriff's party using hooks to pull Ben and the other corpses to a pyre. Thus, the close of the film fulfills the worst fears of all the participants in the futile struggle of the preceding night: everyone is destroyed.

One of the few good examples of unremitting horror in the nightmare genre, this film permits no moments of emotional rest, for the danger remains continually present in the environment. The television newscasts watched by the group in the house give little hope. They present no scientific explanation, though one is proposed: an excessive level of radiation from a returning space probe rocket—but this is a nonexplanation that even the announcers do not seem to believe. The source of the nightmarish terror in this film does not spring from the hideously distorted faces of the living dead, nor from the film's premise that such creatures exist. Even those of us who might believe in the return to life of dead people do not picture them as this kind of threat—certainly here they are cleared out rather easily by being shot in the head (they move more slowly than the living) and by fire. And the matter of cannibalism is more disgusting than frightening.

The fears generated by the film have to do with the continuous efforts of the living dead to achieve their goal—an apparently insatiable need to eat flesh that manifests itself by their refusal to turn away from the house, no matter how many of them are shot or killed by those inside. Thus, their persistence signifies that the horror will succeed eventually in getting into the house. We are also emotionally engrossed by the manner in which the sense of panic precludes useful cooperation among the group of the living. Aside from Ben, the main source of rational response, the others have no sound ideas for avoiding or fighting against the enveloping horror. Fear turns Cooper irrational, and finally seems to affect Ben that way too as he kills Cooper. The genre seems usually to suggest that in the ultimate confrontation between reason and unreason, the former will win out, but in *Night of the Living Dead* the irrational wins and the nightmare endures.

148

ROSEMARY'S BABY
(1968)

Director	Cinematographer	Script
ROMAN POLANSKI	WILLIAM FRAKER	ROMAN POLANSKI
Producer	Technicolor	Based on the novel by Ira Levin
WILLIAM CASTLE		
For Paramount		

PRINCIPAL CHARACTERS

MIA FARROW	JOHN CASSAVETES	RUTH GORDON
Rosemary Woodhouse	Guy Woodhouse	Minnie Castevet
SIDNEY BLACKMER	MAURICE EVANS	RALPH BELLAMY
Roman Castevet	Hutch	Dr. Sapirstein
ANGELA DORIAN		
Terry		

Length: 136 minutes

Polanski's vision of the nightmare world resembles Hitchcock's in that certain sources of horror contain elements of the ludicrous. The overt subject matter of *Rosemary's Baby*—modern-day witchcraft—is engagingly comic throughout, though the gradual terror it evokes in the heroine produces an atmosphere of horror for the audience. Since the whole film is presented from Rosemary's perspective, and her dread is both genuine and justified, the comic undertone of the film remains muted and adds to the sense of the grotesque that is prominent throughout the narrative.

149

The central horror motif is the increasing isolation of the young wife, as she grows suspicious that the child she is carrying will, upon its birth, be taken from her for some unspeakable blood ceremony of the witches' coven she has discovered in the next-door apartment. Rosemary is quite wrong in her apprehension, as she and the audience find out at the end, for the secret kept from her throughout is that the baby is Satan's child, worshiped as the anti-Christ by the coven. The actual ritualistic impregnation of Rosemary is shown as a series of dreamlike impressions noted by the semiconscious victim—so fantastical in design that the audience is not likely to accept the sequence as anything but Rosemary's nightmare, though in fact much of it is real. Nevertheless, the suspense of the narrative derives from Rosemary's awareness of a conspiracy surrounding her pregnancy and her inability to reach anyone who can help her. Her perceptions are obscured by the fact that her husband Guy has joined the conspiracy, but she cannot grasp this most terrifying of facts until very late since she

is deceived by the scorn Guy projects for her fears and anxieties over the problems of her pregnancy.

The extent of her separation from all sources of help is displayed by Polanski as a developing process because we as viewers are limited by our own disbelief in witches. The film begins with a marvelous long panning shot across much of Manhattan, culminating with a ninety-degree downward tilt to the street in front of the apartment house that Rosemary and Guy, as prospective tenants, are being shown by the rental agent. In a crowded urban community, in a New York apartment, the nightmare situation seemingly could not develop—yet a coven of witches exists in the neighboring apartment, made up of a collection of oddball characters who individually appear mild, eccentric, and well-meaning. The menace grows evident only in regard to the claustrophobic atmosphere Polanski sets up, as Rosemary is led innocently into an increasing reliance on Minnie and Roman Castevet, the strange, garrulous old couple next door, and her obstetrician, Dr. Sapirstein, whose reputation hides the fact that he is one of the witches' group.

Drinking a natural vitamin diet of a liquid herb concoction recommended by her doctor and prepared by Minnie, Rosemary develops pains that would indicate a serious problem, but her husband insists that she stick with Dr. Sapirstein and not venture to get a "second opinion" from another, less prestigious obstetrician. Under her husband's influence she spends considerable time with the much older Castevets rather than with friends of her own age. The one reliable long-time friend and advisor, Hutch, mysteriously lapses into a coma when he is on the verge of investigating the herbs supplied by the Castevets. When he dies some months later, he leaves Rosemary a book on witchcraft that reveals the parentage of her neighbors, who were famous among witches. Evidence of this sort and a steadily developing fear of sacrificing her infant lead Rosemary to the climactic escape sequence. She flees to Dr. Sapirstein's office, but in the waiting room learns accidentally that he too is a member of the coven. In desperation she persuades another obstetrician to listen to her story, but the tale she relates defies credibility, and the obstetrician betrays her back into the hands of her husband and Dr. Sapirstein.

The horror aspect of the film, then, consists of a series of narrowing alternatives, the final one being Rosemary's attempt to lock herself in her apartment, which the others then enter through a secret door. Ultimately subdued, she gives birth but is told that the baby died, a statement she never accepts. In the ironic ending of the film, the one alternative not anticipated by the audience is chosen by the heroine. Rosemary discovers her child, a baby devil, and horrified though she is, she immediately comes to terms with the situation and, with the sense of motherhood sustaining her, begins to rock the baby carriage, to the delight of the aging troupe of witches who have come together to pay the new anti-Christ homage. This ending is a joke, presumably, and it reverses some of the nightmarish implications of the rest of the film, but in another sense it becomes the culmination of horrors to realize that all of Rosemary's struggle leads to this.

151

Those who have read the popular novel on which the film is based may sense a rarer nightmare motif: the potential enemy within. However, whatever danger is symbolized by the unborn child is not depicted in any important way during the film. All the crucial ambiguities in the film are in the compilation of clues that Rosemary perceives. Polanski's structure consists of small bits of circumstantial evidence—each bit offered with both the far-fetched possibility of its pointing to the existence of the witches' conspiracy and the more plausible likelihood of a rational explanation. Rosemary's supposed dream of impregnation by the devil is passed off as a nightmare the next morning, but the scratches on her back seemingly indicate a real experience. Her husband's explanation—that he did it, as a result of mixing passion and alcohol—must be accepted for the moment, for it seems unbelievable that her husband would participate in the ceremonial offering of his wife to the devil. His motivation for doing so—the promise of worldly success—is believable enough in retrospect, but we see it clearly only after the horror is complete. Throughout the film, we share Rosemary's perspective on her predicament, realizing the full extent of her danger only a few minutes before she herself does. As the clues accumulate, the evidence becomes persuasive, but it is Polanski's special consideration to keep us from succumbing to a belief in the witches' conspiracy early in the film. The comic horror of *Rosemary's Baby* lies in its encouraging us to reject the preposterous premise of the conspiracy, and yet all the time supporting it, for after all, that premise does exist as the basis of the film.

THE EXORCIST

(1973)

Director	Cinematographer	Script
WILLIAM FRIEDKIN	OWEN ROIZMAN	WILLIAM PETER BLATTY
Producer	Metrocolor	From his novel
WILLIAM PETER BLATTY		
For Warner Brothers		

PRINCIPAL CHARACTERS

ELLEN BURSTYN	LINDA BLAIR	JASON MILLER
Chris MacNeil	Regan	Father Karras
MAX VON SYDOW	JACK MAC GOWRAN	KITTY WINN
Father Merrin	Burke Dennings	Sharon
LEE J. COBB		
Lt. Kinderman		
	Length: 122 minutes	

The extraordinary commercial success of *The Exorcist,* even surpassing that of the novel, makes this an important case study of the sociology of our era. Its controversial nature has led many critics to speculate about the sources of its popularity and often suggest negative valuations of a society that would become fascinated by such a subject. Yet this film is clearly of its genre, and part of its affective power must be explained by its partaking of the genre's formulaic patterns. For example, the first sequence to employ elements of horror is the old standby of the woman searching the darkened house by candlelight—even though to us the house at first seems hardly likely to afford the usual terrors of

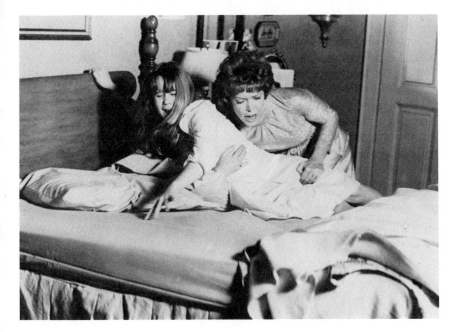

the genre. It is a city house, which provides no secret recesses, so
the attic, which is not electrically wired, of the otherwise ultra-
modern townhouse is the scene of the exploration.

The horror motifs at the heart of *The Exorcist* are possession
and the endangerment of children. In regard to the latter category, we note that the typical film effects of horror in regard to
children have more to do with the dangers that children create for
adults than the other way around. For comparison, two fairly well
remembered, relevantly structured films will shed some light on
the way in which Friedkin operates within this cinematic tradition. In Wolf Rilla's British science fiction film *Village of the
Damned* (1960), women are impregnated by unseen creatures
from an alien planet, and their children grow to be mysteriously
unemotional, totally intellectual young people who are destined
to take control over the earth, by force if necessary. An entirely
different type of threat from the child appears in Mervyn LeRoy's
The Bad Seed (1956), which is realistically based, its horror
emanating from the evil perpetrated by a little girl. Both films
may also be connected to the category of possession, but nothing
is made of that possibility; the two films deal with the capacity of
normal-looking, "sweet" children to destroy adults. Friedkin presents his dangerous child from neither a science fiction nor a
naturalistic viewpoint—rather from a supernatural basis that
has an established credibility within several major religious traditions, here very specifically that of the Roman Catholic Church.
It is on this unusual level of the supernatural, where hardly any
American film has ever succeeded, that Friedkin's film and

Blatty's novel have apparently hit on some current (or perhaps enduring) widespread interest in a rather esoteric way of accounting for abnormal behavior.

The other generic source of horror in *The Exorcist* is the matter of possession in general, which of course calls to mind first the "living dead" motif, the zombies or vampires that inhabit bodies that are otherwise externally human. In *The Exorcist,* Satan himself takes up residence in the body of twelve-year-old Regan. Possessions in most films culminate in a "permanent" death, whereas the essence of *The Exorcist* is the hope of a curative ritual, the return of control over Regan's body to her imprisoned spirit. This horror motif is also related, however indirectly, to the concept of existing under the control of a master, a Count Dracula or a scientist or a hypnotist who determines the will of the victim; yet the idea of an external or remote master seldom succeeds in generating as much horror as Friedkin produces here. The film's tone of hysteria, however, helps implant the attitude of seriousness in us while we watch *The Exorcist,* and the demonic possession of the child is characterized by vicious or malignant attacks on adult sensibility. Possession as a horror motif is effective in two directions: getting the audience's sympathy for the mother, who along with the adult community is the object of the devilish animosity of the possessed girl, and for the girl herself, who is utterly submerged except for occasional pleas, made in calm moments, to be restored to normality.

154

Some of the adverse criticism aimed at the author and the director for the film's horror was made on the basis of the film's sensationalism and graphic shock effects, which are probably charges that could be leveled at most films in the genre. Religious symbols are much in evidence and are deliberately put to perverse use by the devil while he is in the girl's body. Satan in the child's form utters obscenities to priests and uses a crucifix in a bloody masturbation sequence, but as if to compensate for that, he shows an unusual aversion to holy water. Other than this, the horror consists of spitting and vomiting and much shaking of the bed. One murder occurs, which we do not see on screen, and at the end of the exorcism, when the devil apparently moves from the body of the girl to that of the surviving priest (the other dies, evidently of natural causes, during the rites of exorcism), the priest throws himself out the window to his death.

If there is any manipulation, it has to do with Friedkin's insistence on maintaining a level of frenzy to sustain the horror; but the alternative to this would have produced an entirely different kind of film. Without the consistent frenzy the audience might begin to draw back and objectify certain elements of the horror that are pictorially perhaps much less than horrific. For instance, the physical image of levitation or of a head turned 360 degrees with no ill effects might fit just as well in a Mack Sennett or Abbott and Costello film as here, yet no one in the audience laughs at these scenes in *The Exorcist*. This tone is also kept up by the mother's frantic anger at the futility of the medical men examining her daughter (the mother also sustains the tone of obscenity, for a similar purpose). In real life, the mother would surely bow to the pressure of a psychiatric group and commit her daughter to a term of observation and treatment—much more plausible than tying the extremely powerful child to the bed. But such rational objections at each stage of the film are irrelevant to the thrust of *The Exorcist*, which is toward the analysis of a peculiar aspect of life. It is not a film in which the ambiguities lead to a tragicomic view of life, as Hitchcock might have developed it. Friedkin's film is humorless except for the flagrant obscenity of the devil, which Satan may intend to be funny, but which the characters in the film always either are shocked by or ignore. It is a film about the phenomenon of possession, not about the responses of skeptics to it. In fact, in the film, the psychiatrists themselves suggest the exorcist, and the Church exhibits some skepticism. Nor is it a theological film, though the author has stated an opinion about the film's dealing with such matters as redemption. The theology of the film is unacceptable within Christian philosophy or literary tradition; the Great Adversary who confronts Christ in the desert in the New Testament and the imposing figure of Satan in Milton's *Paradise Lost* are reduced in *The Exorcist* to motiveless malignancy, enfeebled to the point of being capable of little more than parlor tricks, bed shaking, a little extra strength (but not stronger than two people), a few curse words, and even fewer latinisms. While neither the scholarship nor the power of the devil is imposing in this film, the mere possibility of his being in possession of a human being's physical identity keeps *The Exorcist* very close to the tradition of the psychological horror of the nightmare world.

155

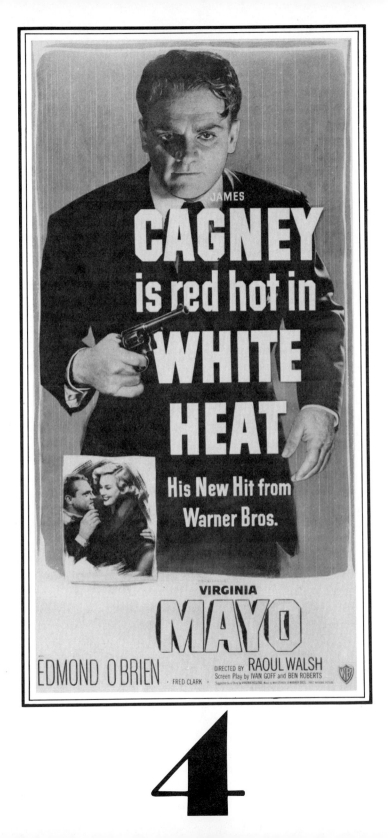

4

THE LIFE
OF CRIME

THE CATEGORIES OF CRIMINAL FILMS

Among the oldest and most often revitalized cinematic genres, the criminal film derives its mass appeal from several sources. Its mythic dimensions frequently lie just below its surface story. Its motifs can be traced to the origins of any culture; these motifs were used (or exploited) by Hollywood in the 1930s in some of the same ways they were used in ancient forms. The moral lesson of Cain and Abel or the ethical problems of justice and retribution in Aeschylus' plays are direct antecedents of the criminal film.

But of more immediate interest to us in the cinematic treatment of the generic themes is the apparent fact that much of the criminal film's mass appeal originates in our appreciation of the vicarious experience of continual action, violence, social deviation, corruption, and a determined drive for power. The life of crime as depicted in film provides the public with a textbook on the nether world of contemporary civilization, and thereby fulfills the prime function of what must have been the basic concept of cinema in its formative era: to give us a window on the world, to allow us to see beyond the walls enclosing our normal perceptions of the reality around us.

Although not as prolific a genre as the Western, the crime film is older and in one sense probably the source of the Western: an early Western film such as Edwin Porter's *The Great Train Robbery* (1903) was likely to have been first perceived by audiences as establishing the crime genre rather than the Western. In any case, silent films provide many and varied examples of the crime genre. D. W. Griffith produced many crime films prior to his mini-classic, *The Musketeers of Pig Alley* (1912), and by the time he included a modern crime story in *Intolerance* (1916), the type was fairly well recognized in feature-length films. Even before the sound era, the genre had developed distinct categories that showed the basic division used in this study: films that deal primarily with people plotting and carrying out criminal activities and—to be discussed in the next chapter—films that feature people preventing crimes or apprehending criminals.

The genre of the crime film is readily identified by the overall activities and milieu of its characters, but we can divide it into primary categories in terms of four relevant criminal types. (1) The gangster or syndicate member: an overt criminal, whether the great Don Corleone or a hoodlum like Scarface. The police in the film and the representatives of the civilized world in general can immediately identify the movie gangsters and their social milieu. (2) The concealed criminal: an infiltrator of the normal world, he or she is a figure of corruption, existing on the surface as a law-abiding citizen but completely involved in dishonest enterprises. This character is sometimes known by many to be corrupt (for example, a union leader or politician) but still presents a facade of legitimacy difficult to penetrate. (3) The prisoner: although the criminal's activities here are confined among other prisoners and guards, he or she is understood to be capable of violence and to retain many of the values of those in the first category. (4) The swindler, con man, or "big caper" organizer: the thief, engaged in accumulating money by outsmarting those people or institutions that have wealth.

Considering the intention of their chief activity, we may more properly assign murderers to film classifications other than crime. Elements of revenge, intrigue, mystery, detection, and horror fit various genres more revealing of the nature of the murderer than does the crime film. Some gangsters are murderous, but in terms of occupation, even hired killers who work for criminals are not, cinematically, occupational murderers but simply lower-echelon gangsters. The exception to this classification, however, happens to be perhaps the greatest work in the genre, Charles Chaplin's *Monsieur Verdoux* (1947). Still, even Verdoux, the most professional of murderers, operates essentially in the realm of the confidence man. If, generically, mass murderers belong to the nightmare world, the reasonable Verdoux by contrast contrives his murders in the rational fashion of a dispassionate swindler pursuing any ordinary illegal enterprise.

Another way of categorizing criminal types is to use two broadly perceived patterns: the characters' psychological orientation as purveyors of violence or as thieves. The first group can be further divided into its most interesting manifestations: films about traveling gangs (Raoul Walsh's *High Sierra* [1941]); bank robbers (Joseph Lewis's *Gun Crazy* [1949]); criminal organizations such as the Mafia, the syndicate, or the underworld (Samuel Fuller's *Underworld USA* [1961]); and gangster biographies (Richard Wilson's *Al Capone* [1959], John Milius's *Dillinger* [1973], or fictional lives such as Michael Curtiz's *Angels with Dirty Faces* [1938]). As for biography, two separate types of films are common: those that deal with the sympathetic criminal who,

159

for reasons detailed at some length, has chosen crime out of necessity or has been accidentally condemned to live that way (Nicholas Ray's *Knock on Any Door* [1949], Fritz Lang's *You Only Live Once* [1937]); or those that depict characters well suited by nature for a vicious career (Don Siegel's *Baby Face Nelson* [1957]).

Films about thieves differ considerably in tone from films about violent criminals. Thieves either come from or aspire to an upper-class environment, and generally they shy away from violence, at least in their plans. The two major types of movie thieves are the lone operators, who perfect skills that enable them to steal or cheat repeatedly, and the organizers, who plan the type of crime often called "the big caper." In films that deal with big capers, the entire film typically leads up to and away from a single, ingeniously conceived crime that is supposed to net the group of thieves enough money to retire. This type of crime invariably attracts noncriminal characters, amateurs, or retired master criminals, but always people with brains and sometimes with great style (for instance, Fred Astaire once played one). What frequently distinguishes big caper films, and to a significant extent all films about stealing, is humor or comedy. Some of these films successfully mix their serious or dramatic elements with comedy, as in Hitchcock's *To Catch a Thief* (1955), but more often than not, once comedy is introduced it determines the whole tone of the film. The comic pattern of the big caper film was established by an Italian film, Mario Monicelli's *Big Deal on Madonna Street* (1960), which stressed the plausible concept of criminal incompetence, parodying an earlier French film, Jules Dassin's somber *Rififi* (1955), which popularized the category by detailing the fascinating skills needed for this type of work. The typical comic pattern of the thief film, while frequently European in its inspiration, probably achieved its artistic culmination years ago in the American work by Ernst Lubitsch, *Trouble in Paradise* (1932).

The generic relationships among all the categories of crime films are found in the main characters' illegal enterprise and the inherent dangers of their existence. As long as criminal activities are not tolerated by the community, the possibility of arrest is usually a pressure motivating the criminal's patterns of behavior and his usually neurotic attitudes toward his surrounding environment (though some films concern themselves only with criminals, and the actual threat of outside intervention by the police is minimal). Perhaps more generically important, criminal planning must be done in confidence. We often note the fear of "leaks" and the occurrence of "tips"—passed on to rival groups or to lawmen. "Stool pigeons" are probably more common in police films, but they appear in the crime genre too; there are also the

160

disloyal colleagues of the criminal enterprise who through intimidation, greed, or envy betray the plans and destroy the hopes of the main characters.

THE GANGSTER MIND

Along with musical film, the gangster film was the first major category of the era of the talking picture, taking advantage, as critic Arthur Knight has noted, of the possibilities of a realistic, clipped dialogue, not at all literary but perfectly suited to the cinematic materials at hand. Conceived as sustained action dramas in an urban setting, the early films displayed impressive street sets that captured naturalistic elements of the city, with the camera sometimes exploring this environment and singling out conditions of crowded poverty (as in William Wyler's *Dead End* [1937], constructed on a huge studio set)—which immediately implied a reason for the criminal life style. The setting did not explain everything, but it took audiences instantly into the familiar stratum of the inner city and made essayistic discussions of the issue of survival unnecessary.

161

If the early gangster film often appeared to be excessively simpleminded, with its appeal aimed at the lowest levels of audience gratification, this was so only because its creative artistry came close to pure cinema—a clearly linked pattern of visual images, an eminently coherent narrative, dialogue that almost always seemed perfectly appropriate for the emotions generated within the dramatic sequence. More than that, the underlying myth of the gangster film, which may not have been noted at the time, had much to do with 1930s cinema's increased interest in the significance of urban life. Robert Warshow sees the gangster as a surrogate hero for the contemporary man suffering the depersonalizing pressures of the city:

> . . . we are always conscious that the whole meaning of the [gangster's] career is a drive for success: the typical gangster film presents a steady upward progress followed by a very precipitate fall. . . . the initial contact between the film and its audience is an agreed conception of human life: that man is a being with the possibilities of success or failure. This principle, too, belongs to the city; one must emerge from the crowd or else one is nothing. On that basis the necessity of the action is established, and it progresses by inalterable paths to the point where the gangster lies dead and the principle has been modified: there is really only one possibility—failure. The final meaning of the city is anonymity and death.*

*"The Gangster as Tragic Hero," *The Immediate Experience* (New York: Atheneum, 1971), p. 132.

Whatever the contemporary public's perception of the gangster role was, the gangster was—and often still is—portrayed as an admirable figure in spite of the violence of his occupation. Given the value system of our society, the outcry for censorship of the genre in the 1930s seems rational enough, for there was no critical distinction between the portrayal of admirable aspects of the criminal type and the glamorization of crime itself—the latter not necessarily being a corollary of the former. Our tendency to admire or sympathize with the gangster has much to do with our general interest in any main character in a narrative. For one thing, we know the main character better than we do others in the film; for another, we believe that few people are totally despicable anyway. The rare good actions of a bad man, which in reality cannot balance out a life of misdeeds, can in the cinema register graphically on our minds.

Equally important in explaining the audience attitude toward the criminal, of course, are the magnificent impersonations offered by such actors of the time as Edward G. Robinson, Humphrey Bogart, and James Cagney. It must always be remembered, of course, that in spite of the elements of American realism emphasized in all gangster films, every one of them is a highly fictionalized account of the life of crime. In the 1920s and especially the 1930s, some real-life counterparts of the movies' criminal heroes were made into folk heroes; modern research, however, seems to indicate that they were, as we might have expected, a pretty miserable, vicious lot—though no doubt in some cases the movie characterizations based on the exploits of certain criminals had some reciprocal influence on other real-life bank robbers and Prohibition-era criminals.* Nevertheless, the film gangster always exhibits certain fascinating traits: courage, daring, and an ability to respond quickly to the particular terrors of city life (including the assassins waiting in a limousine on the corner).

Even though it was accused of distorting values by glamorizing the gangster, the film industry did also portray the brutality of criminal life. The presence of charismatic performers could not obliterate the graphic depiction of the activities of thugs, and even when a case was made for a particular criminal, the audience was not allowed to forget the environment in which he thrived, an unredeeming environment of sudden violence and constant revenge. The most charismatic of gangster actors was

---

*This is surely true in regard to such a film as Howard Hawks's *Scarface* (1932): Paul Muni's clothes, mannerisms, and general values seemed to gain unofficial gangland approval (supposedly from Al Capone's gang), as did George Raft's "cool" stylization, the counterpoint to his boss's frenetic neurosis. Such movies may have inspired romantic self-images of real-life criminals of the 1930s.

James Cagney, who always conveyed toughness, cunning, and vitality continually evidenced by his fearlessness in hostile environments and his willingness to stand up against physically larger men. Cagney portrayed the full range of gangster roles, from the hopelessly vicious killers of William Wellman's *The Public Enemy* (1931) and Walsh's *White Heat* (1949) to the sympathetic, victimized-by-environment criminals of *Angels with Dirty Faces* and Walsh's *The Roaring Twenties* (1939). His special quality in the sympathetic roles was his humor, which plainly indicated that the toughness his character adopted within the criminal environment was self-conscious; he always seemed to know how his physical presence, particularly his entrances and exits, affected his enemies and his followers.

The implicit question of the genre—and the explicit question of many analyzers of the subject—is how a potentially likable character (and in many instances an admirable character) could become a believable villain in the first place. Normally, the film gives us a few pieces of information to consider, though in a certain sense Warshow's generalization is correct:

163

> Usually, when we come upon him, he has already made his choice or the choice has already been made for him, it doesn't matter which: we are not permitted to ask whether at some point he could have chosen to be something else than what he is.*

Warshow, however, glosses over the often-crucial distinction between freedom of choice and accident in the determination of a gangster's career. Our own attitude is surely affected by whether a man engages in crime for one reason or another, whether he is a victim or a victimizer. The genre itself may have been slow to realize this fact. Colin McArthur notes a shift somewhere in the mid 1930s:

> Up to this point in its development, the explicit attitude of the gangster film to the criminal had been a simple one. Criminals are born, not made; they are incapable of reform and can be stopped only by being destroyed. It is true that *The Public Enemy* . . . has the materials for a statement about the social origins of crime, but this is not developed. The possibility of such a statement does not reappear until William Wyler's *Dead End* (1937), marking the beginning of the next phase of the genre.†

Interestingly, the introduction of social theory, with its implicit plea for an understanding of the criminal's motivation,

---

*"The Gangster as Tragic Hero," p. 131.
† *Underworld U.S.A.* (New York: Viking, 1972), p. 39.

does not affect the plot structure of the genre's films. Cagney as unregenerate killer is gunned down not only in *The Public Enemy* and *White Heat*, but also in *The Roaring Twenties*, where a good deal of time is spent in the beginning of the film to show Cagney first as a good soldier in battle, next as a returning veteran unable to find a job, and then as an innocent victim falsely arrested and facing two months in jail because he does not have $100 to pay his fine. When he is bailed out by a woman who operates a speakeasy he simply slips into a criminal existence. Nevertheless, his aggressive nature and his abilities assure that he will rise to the top in this enterprise. A life of crime for Cagney is almost a matter of survival. (Prohibition criminals operating on the lower levels of the organization often had social approval in that era.) But from that point on in the film, Cagney sees that he can regulate his own destiny in the world of crime, limited only by his own decisions, whereas when he tries to find an honest existence for himself he is entirely at the mercy of an indifferent, sometimes cruel society.

164   Yet the theme of the doomed hero is as operative in *The Roaring Twenties* as that of the doom of the rising hood is in *The Public Enemy*. It is not the criminal act, but the whole pattern of a life of crime that the gangster follows through progressive stages to his inevitable downfall. In *Angels with Dirty Faces*, Cagney is presented as a good man in a bad business, and he refrains from acts of murder until the end of the film. Even then he kills only the craven villains who were plotting to kill a priest (the most craven is played by Bogart, who will be cowardly again in *The Roaring Twenties* the following year and again will be shot by Cagney). Thus, it is Cagney's destiny that ultimately controls him, and we do not feel that his ending up in the electric chair carries with it the same moral justification we feel at the demise of other Cagney-played criminals, such as Cody Jarrett in *White Heat*.

Curtiz in *Angels with Dirty Faces* uses the fatalism implicit in the genre to promote our sympathy and pity for his hero because in this case we realize that the "hero" could have been something finer than he was, had he lived in a better world. The parallel is drawn between two childhood friends—Cagney, who became a big-time gangster, and his former juvenile-delinquent sidekick (played by Pat O'Brien) who reformed and became a priest. Cagney serves a prison term for a crime that O'Brien shared in. The film exhibits an insight into an aspect of the genre that had existed previously, but had been developed on a much less self-conscious level: the appeal to the gangster's better nature, if persistent enough, will activate the soft sentimentalism that is usually the core of his being but that he has made great efforts to hide or destroy. The gangster is perhaps aware that his sentimental secret nature is in itself a destructive element for a man who makes his way by punching or shooting people routinely. Bogart's Duke Mantee displayed this quality memorably in Archie Mayo's *The Petrified Forest* (1936), but indications of it can often be found, though they are seldom exploited, in almost all crime films of the 1930s.

In *Angels with Dirty Faces,* however, Curtiz draws out this quality by showing two paths open to the criminal from the urban slum environment. When Cagney returns to his old neighborhood, he discovers that he has become a folk hero to the local youth gang, but at the same time that he begins to inspire, almost to teach them, he gets reinvolved with his old friend O'Brien, now the priest. The priest asks the criminal's assistance in transforming the youths from potential thugs to solid citizens, and Cagney does what he can, asking nothing in return. As he becomes a more notorious criminal, and thus a greater idol to the neighborhood youths, he does not forget his deeply rooted childhood ties with the priest, his surrogate family (in gangster films, the criminal is usually good to his family). At the end of the film, a few minutes before he is to be sent to the electric chair, Cagney is visited by O'Brien, who urges the undaunted hero to pretend to die a cowardly death so that the report of it will undermine Cagney's reputation in the eyes of the youth gang. Cagney (and perhaps the movie audience too, as witnesses to the victimized life of an essentially noble man) is shocked by his friend's appeal. He refuses to give away this last shred of human dignity, but as he walks toward the execution room he changes his mind. Curtiz films the sequence indirectly, showing only the shadow of Cagney falling to his knees and screaming his pretended fear to the guards. Naturally the plan works, and the neighborhood kids convert to a "clean" life out of disillusionment with their hero. The end result of the sacrifice on Cagney's part, however, and the corresponding lie the priest utters when the kids ask him if their hero really died a coward, is that the overt moral conclusion is reversed, as Curtiz no doubt intended: Cagney emerges as a hero to us, the audience, in a way that surpasses the feelings we have for him in other films where he is an exciting, courageous criminal but not so surely a victim of society and his own inner goodness.

165

The genre, therefore, accommodates stories about both criminals who deserve their violent deaths and criminals who do not, within essentially similar story lines. If we feel that Cagney in *The Public Enemy,* Muni in *Scarface,* Edward G. Robinson in Mervyn LeRoy's *Little Caesar* (1930), Bogart in *Dead End,* and Mickey Rooney in *Baby Face Nelson* deserve to die, we probably feel that there is less moral justification for the deaths of Cagney in *The Roaring Twenties,* Bogart in *The Petrified Forest,* Henry Fonda in *You Only Live Once,* and Burt Lancaster in Robert Siodmak's *The Killers* (1946).

CRIMINAL VALUES

The daily activities of the master thief, swindler, or organizational wizard who designs the perfect robbery naturally differ from the routine of the gangster; however, they all are professionally preoccupied with the life of crime, devoted to perfecting their skills and deservedly, they feel, enriching themselves at the expense of a society that they regard as the unworthy guardian of the sources of wealth. Yet ultimately not the wealth itself but the procedures of acquiring it mark the professional character of the criminal. Each criminal type is dedicated to its own set of standards of excellence. Murder as a crime of passion, rather than of necessity or revenge, would signal weakness since it detracts from professional activities; thus "occasional" or passionate murderers do not figure in the genre. Mass murderers, as distinct from syndicate-contract murderers, belong to the psychologically oriented genres of either horror or police detection. To engage in a life of crime, the criminal dedicates himself to the primary task at hand. Indeed, gangsters are particularly ascetic in their concentration, having just as little time for sidelights like romance as has the other most dedicated group of movie professionals, the detectives. It is no wonder then that criminals seem to have been—and to continue to be—glorified in films: proficiency in any job seems admirable when we are not directly threatened by it. Usually, though, the movies have also depicted the more gruesome aspects of criminal life so that it surely is an oversimplification to accuse the genre's filmmakers of deliberately creating heroes out of villains. After all, not only is the gangster usually gunned down, but a kind of justice is arrived at through the ultimate brutalization of his existence and his death.

There is, however, one kind of criminal who generally does not die and in fact often succeeds, though love or carelessness might trip him up at the end: the big-time thief. Unlike the bank robber or the member of an underworld organization, the thief is essentially not vicious and exists behind a facade of respectability or a disguise of innocence. Of particular interest are two types, the charming professional, usually a jewel thief—a Herbert Marshall (in *Trouble in Paradise*) or a Cary Grant (in *To Catch a Thief*); and the ambitious amateur who devises the big caper such as Steve McQueen in Norman Jewison's *The Thomas Crown Affair*

166

(1968) or Melina Mercouri in Jules Dassin's *Topkapi* (1964). Our interest in the thieves can be generated simply by our desire to see the successful execution of an intricate plot. Yet often it has much to do with our sympathy for the criminals themselves, a sympathy that is not like our feelings for those doomed gangsters whose virtues are courage, persistence, and a realistic fatalism about themselves. Thieves are barely akin to gangsters: like us, thieves exhibit an underlying fear of encounters with the law, of arrest. The reason for their cunning and skillful planning is precisely to avoid danger as much as possible, given the nature of their enterprise. The gangster's sense of survival is not so profoundly rooted as to prevent his occasional recklessness. But the thief's very pronounced sense of survival is typified by his caution.

One of the peculiar attributes common to most films both about gangsters and about thieves is the relative ethical standing of the criminal activity. As immoral as crime may be in the abstract, in a particular film it is usually measured against an even less appealing alternative. As a result the criminal act performed by the main character in comparison to what others are doing in the same film often creates the necessary sympathy on the part of the audience. If the criminal is confronted with others of the same profession, we want the main character to succeed because the others represent a worse system of values or a potential viciousness unjustified by the prevailing circumstances. In Francis Ford Coppola's *The Godfather* (1972), we side with one gang against all its opposition not because we approve of the gang's murders, but because the opposing criminal factions are more chaotic, less scrupulous, and apparently less skillful at organizational crime. If in some crime films the major opposition to the main characters is the police, the portrayal of "the law" is almost always highly negative: the police are less adept at their profession than the criminals at theirs, and frequently ruthless, immoral, inept, or corrupt besides. It would be artistically destructive to the genre if the police were treated so favorably that the audience wanted them to capture the criminals.

167

Thus, crime films operate in a specially constructed moral universe that in many ways resembles the real world but does not attempt to cope with the real world's value systems. These films could not deal precisely with the moral issue of crime without becoming, on the one hand, social documentaries of considerable magnitude, or on the other, mere case studies. The gangster biography, which comes closest to the latter, is itself only a purported case study: it is essentially fictional narrative. We may note that the precedent for the moral relativism of the crime genre is its historical development in seventeenth- and eighteenth-century fiction, notably in the works of Daniel Defoe. The prototype novel is Defoe's *Moll Flanders* (1722), in which the heroine, a whore and a thief, emerges constantly as morally justifiable in spite of her frequent and acknowledged wrongdoing, primarily because she is more intelligent and likable than the rest of the characters in her environment. Her advantage is the same as that of all the gangsters and thieves to follow her in American films: superiority to the others depicted in the limited world of the fictional narrative. If the world at large were ever depicted in a genre film, moral outrage would be generated by the criminal activity, and we would lose our comparative sympathy; the glamor of crime would disappear in the everyday reality of penniless widows and orphaned children. But the purpose of filmmakers working in the genre is certainly not moral criticism of criminal life, which is only a small factor, a byproduct of certain crime films. Often the possible moral criticism is completely muted by removing from our attention any real representatives of noncriminal life. Thus, in films like *The Godfather*, there is nothing for us to condemn in the film itself (though of course many viewers deplore the violence of it) because the incessant criminal activity is directed at other criminals.

168

Like Moll Flanders, the professional criminals of the American cinema demonstrate superiority to their brethren not only by being more skillful in their trade but by holding moral views about what they are doing. In company with thieves and big caper organizers, who generally come from the middle or upper class, are not forced to participate in crime, and try to avoid violence, even the most unregenerate criminals, like Cagney's Tom Powers in *The Public Enemy*, are by contrast some small degree less reprehensible than their enemies. In one of the best of the 1970s films about criminals, *The Friends of Eddie Coyle* (directed by Peter Yates, 1973), the title itself expresses the implicit irony surrounding Eddie's death: a small-time hood like Eddie is doomed by the environment he cannot escape, and his little decencies are merely weaknesses in comparison with the qualities of his ruthless friends.

George Roy Hill's *The Sting* (1973) provides a brilliant example of how the genre creates a reasonable facsimile of moral order within a situation that—in a real-life equivalent—would be completely beyond moral considerations. Virtually everyone in this film is a professional criminal, from the extortionist policeman to the rackets head to the contract murderer. Within the fictional universe of this film, so determinedly given over to violence and corruption, it is no wonder that the affairs of two skilled con men should provide splendid relief from the more serious criminal activity surrounding them—and this would be true even if the con men were played by a couple of professional thugs, let alone the extraordinarily popular Robert Redford and Paul Newman. But with the charismatic charms they bring to their roles from their previous films, and the comical and humane characterizations they undertake, they immediately convert their roles into types of folk heroes.

This film seems particularly successful in establishing a hierarchy of moral values, a tendency typical of the genre. Redford and Newman as partners work a con on the devious and clever underworld kingpin, who is depicted as both vicious and proud. His deception is therefore both deserved and comically deflating, especially since in addition to being a villain with notable vices (such as having people he dislikes murdered), he too is a con man. While participating in what he believes is a scheme to defraud Newman he is completely fooled by the two partners. Furthermore, the moral issue is raised early in the film by the murder of Redford's old and poor black colleague (black because the film utilizes all opportunities to draw the lines between the good guys, who are not racially prejudiced, and the bad, who are). 169 The man is murdered for committing a relatively small fraud, accidentally directed against the organized numbers racket. Thus, Redford's motivation is revenge against the man who ordered his colleague's murder; the way he sets about obtaining it increases our admiration. He seeks out a famous con man, Newman, and asks to be taught how to work the "big con" against his all-powerful enemy (who throughout the film maintains a "contract" he has taken out on Redford's life). Indeed, the film's surface is so complicated by motivations, cross-purposes, and deceptions that the plot is almost as difficult to describe as the incomprehensible plots of some private detective films. Yet the overriding issue is kept clearly in focus: Redford and Newman risk their lives to pull off their confidence game, not for the huge sum of money they can gain from it but, on Newman's part, for the sake of the artistry of his plan and his affection for Redford and, on Redford's part, out of a desire to revenge his murdered friend.

The world of *The Sting*, like that of other criminal films, is a limited and stylized microcosm, free from the concerns and the pursuits of noncriminals. The chain of events in crime films deserves our attention exactly because this action depicts the lives (not just the life styles) of the characters, played out against a background of values and codes of behavior fascinating in the degree of their intricacy and deviation from normal life. For instance, everyday experience tells us that the desire for wealth is a powerful motivating factor in human life; yet in crime films the leading characters generally display only vague desires of this sort. The usual motive for crime outside the criminal genre is certainly money—as we see in the detective genre, in which films, however, the emphasis is on the sleuth, not the criminal. When the movies offer us an analysis of motivation in the criminal film, money ceases to be an important factor. In the most brutal films about crime, money is always much in evidence, tossed around by the criminals as part of the paraphernalia of the profession. But the richest criminals, for example the "family dons," often seem concerned mainly with family honor and preserving the peace—that is, ruling over an orderly little kingdom. Such criminals are largely depicted as conservative businessmen, and they do not flaunt money. Bank robbers and other vicious criminals who seem to make a very good income may indeed exhibit hedonistic qualities, which usually just reflect another form of their fatalism, but by and large the Bonnies and Clydes do what they do because there is nothing else to be done. Robbing and shooting is what they know, and alternatives for them are always abstractions. The Prohibition bootleggers of 1930s films seem motivated by a desire to push others around, which may have been psychologically caused by impoverished childhoods in which we sometimes see them pushed around by their parents and society. In most cases, if money is a factor at all, it is so only in the sense that it provides a much-needed status. Deprived of the possibility of achieving honest status by the Great Depression, the criminals of the 1930s films climb to the top of the underworld by their perverted idea of American values. With money, criminals could force people to notice them; without money, they might sink back into the anonymity they desperately need to escape. Becoming notorious desperadoes or working their way up through the ranks of an organized criminal operation, gangsters discover their identity. Faced with arrest, like Rico in *Little Caesar,* they intuitively sense a loss of identity, a depersonalization that is a prospect worse than death. Thus, with no sensible alternative, a Rico or a Cody in *White Heat* will never let himself be taken alive.

Money in the hands of jewel thieves is simply another material of their trade. They need to mingle with wealthy people in order to operate successfully, and of course they always seem to have adopted the life style of their potential victims. Only rarely, as in the case of Hitchcock's master jewel thief in *To Catch a Thief,* do we have an example of someone who has made enough money to retire—and in this film he is forced out of his peaceful withdrawal to catch another thief who is copying his former modus operandi. All other jewel thieves seem only moderately successful; they have to expend their ill-gotten gains to live among the truly wealthy.

The one subcategory of the crime genre in which money may be a major motivation is the big caper film, where obviously the raison d'être is to steal a significant sum. Yet even in this group, money is sometimes a nebulous factor. The hero of *The Thomas Crown Affair* is so well-to-do already that his motive is more the perfection of his plans than the sum stolen.

"You're not a criminal," the Scotland Yard inspector says to the hero of Jack Smight's *Kaleidoscope* (1966), demanding an explanation of why the wealthy young playboy (Warren Beatty) should have engineered his master crime: marking the Kaleidoscope playing card design so that he could win at gambling casinos throughout Europe. The only answer the inspector gets is that once the hero had thought of the crime, the desire to practice it became "irresistible." Crime, then, can become the hobby of the otherwise-idle rich. Since big caper crime is always aimed at the institutions of the rich such as banks, casinos, or corporations that have huge amounts of money, film audiences are remote from any sense of involvement in the security of valued property. We almost always want the criminals to succeed; so to prevent the category from becoming merely the means of dramatizing an audience's fantasy, filmmakers endow the hero with certain qualities that will compensate morally for his criminal acts, as in John Huston's *The Asphalt Jungle* (1950), where Dix (Sterling Hayden) is seen to be thoroughly honorable and motivated by a nostalgic desire to return to the farm of his youth; or else they have him outmaneuver an organization more disreputable than he is (as in *The Sting*). In *Kaleidoscope,* the captured hero is made to work for the police against a wealthy gambler who makes his money from narcotics. Thus, the hero's relatively harmless cheating in gambling casinos can be forgiven (if the money is returned) because he will later risk his life in a major deception leading to the ruin of a narcotics empire.

171

PRISONERS

A few years ago a popular television commercial parodied a prison scene typical of the crime genre as found in such a film as Walsh's *White Heat:* in the commercial, prisoners in the mess hall—prominently among them George Raft—rhythmically pounded their metal cups against the table shouting "Alka-Seltzer! Alka-Seltzer! Alka-Seltzer! . . ." The point of the commercial, presumably, was that confronted by penitentiary food, the inmates were staging a protest in the form of a demand for stomach relief—symbolically depicting not an incipient rebellion against the institution but a claim to an alternative system of justice to be supplied by the sponsor's product.

In addition to being an effective parody of the prison film, the commercial managed to suggest the thematic essence of the genre by fastening on a familiar element. Prison rebellion is endemic, regardless of where in the prison it takes place or in what degree of violence it ultimately erupts. Films with long prison sections represent the only important category of the crime genre that emphasizes social protest, and has done so from its first major example, George Hill's *The Big House* (1930), to Stanley Kubrick's English film, *A Clockwork Orange* (1973). This theme of protest organizes the dramatic material of the category into both of its major plot situations: the attempted escape and the internal conflict between prisoners and guards. Theoretically, it seems feasible to make a film in which a group of villainous prisoners makes life difficult for the authorities, who are good-natured and aware of their social responsibilities in regard to the inmates. But such a plot has not been turned into a memorable film. The Alka-Seltzer commercial links up with our general impression of the category: men in desperate circumstances resisting the oppression of the institution.

Even in films in which men are unjustly imprisoned, films that do not truly belong to the genre of criminal life, such as Hitchcock's *The Wrong Man* (1956), we note how spiritually deadening and genuinely oppressive are the conditions of imprisonment, though the plot emphasis in these films falls on the rectifying of a gross mistake. In addition, films that deal with criminals deservedly serving time for an assortment of criminal acts, including murder, almost invariably direct our sympathy toward these men and away from either their immediate oppressors (the guards) or society in general (whose indifference has created the conditions the prisoners seek to change).

The outward complaints of prisoners, whether about bad food or inadequate cells, really relate to the inward process of dehumanization, a process that more often than not is a deliberate strategy of the institution, the chief guard, or the warden himself (or all three, as in Stuart Rosenberg's *Cool Hand Luke* [1967]). When a single person embodies the social evil of the prison, there is usually accompanying evidence that he has a sadistic mentality, sometimes overtly cruel to the point of perversion. In Jules Dassin's *Brute Force* (1947) the prisoners planning an escape are motivated by their hatred of a guard (memorably portrayed by Hume Cronyn), a fascist psychopath who tortures inmates and is ultimately thrown to his death during the unsuccessful breakout attempt. Another subcategory features the prisoner-leader as the source of evil: he may appear as a simple brute bullying the others with his physical superiority, a gangster with connections to the outside, or a surrogate of the guards, supported and encouraged by them as another means of controlling the group. In comic prison films the bully is usually vulnerable because he is stupid: the little hero's large cellmate in Charles Chaplin's *Modern Times* (1936) is not much of a danger after he is shown sewing. But the sadistic criminal bent on subjugating others provides a recurring motif in the more recent additions to the category. In *Scarecrow* (directed by Jerry Schatzberg, 1973), for example, the present-day emphasis on the penal problems of homosexuality and related abuses is made the focus of attention in the sequences depicting prison life. Generally, the humiliation of men (or women, in the few films depicting women's prisons), no matter what crimes they committed prior to their incarceration, remains the essence of the social protest in the prison film.

In certain cases, the sympathetically portrayed warden (or prison psychiatrist or guard) establishes some balance in the conflict; nevertheless, the purpose of a prison film most commonly is to give a full portrait of the prisoners. The point of the film, after all, evolves from the condition of these men: they are potentially dangerous and they have been forced into an unnatural community from which there is no relief. Left with continual thoughts of escape or parole, in the most tedious circumstances, how will they cope with the situation? How much will they take of the demeaning tasks and overt brutality of the institution? Solitary confinement, the institution's typical mode of enforcing its policy of dehumanization, is fairly common (though, as demonstrated repeatedly in *Cool Hand Luke,* it never really accomplishes its intention of breaking the spirit of the rebellious prisoner). Thus, while we might see one or two concerned representatives of the prison and hundreds of hardened criminals, the visual elements of these films stress the bad conditions that lead to the prisoners' actions, and inculcate audience sympathy for those suffering repression.

173

THE PUBLIC ENEMY
(1931)

Director	Cinematographer	Script
WILLIAM WELLMAN	DEV JENNINGS	HARVEY THEW
Produced by		Based on a story by
WARNER BROTHERS		Kubec Glasmon and
VITAPHONE		John Bright

PRINCIPAL CHARACTERS

JAMES CAGNEY	JEAN HARLOW	EDWARD WOODS
Tom Powers	Gwen Allen	Matt Doyle
JOAN BLONDELL	BERYL MERCER	DONALD COOK
Mame	Ma Powers	Mike Powers
MAE CLARKE	LESLIE FENTON	ROBERT EMMETT O'CONNOR
Kitty	Samuel ("Nails") Nathan	Paddy Ryan
MURRAY KINNEL	RITA FLYNN	
Putty Nose	Molly Doyle	

Length: 83 minutes

174

The Public Enemy is probably more important evaluated from a historical view of the genre than from an artistic one, but James Cagney's portrayal of the gangster Tom Powers is virtually archetypal in the cinema's treatment of the life of crime. In some ways this seems the least insightful of Cagney's criminal characterizations, for much more depth and complexity seems to be conveyed in films like *Angels with Dirty Faces, The Roaring Twenties, White Heat,* and *Love Me or Leave Me.* Yet the images associated with Tom Powers linger in the memory longer than any of the others, perhaps because this gangster is presented entirely from the outside. Tom has no psychological reality, merely a set of gestures, voice mannerisms, and a stance (proclaiming the self-confident image of Cagney the dancer, who would portray George M. Cohan years later). Practically every gangster film that came after this one made at least some crude effort to explain the inner workings of the criminal, but the hidden strength of this film probably consists in the very fact that Tom Powers is at essence nothing, an unthinking "power" unleashed on society to wreak destruction for the simplest of self-serving motives, greed and ambition.

Nevertheless, Tom Powers represents some complex factors that Wellman apparently felt the need to explain. *The Public Enemy* depicts the childhood of this hero-villain, showing him as a young boy already fully rebellious and engaged in minor criminal activities. The environment is lower-middle-class and urban, with easy access to beer and saloons. Although Tom's good brother comes from the same background, we never really receive any insight as to why one brother works hard, studies at night, and enlists in the army, and the other turns immediately toward a criminal life. But perhaps that is exactly the film's point—one's life choice is chancy if one comes from this environment. In any event, Tom remains unredeemable to the end, operating with little thought for anyone else except for an affectionate regard for his mother, some respect for one of his girlfriends (played by Jean Harlow), and a commitment to his friend Matt. Tom is told early in his career that it is essential to have friends, and he seems inseparable from his lifetime buddy Matt—though their relationship is depicted as, primarily, simply being together. When Matt is killed in an ambush from which Tom escapes, Tom's immediate response is a murderous desire for revenge—which, however, requires an almost suicidal one-man assault on the rival gang's hangout. Out of camera range, Tom shoots down several of his enemies (as we assume from their screams), but seriously wounded in return, he lunges out into the rainswept Chicago streets, defiantly throwing his guns back into the building he has just stumbled from, and collapses, with the peculiar self-addressed line, "I ain't so tough." We do not know whether this insane vengeance was motivated by a sense of loss over his friend's death or by a determination to work out his fate, in fulfillment of a code demanding that he attack his enemies.

175

We see Wellman's view of Tom and his criminal society only through an objectified, almost documentary technique, in which each short sequence (ended neatly by a fade out) encapsulates a moment in the inevitable development of the character—from a young tough to a murderous hood and ultimately to a slaughtered gangster. Even in later examples of the genre developed along similar lines, we find very few other films depicting lives of criminals who never amounted to much and ended up ignominiously. Rico, for instance, gets to control the gang in *Little Caesar,* but Tom never even aspires to that position. Even when Nails Nathan, Tom's immediate superior, is killed in a fall from a horse, Tom goes down to the stable, pays for the horse, and shoots it, instead of rushing out to stake claim for a promotion. Here again the code of revenge works powerfully on him—though in a ludicrous context—but Tom is not driven to achieve the status of leader; he appears content with his identity within the organization as a loyal retainer. His self-image encompasses merely the outward signs of wealth—cars, clothes, girls—and a reputation for toughness.

In this latter sense, we note the beginnings of a complexity of characterization not truly pursued here, but probably inherent in the genre. Tom fears being thought of as a fool. He seems to

despise his brother (although he may secretly admire him) for working for an honest but poor living. Even as a child Tom has to pretend disdain for the ritualistic strap beatings delivered by his father. In the most brutal sequence of the film, he takes revenge on a former associate who, Tom's friends inform him, considers Tom weak for not taking revenge when denied shelter after an abortive robbery a couple of years earlier. Even Matt seems taken aback by Tom's single-minded obsession with killing the pitiful, helpless Putty Nose. Defenseless and aware that he deserves punishment, Putty Nose pleads on his knees, then runs over to a piano and plays a song he used to sing to Tom and Matt when they were kids learning crime from him. Smiling and calm in his determination, unaffected by Putty Nose's attempts to evoke nostalgia, Tom walks up behind him and shoots him as he sings. Revenge, to Tom, means preventing others from thinking they can take advantage of him and thus consider him a fool.

Two other sequences in this film helped shape the category of criminal biography, though they are so individualized they could never be exactly duplicated. At one point, sitting at the breakfast table with his girl Kitty, Tom becomes annoyed with her nagging and shoves half of a grapefruit in her face. He is not above slapping girls either, but the ultimate tough guy attitude toward women symbolized by the grapefruit scene reflects the condescension and arrogance of a superior toward a mere pretty accessory. In the 1930s, slapping a woman meant simply masculine brutality, but in films, the equivalent action with an element of humor was a sign of gangster stylization and individuality. The other sequence, perhaps the most famous image in all gangster films, is our last view of Tom, almost totally bandaged, kidnapped from the hospital and delivered to the family porch tied and dead; his brother opens the door and the corpse falls straight forward toward the camera, which is filming from a low angle. The influence of this scene on later films was in the devising of some horribly violent forms of death: gangsters usually are not merely killed by a couple of bullets but annihilated, as in the final spray-of-bullets sequence of *Bonnie and Clyde* or the tremendous fire at the chemical plant in *White Heat*. In any case, *The Public Enemy*, like *Little Caesar* and *Scarface*, established the generic structure whereby certain death awaited the gangster as an inevitable balance to the glamorous life style he envisioned for himself during his career.

177

FORCE OF EVIL
(1949)

Director	Cinematographer	Script
ABRAHAM POLONSKY	GEORGE BARNES	ABRAHAM POLONSKY
Producer		IRA WOLFERT
BOB ROBERTS		From his novel
For MGM		*Tucker's People*

PRINCIPAL CHARACTERS

JOHN GARFIELD	BEATRICE PEARSON	THOMAS GOMEZ
Joe Morse	Doris Lowry	Leo Morse
ROY ROBERTS	MARIE WINDSOR	HOWLAND CHAMBERLIN
Ben Tucker	Edna Tucker	Fred Bauer

Length: 76 minutes

Crime as a corrupting influence on the individual has not, oddly enough, served as a major theme in the genre of crime films. However, one still-neglected classic of the American cinema, *Force of Evil*, probes the implications of this theme in regard to the pursuit of materialistic goals, thereby relating the American dream to the process of crime. In one of the most richly textured and literate films, Polonsky endows Joe Morse, the spokesman for materialism, with a verbal gift for persuasively expressing the attractions of money gotten by any means—and at the same time, the author-director gives his main character the ability to articulate the underlying anxieties of fear and guilt. The ambiguities and tensions springing from this characterization of Joe, the fast-rising numbers syndicate lawyer, produce a series of ironic consequences, ultimately leading him to recognize the futility of evil.

Evil itself, as the title seems to suggest, is one of the pervasive elements of modern life, its source seeming to lie within man. It is not quite identical to greed, though its object usually is the accumulation of wealth, for it also involves the desire for success and status at any cost; it is ambition pursued without the restraint of any other values. Joe Morse would argue that evil is a normal condition of life, and that success in life means manipulating this force, since it motivates so much of personal achievement. The film, however, obviously does not support his claim because he himself proves that the exertion of his will at the proper time can free him of his association with the criminal world and restore to him his better self.

The urban society observed in the film is entirely preoccupied with making money, principally through gambling. Although Joe's law office is on Wall Street, money speculators and brokers play no part in the film, and in fact the film's range of characters is exceedingly narrow. Polonsky's tendency toward symbolic abstraction serves him well, for he manages to convey a general sense of the drive for wealth without depicting more than a few of its forms. The numbers racket is based on nickel and dime wagers, small bets by people who stake very little for the chance to be lucky once in their lives. (Surprisingly, Polonsky has no particular understanding of, or even interest in, the motivation of the bettors, but the film's artistry does not depend on this issue.) Joe has no sympathy for the gamblers, though he has a very clear idea that their activity is itself evil, evidenced by the etymology he gives of "policy" (the common term for the numbers game): betting by the poor with money supposedly intended for their life insurance premiums. His scorn for the "sucker" mentality that bets on the one-thousand-to-one odds of the game is a reason behind his decision to engineer, for the rackets boss, Tucker, the large-scale swindle that forms the basis of the film's plot.

A change in Joe's attitude is brought about by his relationship with Doris, his brother's secretary, who refuses to accept the philosophy of corruption that he propounds to her. At the same time, Joe has failed to convince his brother Leo to join the betting

178

syndicate. During a taxi ride, Joe argues to Doris that human nature is selfish, that it is a "perversion" on Leo's part not to take money just because the source is tainted. Later he shouts at Leo, "Money has no moral opinions." Nevertheless, Joe is reduced to defending his position in front of Doris; even though he explains his views forcefully enough, he evidently needs to reassure himself by this process of articulation, and thus seems to undermine his own theory that selfish interests are natural motivations for everyone.

The story of the two brothers lies at the center of *Force of Evil,* but it does not seem to relate substantially to the Cain-Abel myth, as the few critics who have bothered to write on this film suggest. The brothers do not get along; they have not seen each other for years prior to the beginning of the narrative, yet they harbor an abiding affection for each other that throughout the film struggles to overcome a scorn for each other's life style. Leo, who sacrificed his own early hopes to put Joe through law school, suffers from a sense of his brother's moral failure and his own career disappointments, which he attributes partially to his sacrifice for Joe. Joe, for his part, despises the tone of moral superiority Leo uses with him, though at the same time he recognizes that perhaps he is indeed inferior to Leo. Leo maintains some degree of integrity by independently running a small-time numbers operation. There is regret and guilt in the way each views the life of the other. Leo dies at the end of the film because of his involvement with the syndicate, after Joe finally does cajole Leo to come in with him, and Joe accepts the responsibility for his brother's death. The death causes Joe to cooperate with the authorities and destroy the syndicate, though to do so will surely involve his own disbarment and probable imprisonment. The relationship of the two brothers, even without any motifs from Cain and Abel, takes on some of the dimensions of a myth, but it is love, not envy, that determines their major decisions.

Within the category of organized crime, *Force of Evil* is notable for the moral complexity of its basic pattern: a person attempts to limit his association with a criminal element or mob to one particular activity (here, in executing a scheme to destroy financially the private operators of the numbers game and force them into syndication), but finds that he has inadvertently extended his association to the point where he detrimentally involves others whom he cares for. Trying to protect his brother, to clear his conscience after a lifetime of guilt in regard to Leo (and yet perhaps to bring Leo down from his position of moral superiority), Joe convinces Tucker to make Leo the chief banker for the syndicate. This scheme works disastrously, crushing Leo's image of himself as a man of integrity and finally leading him to his death as he is abducted by a rival mobster. In a minor way Doris too is victimized, being arrested twice in police raids. Even Joe's law partner is affected, since in helping the authorities to tap Joe's phone, he compromises his integrity. Leo's bookkeeper, already fearful of the gangster environment in which he suddenly finds himself, is brutally murdered because he witnesses Leo's abduction. And finally Tucker and his rival die violently in a three-way shootout with Joe Morse. As a "smart lawyer," Joe has spent his career building up a facade of slick legality as he concocted his scheme, but to protect his brother he has to become overtly involved in the administration of the operation, thus jeopardizing his alibi of fiduciary privilege (which twenty-five years later became a prominent issue among lawyers involved in the real-life Watergate case). He can at last extricate himself only by surrendering to the authorities in revulsion against the web of corruption he has spun around himself.

Although it is too late to save others, Joe saves himself at the end. In a sense *Force of Evil* retains some of the idealistic optimism developed in the ending of Polonsky's earlier filmscript for Robert Rossen's *Body and Soul* (1947). The later film is grimmer, but it is essentially another, more realistic, accounting of the human propensity to seek obsessively materialistic goals and the assertion of moral redemption as a plausible response to one's tragic awakening in the midst of material ruin. Joe Morse at the end seems to have gained that strength to resist evil he earlier

180

told Doris he lacked. The force of evil in the form of temptation has driven him for most of the film. When cornered, he gives up his opportunity to escape punishment and flee with a considerable amount of money. His choice not to do so is based on his observation that yielding to corrupt impulses produces further corruption. Descending to the "bottom of the world" to retrieve his brother's corpse, dumped by the mob at the foot of a bridge, Joe abandons his cynical philosophy with a simple affirmation: "I decided to help."

WHITE HEAT
(1949)

Director RAOUL WALSH	Cinematographer SID HICKOX	Script IVAN GOFF BEN ROBERTS
Producer LOUIS F. EDELMAN For Warner Brothers		Based on a story by Virginia Kellogg

PRINCIPAL CHARACTERS

JAMES CAGNEY Cody Jarrett	VIRGINIA MAYO Verna Jarrett	EDMOND O'BRIEN Hank Fallon
MARGARET WYCHERLY Ma Jarrett	STEVE COCHRAN "Big Ed" Somers	JOHN ARCHER Philip Evans

Length: 114 minutes

Although partly conceived in terms of two other film categories—police detection and prison films—*White Heat* remains memorable primarily as an episodic criminal biography. In the volatile, neurotic Cody Jarrett we have one of the most interesting antiheroes of the genre—whose most significant motivations stem from his devotion to his mother! Played frenetically by James Cagney in one of his classic roles, Cody constantly veers toward the edge of sanity, but only at the very end can he be seen to have gone over. There are moments when he is saved from turning psychotic only by lapsing into seizures of intense headaches, which are diagnosed by Treasury Department agents as the psychosomatic result of his childhood need to claim his mother's attention. (We have no sustaining evidence for this opinion, nor are we able to make anything of other evidence mentioned prominently throughout—such as the fact that Cody's father died in an asylum.) Actually, Cody Jarrett is a skilled, efficient, exceedingly brutal criminal, and all his murders make sense from his point of view; he commits them either to save his own neck or to take revenge on his enemies. He holds his gang together, though members of it express the view that he is insane; yet the logic of his schemes and his forceful leadership prove that he is indeed clearsighted.

Throughout the film Cody is pursued by agents of the Treasury Department, who continue to plot against him even when he surrenders to serve time for a state felony (to which he falsely confesses in order to avoid much more serious federal charges). The T-man Fallon poses as a prisoner and insidiously gains Cody's friendship in order to find out where Cody has hidden the money from a previous robbery, though this subplot is forgotten—as are many others—as the film progresses.* The persistence of the T-men, their characterless faces, and Fallon's treacherous behavior arouse our sympathy for the gangster since he, in contrast, remains so vital a figure. Cody's problem throughout his life has been his inability to trust anyone other than his mother. But since we see his wife running off with Big Ed, a member of his gang, Fallon ingratiating himself as a mother substitute only to deceive him, and cops and gangsters trying to kill him, the visual imagery provides valid reasons for Cody's choice of self-isolation. Near the end of the film he strolls in the woods, talking to his dead mother (as he later tells Fallon), conscious that his image would be harmed if he were seen, but he is surely not insane at this point, merely pathetic in his loneliness.

Merely as a study of a psychopathic personality, *White Heat* would not retain its high place in the history of the gangster category. Walsh has, however, filled his film with a surprising number of the most vivid, memorable images in any crime film. The terrible coldness of gangster vengeance is most effectively displayed when a captive whom Cody has concealed in the trunk of a car complains of a need for air, and Cody accommodates him by firing several shots into the trunk. And yet Jarrett's typical sadistic humor—because of a minor grievance he kicks his wife off a chair she is standing on—seems less shocking when we remember that he is played by an actor who in one 1930s film pushed a grapefruit into a woman's face and in another film dragged a woman by the hair.

The sequences relating Cody's relationship with his mother also contain some remarkable imagery. The first is a startling

---

*Spraying bullets throughout the film, Cody riddles not only a sizable number of victims but possibly the script itself, which has more holes in it than almost any other major filmscript in this category.

view of Cody, following a seizure, sitting on his mother's lap and being comforted by her, while his entire gang is in the next room. When he goes to prison, his mother takes over the leadership of the gang, and while visiting him one day she reveals that his wife has betrayed him with Big Ed. We are then treated to the peculiar sight of the kindly mother herself announcing that she will personally perform the usual gangland vengeance! Perhaps the most famous sequence in the film occurs in the prison mess hall when Cody learns of his mother's death. He goes into a fit, racked by physical pain and mental agony, stumbling wildly along the rows of crowded tables, attacking every guard who attempts to stop him. The sequence achieves a wild pathos unusual to the genre.

The ending of *White Heat,* however, remains faithful to the conventions of the genre, and ties together the thematic strands of an otherwise loose structure. During a huge chemical plant robbery, the Jarrett gang is cornered when Fallon manages to leave a message for the police and T-men. As a virtual army of law enforcers arrives, it becomes clear that the gang has no chance. Cody knows this too, but now, crazed by the excitement of his predicament, he climbs to the top of a storage container of flammable chemicals, from where he exchanges futile shots with the authorities. Fallon shoots him several times with a rifle, but Cody seems almost invulnerable. His laughter and taunting of his enemies is partly madness, but it is also a final determination to make his death a symbolic achievement. No good movie gangster, of course, would surrender in this kind of setting, a maze of modern industrialization with a huge audience of hateful but admiring police beneath him. Staggering from his wounds, he shouts to his dead mother, "I made it to the top of the world!"—a phrase she had often used to tell him where she thought he belonged. He then fires his gun into the storage tank on which he is standing. The resulting explosions and gigantic swirls of flame end the film in a magnificent image of violence, the perfect summation for Cody Jarrett's career and one more marvelous gangster death for James Cagney, who died so well and so often in the service of this genre in the past.

RIOT IN CELL BLOCK 11
(1954)

184

Director	Cinematographer	Script
DON SIEGEL	RUSSELL HARLAN	RICHARD COLLINS
Producer		
WALTER WANGER		
For Allied Artists		

PRINCIPAL CHARACTERS

NEVILLE BRAND	EMILE MEYER	LEO GORDON
Dunn	The Warden	Carnie
FRANK FAYLEN	ROBERT OSTERLOH	PAUL FREES
Haskel	The Colonel	Monroe

Length: 80 minutes

Although at the time it appeared *Riot in Cell Block 11* received much praise for its violent realism (it was filmed in Folsom Prison, California, with many actual convicts participating), to the post-Attica generation it seems a relatively civilized drama of social protest—and even the imprisoned psychopaths of the 1950s seem restrained by comparison with today's ordinary street mugger. It is obvious in the film that Siegel's interest lies primarily in the conflict between different theories of the purpose and functioning of penal institutions. There can hardly be a better example of how genre patterns enable a good filmmaker to dramatize some otherwise abstract concerns.

The film fits into a documentary framework that includes an
introduction in newsreel style, emphasizing contemporary discontent among jailed men and utilizing apparently-real footage
from riots of the 1950s. There is no attempt at a prolonged cause-
and-effect buildup, and rather early in the film a guard
announces, "there's a riot in cell block eleven." The source of
tension throughout the film revolves around the question of
whether the authorities will meet the rioting prisoners' demands
for better living conditions, but the structure of the film does not
force us so much to confront the human dilemmas arising from
this question as to perceive alternative responses to a crisis situation. It is not a film of characterization, as many lesser prison
dramas tend to be; instead, the social issue is presented through a
dichotomy developed between two groups of inmates and two
factions among the authorities and presented in parallel structure. In both cases the structure presents men behaving reasonably in conflict with men acting irrationally. Therefore, the audience retains a degree of neutrality while observing the progress of
the conflict; we are not asked to side with all the prisoners against
all the forces of law, but rather with the more rational prisoners
and with the reasonable authorities—in opposition to both the
psychopathic inmates and their counterparts, the unreasoning
authorities who advocate oppression and revenge.

On the prisoners' side of the conflict, one group is represented
by Dunn, the overall leader, a spokesman for reason (but a tough

convict all the same, and described more than once as a psychopath himself), and on the other by Carnie, second in command, a man bordering on insanity. When Carnie is in charge he threatens to execute the guards held as hostages and thereby precipitate a bloodbath if the state police should react in kind against the prisoners. Carnie, however, controls his urge to kill his captives as long as Dunn exercises authority in cell block 11. Interestingly enough, one of the prisoners' demands is that the mental cases now incarcerated along with them be segregated, though the mentally ill prisoners themselves are presumably taking part in the demonstrations favoring that demand (but perhaps individually, each one is unable to recognize his own insanity). The other demands, including the inevitable call for amnesty for the rioters, seem on the face of things equally reasonable, and the abuses (such as overcrowding) leading up to the riot are not even depicted in much detail. Dunn is not presented as a socially conscious reformer; rather, he is simply an articulate and brave spokesman for a series of remedies to correct constant, unjustified, and universally deplorable conditions. At one point in the film, someone notes that the prisoners' demands are practically identical to the warden's own requests of the previous year. Siegel shows us that the warden, as he signs the prisoners' list, is aware of the irony involved in seeing his own plans tentatively approved by the governor only as a result of a riot; the riot would have been avoided if the acknowledged conditions had been changed as he had recommended.

186

As for the authorities' side, the warden represents the same attitude as Dunn, and as a reasonable voice amidst the confusion and turmoil he resembles Dunn in another way: the warden is tough and brave too, acceding to the prisoners because of a desire to avoid violence, but also subjected to pressures from the unreasonable and uncompromising elements advising him not to yield. The governor's agent, Haskel, constantly urges a tyrannic response to the prisoners—demanding that the riot be put down by force. A confrontation between Haskel and his irrational counterparts among the inmates leads to his receiving a shoulder wound when a knife is thrown at him. Thereafter, the lines are drawn, and the irrational forces on both sides seem to gain the upper hand. Haskel's authority, because he is acting for the state, supersedes the warden's, and he has explosives implanted in the wall of the cell block. When Dunn is injured in a fight with one of the psychopathic inmates, Carnie takes over and prepares to kill the hostages. Only at the last minute is violence averted: Dunn regains his leadership and the governor signs an agreement with the prisoners.

Siegel's ending takes the form of a reversal of the premises of the conflict, but it works with unusual effectiveness because the emphasis throughout has been on the nature of the contending social forces rather than on the outcome of the action. A few days after the seeming victory of the prisoners, when the penitentiary has returned to normal, the warden calls Dunn in to tell him that the state legislature has repudiated the terms of the governor's agreement. Not only will nothing be done to alleviate the bad conditions, but the promise of amnesty has been thrown out, and Dunn faces prosecution that is likely to add thirty years to his sentence. This ultimate victory of injustice and unreason is as bitter as it is unusual in the American cinema, but it is consistent with the stylistic realism of the category in general and its typical sympathy for the victims of a system inherently oppressive and dehumanizing.

187

ON THE WATERFRONT
(1954)

Director	Cinematographer	Script
ELIA KAZAN	BORIS KAUFMAN	BUDD SCHULBERG
Producer		From a story by Budd Schulberg, based on articles by Malcolm Johnson
SAM SPIEGEL		
For Columbia		

PRINCIPAL CHARACTERS

MARLON BRANDO	KARL MALDEN	LEE J. COBB
Terry Malloy	Father Barry	Johnny Friendly
ROD STEIGER	PAT HENNING	EVA MARIE SAINT
Charles Malloy	"Kayo" Dugan	Edie Doyle
LEIF ERICKSON		
Glover		

Length: 108 minutes

Deriving from the categories of crime organization films of the 1930s and the social corruption films of the 1940s, *On the Waterfront* gathers most of its force from the developing moral consciousness of its hero, Terry Malloy, as he begins to comprehend how his relationship to his criminal environment has drained him of his ability to exercise choice and determine his own identity.

Terry is far less articulate than Joe Morse in *Force of Evil*. Faced with a similar predicament, Joe finally rebels against the underworld figures controlling him. But both Joe and Terry ultimately stake themselves in their own fashion—redeeming their spiritual lives by endangering their physical lives. The criminal organization in *On the Waterfront*, the local longshoreman's union, is a pervasive threat, ruling by fear and violence, having subdued almost all its two thousand members into acquiescence to the tyrannic labor leader, Johnny Friendly. Given status, friendship, and preferential work assignments by associating with the union hierarchy, Terry—a former boxer who ruined his career by "throwing" his big fight—takes his identity from the power structure, suppressing occasional insights into the essential nothingness of his existence. For Terry to break away from his own habitual complacency toward the violence around him and his criminal connections, which are developed primarily through his brother (a member of Friendly's inner circle), he needs a new perspective to change the drift of his life.

The source for this change eventually must be internal, but the agents who bring about a new awareness are Father Barry and Edie, the sister of a longshoreman murdered by the union leaders. Father Barry operates on Terry in a manner similar to the way Pat O'Brien as a priest worked on Cagney in *Angels with Dirty Faces;* in each film the social consciousness of the priest awakens a slight moral sensibility on the part of his criminally involved subject. Cagney finally does succumb to the plea for social responsibility when he agrees to go to the electric chair playing the coward, for the purpose of ruining his image among his young admirers. But Terry is less susceptible to social causes; he eventually agrees with Father Barry to help his fellow dock-workers, but his motive is mainly a personal feeling of repulsion for what he has become and what Friendly has done to him. Father Barry's success in raising Terry's consciousness lies in making Terry's brooding discontent surface as hostility to what Friendly has represented: the materialistic attractions of selling out.

Terry's selling out has been a casual but increasing involvement with the union mobsters, which in turn has undermined his relationship with Edie. At the beginning of the film Terry, obeying a request from his brother and Friendly, "sets up" Joey, who is testifying before the Waterfront Crime Commission. Terry believes that the union is merely going to "lean on" this informer, but instead, Joey is thrown from a roof and killed. Terry responds with both anger and guilt (for the rest of the film he takes care of Joey's pigeons), but being used in such a way does not by itself cause him any moral revulsion that might lead him to break with the mobsters. When he falls in love with Edie, his secret involvement in her brother's murder makes his position as possible lover untenable. Admitting this involvement to Father Barry, Terry is urged by the priest to confess it to Edie. When he does, the subsequent breakup of their relationship becomes the first step in Terry's psychological separation from his comfortable association close to, but not part of, the power structure of the union mob. He wants Edie more than he wants to remain on the fringes of the mob's inner circle.

189

The personal motivation for Terry's change is compounded by the social issue of corrupt union control of the docks, which Kazan keeps in the forefront. When Father Barry continues to try to rally support for union members to testify before the commission, the union leadership overreacts and murders another potential witness. Terry observes this and becomes more cynical about the union. Yet it is not until Friendly begins to threaten him that Terry prepares himself for an irrevocable split with his friends. In a famous automobile sequence (recalling a similar sequence in *Force of Evil*), Terry's brother warns and attempts to persuade him to come back to the fold before it is too late. Terry then articulates his failure in life, his selling out to Friendly when he was still young enough to have a future, his throwing of the fight. "I could have been a contender. I could've been *somebody!*" He blames his brother for the advice that has led him to be, in his own words, "a bum." His brother recognizes the truth of Terry's words and, for once jeopardizing himself, does not deliver his brother to the gang. For what the mob considers a betrayal, Friendly has the brother killed.

After Terry delivers damaging testimony to the commission, implicating Friendly in Joey's murder, the emphasis in the final part of the film is placed on rousing the collective awareness of the union members, to get them to rebel against their leadership. The waterfront code of noncooperation with authorities is at stake. At first Terry is isolated by the union members because he testified and because they continue to fear their leadership. But their resentment of Friendly is surfacing. What they need is an act of courage to inspire them (though at this point their cravenness has perhaps alienated them from our sympathy no matter what they decide). Symbolically challenging the power of the whole criminal structure of the waterfront, Terry risks everything in a fight with Friendly, but is beaten up by the leader's henchmen. Inspired by Terry's courage, the men indicate that they will work only if Terry is given work too—expressly countermanding Friendly's order that Terry is never to work the docks again. Another symbolic action on Terry's part is needed to destroy Friendly's reign of fear. So, rising from his terrible beating, Terry struggles to stand and walk ahead of the men, leading them to work in spite of Friendly's ranting threats to all of them as they walk past him. With this gesture of defiance, Terry and the men free themselves from their involvement with corruption. Terry is a new man, redeemed from a useless life, and his reconciliation with Edie seems inevitable.

190

BONNIE AND CLYDE
(1967)

Director	Cinematographer	Script
ARTHUR PENN	BURNETT GUFFEY	DAVID NEWMAN
Producer	Technicolor	ROBERT BENTON
WARREN BEATTY		
For Warner Brothers-		
Seven Arts		

PRINCIPAL CHARACTERS

WARREN BEATTY	FAYE DUNAWAY	MICHAEL J. POLLARD
Clyde Barrow	Bonnie Parker	C. W. Moss
GENE HACKMAN	ESTELLE PARSONS	DUB TAYLOR
Buck Barrow	Blanche Barrow	Malcolm Moss
DENVER PYLE	EVANS EVANS	GENE WILDER
Capt. Frank Hamer	Velma Davis	Eugene Grizzard

Length: 111 minutes

The gangster film has always been premised on the criminal's role playing, but seldom is that motif elevated to the thematic level of the crime genre, as it is in *Bonnie and Clyde*. Little Caesar or Tom Powers in *The Public Enemy* no doubt relies on his public image as a means of disguising his insecurities and inadequacies, but role playing becomes natural to him during his rise to criminal distinction. Bonnie Parker and Clyde Barrow constantly have to work on their reputations and even their physical appearance—their Kodak travels with them to photograph not their exploits but their stylized poses, which reflect their impression of what the public wants from its criminal folk heroes.

The 1930s figures from urban mobs, like Duke Mantee in *The Petrified Forest* or Scarface, assume their roles and submerge their weaknesses as they throw themselves utterly into their successful existences as glamorous "star-quality" criminals. Much more pathetically, Penn's Bonnie and Clyde struggle to achieve a dream of glory against the barren landscape of the Great Depression in midwest America. They seem acutely conscious that without continuing such a struggle they will lose their identity and sink into the faceless crowd. Their search for identity, which is presented at the beginning of the film, becomes an attempt to sustain a created public image that is destined to destroy them, but once they are caught up in the consequences of their violence they can do nothing but pursue a hopeless course. When near the end of the film Bonnie asks Clyde what he would do if he had his life to live over, he tells her with straight-faced simplicity that he would not live in the same state in which he

committed robberies. At his level of imagination, the American dream offers no alternatives.

It seems clear that Penn interpreted Newman and Benton's material for their scenario in terms of the tragic inevitability developing from a wrong choice—a choice rooted in the hero's character. Clyde Barrow could not have done anything else as well as he could perform his criminal acts—shooting, robbing, and driving recklessly in flight from the authorities. As for Bonnie Parker, Clyde readily convinces her that her life prior to meeting him was dreadful and boring, and she never attempts to dissociate herself from him once she commits herself to sharing his life style. Equal to him in ambition—they both aim for the status of cult heroes—she creates her own vision of the gangster's moll, posing with cigar and pistol in front of a getaway car. Tragedy develops paradoxically from their need to exist as celebrities: given their public identities as famous criminals, they must eventually be tracked down and killed. To avoid the lawmen determined to corner them, they would have to give up these identities. When Bonnie finally realizes the nature of their predicament, she composes a poem that incorporates her newly comprehended fatalism. But true to their national public character, she and Clyde send the poem to the newspapers. Like movie stars and other media personalities they believe it important for their public to know something about their philosophical views and their emotional lives.

In an earlier version of the Bonnie and Clyde materials, Fritz Lang's *You Only Live Once* (1937), the hunted couple appears constantly victimized by society; so does Penn's couple, in spite of their killing a considerable number of people (all of whom aggressively seek to capture or kill the two robbers and their gang). Both Lang and Penn emphasize the sympathetic point of view of those running from pursuers, an attitude obviously premised on the enormous power associated with the adversaries. At one point in the Penn film, the gang is ambushed at a motel; while escaping from the lawmen Clyde's brother Buck and his wife Blanche are seriously wounded, and Clyde less so. They camp out in a field overnight, and the next morning are ambushed again, this time leaving Buck dying, Blanche blinded (and captured), and Bonnie shot. The duplication of the destructiveness of the two ambushes reinforces the idea that Bonnie and Clyde can never again resume their career with the kind of luck that, up to now, has enabled them to elude innumerable pursuers and achieve their place in the mythology of crime.

Desolate, they find one last refuge in the farmhouse of the father of gang member C. W. Moss, who betrays them (though clearly they would have been found out anyway). The final bloody shootout, another ambush—the most graphically violent in any major cinematic work up to that point, though frequently surpassed since then in many minor films—fairly recapitulates the whole senseless spectacle of their careers, but without doubt the sequence also generates audience regret for the fate of the couple. Here, as in the fashion of the 1930s crime films, society's ruthless determination wins out. Not only is the destruction total; it is also perverse in the sheer number of shots fired at them. Society has decided to punish them even in death, a tasteless vengeance that associates the reckless lack of concern for human values with the victorious lawmen, as it had earlier associated that same lack of humanistic sensibility with Bonnie and Clyde.

Among the notable aspects of this gangster film is its use of rural locations instead of the typical urban environment. It reproduces the barren locales of Depression-worn small towns, and thus helps us to comprehend the dreary alternative life styles that were all that people of Bonnie and Clyde's social class and education could hope for at that time. The wasteland imagery, however, does not work primarily to establish an allegorical landscape equivalent to that which often fostered the appearances of a modern-day rebel or a 1930s gangster blasting his way out of urbanized American ghettoes in other films. Rather, the visual environment of Penn's recreated 1930s rural America seems to suggest the landscape of a failed or limited imagination of a young man and woman deprived of a meaningful cultural heri-

193

tage. Regardless of the historical period of a particular film's setting, the crime genre never really analyzes the criminal sensibility of the past. A 1930s setting here is used to structure an imaginative analogy to America in the 1960s—a society made rootless by events not necessarily alluded to in specific terms. These events have created, however, a generation susceptible to the glamor of violence and daring. The film portrays a society losing most of its ties to the value system passed on by an arid civilization, and living off the dwindling resources of a devitalized culture.

THE GODFATHER
(1972)

194

Director	Cinematographer	Script
FRANCIS FORD COPPOLA	GORDON WILLIS	MARIO PUZO
Producer	Technicolor	FRANCIS FORD COPPOLA
ALBERT S. RUDDY		Based on the novel by
For Paramount		Mario Puzo

PRINCIPAL CHARACTERS

MARLON BRANDO	AL PACINO	JAMES CAAN
Don Vito Corleone	Michael Corleone	Sonny Corleone
RICHARD CASTELLANO	ROBERT DUVALL	STERLING HAYDEN
Clemenza	Tom Hagen	McClusky
JOHN MARLEY	RICHARD CONTE	DIANE KEATON
Jack Woltz	Barzini	Kay Adams

Length: 175 minutes

The overwhelming popular success of *The Godfather* seems attributable not only to the recent great public interest in organized crime, but also to the film's total artistic exploitation of the patterns of its genre. That these conventions should strike audiences and critics as new or controversial testifies to Coppola's skill in combining the most interesting elements of the genre's various relevant categories—criminal organizations, gangsters, gang wars, and syndicate operations—and producing a fictional world wherein a Darwinian struggle for survival plays itself out in the only mode permissible within its tradition: violence employed as the ultimate method of settling all issues.

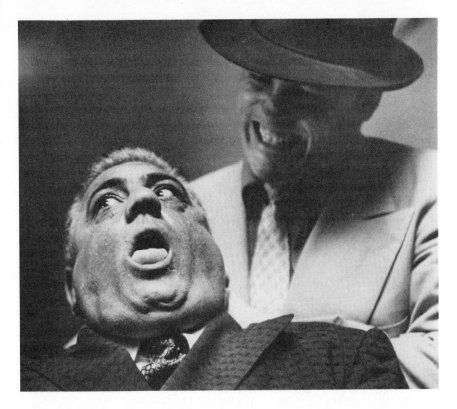

Coppola's insight into the genre reveals itself in his handling of the film's structure, which features a gallery of criminal types with wit, charm, courage, and heroic stature (who never change or develop)—an achievement that can only be accomplished by limiting the film's sphere of life to the criminal element. Coppola certainly understood that if the world of crime obtruded into the realm of society's ordinary activities—if, for instance, the general citizenry were shot at—ordinary moral concerns would dominate our relationship to the figures in the film. But *The Godfather* is populated only by criminals and their relatives or by people corrupt enough to belong to their world. The film is filled with overt moral distinctions, of course, for this is in the nature of the genre. But the moral choices are clearly restricted to the heroic criminals, who are motivated by their loyalty toward the Corleone crime family (this loyalty is actually a form of love), and the treacherous criminals, weaklings, time servers, traitors, and money-motivated scoundrels (all of them perverters of love). *The Godfather*'s power struggles and economic and social conflicts take place in the world of the gutter, but like most films depicting microcosms, the film also operates in the abstract realm, where the believers confront the pagans, and the upholders of order and government clash with the rebels who wish to destroy a hierarchical establishment that has brought a long reign of peace.

Although we are primarily interested in watching the procedures of criminal activity, the film also provides us with a dramatic structure that satisfactorily ties everything together: the rise of Michael to the leadership of the family. At the beginning of the film Michael is a returning war hero still in uniform, who had previously gone to college. During the Old-World-style wedding festivities celebrating his sister's marriage, he explains to his girlfriend (and eventual second wife) that the mob activities of the Corleones do not include him: "It's my family. It's not me." He is, however, perfectly suited to take his place in family circles, showing no moral scorn for what his father, the great Don Corleone, does. Whatever inner life Michael has, nothing in the film suggests much of a struggle against following in his father's footsteps—and the family itself puts no pressure at all on him to join (indeed, the father had hoped to see him become a senator or governor).

The factors that bring Michael to power are undoubtedly linked to his inherent criminal characteristics—but these very characteristics within the confined value system of this film are admirable and sometimes even ennobling. When the Don is gunned down and the family is hard pressed to rally its troops against an invading army sweeping across its territory, Michael naturally enlists in the defense of the regime. Enraged by a subsequent attempt to murder his convalescing father, Michael volunteers to assassinate the opposition's general, along with the opposition's chief ally, a crooked police captain. Without any previous testing, the Corleone "virtues" of determination, self-sacrifice for the family, bravery, and dramatic verve surface in Michael's character. He qualifies for leadership within this society because of his heroic capacity. Later, after his brother Sonny's murder, Michael, who has been groomed for the job, takes over upon his father's death. The mantle passes without dispute to him as the legitimate heir—a determination by character as much as by paternity, since there is another brother living, who lacks the strength of personality to command men. The last part of the film depicts with absolute brutality (but with no emotional emphasis) the killing off of Michael's enemies within and without the organization. Coppola portrays the new godfather's total assumption of his role in a sardonic, almost Hitchcockian manner, though technically he employs the old Griffith device of switchback cutting. Michael, serving as godfather to his nephew, attends the baptismal church ceremony with his family; while the priest incants the traditional service in Latin, and in English asks Michael if he renounces the devil, the film cuts back and forth to the various exterminations simultaneously being carried out by his gang on his orders.

For many viewers, the main achievement of the film lies in Marlon Brando's performance as Don Corleone, a tour de force of acting (and of makeup), so sharply delineated that it led to a year of television parodies. It is easy to see Brando's attraction to the role and how a performer of his talent is able to dominate by his presence, even when the character he plays is only half conscious on a hospital bed (he shares this ability with his gang boss ancestors, Edward G. Robinson and James Cagney, in equivalent roles). Coppola very deliberately emphasizes Don Corleone's magnificence and stature—which are at the same time so obviously like those of a Sicilian peasant in their origins—and the combination of directing, photography, and acting together create one of the decade's landmark portrayals. Don Corleone's dialogue, truly atrocious when taken out of context, distinguishes itself through its spoken rhythms and idiosyncracies from anything heard in the genre before; it becomes a kind of princely poetry from a man conscious of the need to create an aura of respect around himself. That respect is evident from the first sequence in which he appears, in his grand study, dressed in formal clothes appropriate for the wedding reception going on outside. In a raspy voice and an understated manner, he carries on the business of a king or president, seeing visitors who come to him with requests for favors or justice unobtainable in the ordinary world—a villain to be murdered or at least beaten up, a person in need of political intervention, another desperately requiring assistance with his Hollywood career. To all the great Don doles out goodwill and the promise of a favor granted at someone else's expense, sometimes in the form of the film's now-famous threat of violence: "an offer that he cannot refuse." All that Don Corleone ever seems to ask of the world is that it treat him with respect and that it be filled with men who are loyal to their families (he uses this as a moral test of a man's worthiness to have a request granted).

197

The actual criminal business carried on by the Don and his successor Michael is typically vague. Late in the film the family decides to get out of the "olive oil" business and buy a Las Vegas hotel. We are surprised by their ever having been in olive oil, but the gambling operation is simply the genre's traditional enterprise of gangsters. Don Corleone, in fact, tries to keep them out of narcotics, but some accommodation has to be made to the new spirit of commercial enterprise rising in the national organization of crime families. Michael pledges to his girlfriend that in five years virtually all of the Corleone enterprises will be legal—and many critics view the film as a kind of businessman's allegory of American private capitalism. Yet the business operations remain unspecified; the board meetings are really just Sicilian-style family outings, not really for generating corporate strategies. What is symbolized, perhaps, is the nature of corporate competition. The family wars resemble nineteenth-century cutthroat commercial practices energetically pursued by the great "robber barons" of American industry and finance, who engaged in similar violence, but without machine guns. The Corleones are depicted as just on the verge of moving onto that level of American myth. No wonder the film engendered a sequel bringing the family's story up to date as a fulfillment of one aspect of the American Dream.

5

THE SEARCH
FOR CLUES

CATEGORIES OF INVESTIGATION

If the criminal projects an image of a stylized romantic, a daring adventurer rebelling against a grim urban establishment, or a passionate advocate of existing for the moment, the investigator—his counterpart involved equally in the life of crime, though from the opposite angle—conveys an image of cool reserve, detachment, objectivity, and a sardonic intellectualism that seems to require the challenge of dangerous assignments. While the detective is wiser than the criminal, both are perhaps allied at their deepest level by a similar mood of romantic commitment to a life style that forces confrontations, demands testing unto death, and offers possibilities for displays of extreme personal courage. But the criminal and the detective cannot share the same film genre: each is so definitively central to a particular narrative that whenever a filmmaker places an emphasis on one of them, the opposing character becomes peripheral. Since criminals are always present in detective films and detectives of one sort or another (police or district attorneys) are always at least on the fringes of crime films, the life styles of both types of main characters must be considered mutually exclusive: each exists stylistically as a star destined for center stage, and in the presence of the other an inevitable and fatal collision must occur.

Criminal investigation is an extremely broad genre, but this chapter seeks to narrow the area of concern to the two most significant and fertile narrative categories encompassing the search for clues: police investigation films and private detective films. There are many other categories of criminal investigation that may more profitably be viewed in relation to other genres: lawyer investigations, for example, are perhaps more significant as a category of lawyer films, and this is also true of investigative reporter films as a category of newspaper films. Other more specialized investigation categories have produced interesting films (for example, the magazine editor as investigator in John Farrow's *The Big Clock* [1948], or the insurance investigator in Billy Wilder's *Double Indemnity* [1944]), but the categories are either too insubstantial to be evaluated or insufficient in quantity. Closely allied to the police investigator is the district attorney, but even with Humphrey Bogart in that role the category has seldom gone beyond the level of pure melodrama. The reason for its ineffectiveness probably lies in the comparatively abstract visuals (the courtroom) related to the district attorney's profession in comparison with the setting of the police detective's work.

In any case, the criminal investigation categories usually resemble one another in the sordidness of the criminal activities they depict. Petty thefts, after all, are difficult to make into interesting cases for investigators. To justify the efforts of a master professional investigator, the criminal enterprise must be depicted as significant (almost always both murder and grand larceny) and obscure in its motivations: frequently the lesser policemen involved jump on the wrong clues and arrest an innocent person. The detective hero cannot be put to the test by solving a simple crime or catching a stupid killer. In fact, the element of personal danger to the hero probably occurs in ninety percent of such films. Severe forms of human passion, particularly lust and jealousy, are common motifs, and perversions, addictions, and various types of insanity are familiar visual characteristics of both good and bad films of this genre.

201

PROCEDURES OF DETECTION

Since both police detective and private eye films are often classified by critics either in the elusive category of *film noir* or simply as investigative films, it might seem that their generic premises are similar. Actually, there is one overwhelming difference, causing all the notable distinctions that prevent the two main categories of the investigative film from having more than a second-cousin relationship. The gap between the two categories cannot be ignored if either film is to remain true to type because it stems from the essential difference in the two professions of criminal investigation. Although the police detective may indeed be a supersleuth (Inspector Maigret is in most respects the equal of Sherlock Holmes), this unbridgeable gap remains between the approach of the policeman and that of the private eye: the former is a member of an organization, the latter an individual dependent solely on his own resources.

Sometimes the two approaches to the job of solving crimes seem to merge: the private eye may be friendly with some police who help him out, give him inside information, check certain of his hunches, and investigate the more mundane or mechanical clues (such as license plate numbers or criminal records). The police detective, on the other hand, may feel a growing isolation and an alienation from the other members of the force; this can lead to his eventual solving of the case by working with unorthodox methods or against stated department procedure. Two Gordon Douglas films illustrate these mutual tendencies. In *Tony Rome* (1967), Frank Sinatra as the private detective receives help from his detective lieutenant friend, though eventually he has to work on his own because, as is typical, he falls under official police suspicion himself. In *The Detective* (1968), Sinatra, this time a police investigator, finds obstacles in his search for the murderer within his own precinct. He becomes so disgusted with police dishonesty and the attempts to stop his investigation that, on the successful completion of his case, he abandons his career and at the end of the film is apparently about to resign.

Nevertheless, the parallel tendencies do not merge, for the private detective is always ultimately alone, matching wits with a force representing more power than he himself can muster, whereas the police detective in a final sense is always backed up by unlimited resources, larger in fact than even the organized gang can command. Films that deal with the "enemy within" motif, notably Sidney Lumet's *Serpico* (1973), are not films of police detection but belong to the much smaller category of police life (for example, Richard Fleischer's *The New Centurions* [1972] and William Wyler's *Detective Story* [1951]). Such films are characterized by an emphasis on the general routine of the typical police department's day rather than on the search for the solution to a mysterious crime.

The procedural methodology of the two categories provides another noteworthy contrast. The private detective is essentially an intuitive romantic whose brilliant investigatory mind operates on a level often unintelligible to the audience. But it never really matters that most of the time the audience leaves the theater with only the haziest idea of how the criminal constructed his crime; it suffices that the detective has figured it out. Who can recapitulate the cause and effect relationship of events in Howard Hawks's *The Big Sleep* (1946)? However, from time to time we do receive real evidence of the quick thinking of the hero, and we can sense his mind at work even when he says nothing about his procedures. After all, for him to stop and explain himself would lose him valuable time, would force him to articulate what for him is the obvious—the "elementary," as the first great practitioner of the art of detection used to declare to dull Dr. Watson, whose perception of the situation was always as unilluminated as our own.

On the other hand, the police investigator, using the methodology of his profession, sets about his task in a scientific, orthodox way; he has read the manual for proper police procedure, even if at crucial moments he must go beyond his ordinary colleagues' standard methods. Jules Dassin's *The Naked City* (1948), one of the first films to document the ordinary details of police methodology, sets its investigatory process against the background of New York, a location which suggests the need for exhaustive police techniques because (in the words of the film) "there are eight million stories in the naked city." Barry Fitzgerald, as the unheroic, hardworking, middle-aged lieutenant, conducts a team investigation with a fairly sizable staff (six men in three shifts are assigned to shadow one suspect). The film establishes footwork as the fundamental method of investigation, with police going from store to store routinely searching for the retailer of a piece of jewelry. Eventually, the criminal is found because the patience of the pursuing police is unlimited. To apprehend the criminal, in the final showdown sequence on the Brooklyn Bridge, Fitzgerald is backed up by the whole force and never has to confront the criminal face to face. *The Naked City* effectively makes the point that the police force of New York, which represents the soul of the city, brings its massive resources and relentless determination to the pursuit of individual criminals for the purpose of protecting the interests of eight million residents. 203

Most other police detection films, however, do not so entirely deglamorize the methodology of professional investigation. The police investigator very often works on hunches, which might be considered a recognition of the limitations inherent in his own system of investigation; usually, however, such intuition or sheer guesswork accompanies the gathering of clues from the usual traditional sources: evidence, informers, and incessant checking and tracing techniques. When all clues seem to lead nowhere and the police detective turns completely inward, the category loses its peculiar virtues, as in Stuart Rosenberg's *The Laughing Policeman* (1974); for if science, endurance, and logic come to nothing, the police should have hired a private detective to assist them, rather than a powerless policeman. The police investigator that we appreciate is the "good cop," the man who succeeds because he has mastered all the appropriate techniques. If he goes beyond them in his zeal, as in Don Siegel's *Dirty Harry* (1972), he does so because he must reshape the ordinary skills into a strategic new form, adjusting his responses to the criminal's new tactics of evasiveness.

The showdown sequence, though common to both categories of investigation, has distinguishing features in each. At this crucial moment, the private detective is either outnumbered or is about to encounter a lone, but prepared and desperate, killer in the kind of violent encounter he seems destined to lose: he is either in the killer's territory or else on neutral ground awaiting ambush. In every case, he must exercise supreme caution and call upon previously hidden resources of strength. His courage has already been proven from earlier escapades. Therefore, to save himself, the private eye in such moments must exhibit superior intelligence, even in the bloodiest of conclusions (for example, Marlowe in *The Big Sleep* outsmarts a gang leader-killer, who has set him up for ambush, by tricking the gangster's own men into shooting their leader). In contrast, the police detective, at the end of his film, is almost always the pursuer, and the escaping killer is the one who feels trapped. Sometimes the ending is just a matter of shooting down the villain as he flees (Peter Yates's *Bullitt* [1968]); at other times it is a massive shootout in which the ferocity of the police overwhelms the gangsters' own potential for destruction (William Friedkin's *The French Connection* [1972]).

MOTIVATION

The sources of motivation in the detective film do not constitute an area of interest for most film analysts, since the genre almost entirely omits any visual presentation of the subject; in virtually all police films and all but a few private eye films the motivation proceeds from the standardized, unquestioned elements of the milieu. Briefly stated, all detectives hate crime and criminals, but there is a noticeable difference in the two categories: the police detective apparently hates the criminal element because it poses a danger to law and order; the private detective, however, feels a moral repulsion to the nature of crime and the evil character of the criminal.

In practice, the average films of both categories present detectives who never seem to think their own motivations through. This is perhaps fortunate for the genre, for in the scorn, condescension, and frequently violent antagonism of the hero for the underworld we are often expected to endorse pseudofascist doctrines; indeed, we are often compelled by the emotional thrust of the film to adopt several values that we might not intellectually accept in a more reasoned environment. Yet it is not a simple matter of being manipulated away from our own normal attitudes; the films that present detectives as stabilizing forces who uphold traditional values are seldom concerned with examining the moral structure of their hero's society or the motivating factors in the life of the criminals they pursue. Rather, built into the framework of all such detective films is an understanding shared equally by criminal and detective that crime is bad and that the commission of a criminal act inevitably and rightfully sets in motion the process of retribution. The rare police film that raises the issue of the motivation for putting down crime may provoke moral and sociological questions that seem objectionable to many viewers (*Dirty Harry* does this), but the issues are by no means common to the genre.

In a number of police films a second motive somewhat complicates the usual hatred-of-crime motif: personal revenge. The pattern of introducing this secondary motivation, however, strongly links the personal element to the already established reason for the police detective's obsessive desire to destroy an organization of criminals or catch a murderer. For example, in Fritz Lang's classic *The Big Heat* (1953), the police lieutenant's pursuit of the underworld leader results in the usual attempt by the gang to get rid of him, but accidentally his wife is killed instead; from this point on, the detective's main motivation for tracking down the chief criminal is revenge. Yet clearly, the cause-and-effect relationship is virtually reversible, for if the detective had not been fanatically persistent in the first place, the underworld would not have felt the need to strike back at him. As a major filmmaker, Lang deals with certain thematic points that require expansion from the typical genre base of criminal pursuit purely for the sake of law and order, but even lesser filmmakers working in the genre often resort to the personal revenge motif. Interestingly, the motivation for revenge is seldom the death of a friend or loved one (though in private eye films this is more common). It can be a matter of professional indignation over being outsmarted by the opponent-criminal, or of professional pride, as in Don Siegel's *Madigan* (1968), where the hero slips up at the beginning of the film by allowing the killer to escape; he must therefore pursue him to an ultimate tragic encounter at the end. In *Bullitt*, the police detective assigned to protect a witness about to turn state's evidence fails to prevent the murder of the witness; the rest of the film indicates that the detective must stop at nothing to redeem himself by bringing the criminals to justice. His competence is called into question, even though he might not be directly to blame, but in any case he knows his responsibility, not only to society but to the ideal of his profession.

The motif of personal revenge cinematically dramatizes the abstract premise of all police detective films—that crime is a social evil requiring retribution at the hands of the detective. If filmmakers feel that this abstract premise is obvious in the film, they may omit entirely any element of personal motivation, but by doing so they run the risk of sacrificing the sense of the hero's personality. Too often the routine, disinterested dedication of the policeman inadvertently suggests to us a mere mechanized

205

response to the sordid life around him. If the hero is dehuman-ized, and this dehumanization is not deliberately made an ele-ment of the film (as it is in *Bullitt*, but usually not in run-of-the-mill films), then all our attention is focused on the story; this limitation is usually detrimental to the genre simply because the pattern of detection affords a limited number of variant possibili-ties.

Central to all motivation in the detective genre is the implicit sense of mission of both the policeman and the private eye. Whatever their philosophical grasp of the problem of evil, these men are driven by their calling, which is essentially romantic—or even spiritual, in the case of certain private detectives. They are invariably hardworking, regardless of their taste for luxury or desire for leisure. Obviously, the motivation of wealth is not a factor in their existence. They are doing what they like to do, and it is never necessary for them to analyze in much detail why they are so supportive of law and social structure, and so obsessed with the destruction of evil.

206

POLICE PROFESSIONALISM

The abstract notion of professionalism has proven difficult to capture in cinema outside of the detective genre. Probably more than any other figure of a major genre, the police detective exhibits the traits of a professional, having a set of procedures to follow and various levels of authority to report to. The private detective may be equally professional, but his profession is more personal, more mysterious, than the policeman's; much of the private eye's skill is intensely private. In certain other genres, a similar sense of dedication and self-sacrifice appears (the West-ern hero has it), but there is no constant methodology by which we can measure professional performance. The police detective is given a job that has to be done; a set of obstacles arises to thwart those less competent in investigative procedures; ulti-mately he finds the way to success, performs actions that are perhaps unconventional but within the implicit style of the profession, and brings about the reestablishment of justice. The heroes of no other genre succeed in this exact way. Doctors in films come off well in that they manage to save their patients, but their procedures are mechanical. Lawyers are comparable to detectives in the use of imaginative methods, but the profession-alism of the courtroom manipulator is less impressive because it is seen only in the light of the uncreative tactics of the opposing district attorney, who is never as clever as a criminal or murderer tracked down by a police detective.

When the police detective arrives at the scene of a murder, he appears in the company of a group of specialists who are finger-printing and photographing and generally examining every inch of the area for clues. It is, of course, understood that the detective has long since mastered all these obvious procedures and now operates on a level above them. (A truly nongeneric situation would be for the forensic experts to solve the crime from the materials collected at the scene of the murder. This, of course, never happens.) The hero looks over the scene—often arriving just as the covered body is being removed from the area—studies the chalk marks that indicate where the body lay when discovered, asks a couple of questions, suggests some basic procedures to underlings (for example, telling them to question neighbors), assumes from a visual inspection of the premises that no incriminating fingerprints will be found, and then sets off on the business of solving the crime.

In contrast, the private detective usually arrives at a murder scene before the police, and is mainly concerned with erasing his own fingerprints and getting out before he is discovered and suspected of the crime. One other common occurrence at the scene of the murder in a police film is that the detective sometimes picks up an object that has appeared entirely innocent to all the experts who have already gone over the area, but that is actually a significant clue. To a true professional, no objects are merely innocent parts of the setting; they are emblems of the struggle that led to the crime or insights into the personality of the killer. The discovered cigarette lighter is more than a lighter: it is also an illustration of a personality involved in the killing or the conflict that produced it.

A large part of the police detective's professionalism is demonstrated by his emotional control, which is by now codified in the genre. It suggests above all that a familiarity with homicide and brutality has affected his personality in a negative way. What kind of person can become so inured to killing or other forms of violence that he cannot be moved by the latest incident presented to him? The answer, of course, is a person of great experience, someone who has seen it all; a newcomer to the force, unused to such violence, may exhibit great emotional upset (in *Dirty Harry*, the assistant vomits) in complete contrast to the matter-of-fact attitude of the experienced hero. But that in itself tells us a great deal—getting so used to murder is the dehumanizing facet of the job: yet the hero never protests about this aspect of his work. Actually, the typical narrative pattern of the genre never establishes an acceptance of the frequency of murder; rather, it suggests that the detective has a reason for his intense dedication to the apprehension of the criminal. It also suggests that an

207

emotional response would be out of place, since the stimulus of a crime requires the response of an intellectual plan of action. The coolness of the detective informs us of his readiness to begin thinking through the criminal's mode of operation from the moment the detective appears on the scene of the crime. In Otto Preminger's *Laura* (1944), the detective assigned to a murder case two days after the discovery of the crime has so well researched the circumstances and background materials and so carefully studied police photographs that, upon his initial appearance, he immediately seems half-way to reconstructing the crime and also fully capable of assessing the motivations of all the possible suspects.

Especially in recent films, once the level of the hero's professionalism and its relationship to his containment of emotion have been established, we often witness some rather callous, heavy-handed tactics the detective employs in the pursuit of criminals. Informers and other underworld figures common to the genre are sometimes treated with contempt or outright violence; evidence is beaten out of them. Occasionally, the detectives themselves exhibit some criminal tendencies along the way—Madigan does for instance—though this flaw does not change their essential nature or their willingness to risk their lives in the pursuit of killers. The hero of *The French Connection* and its sequel displays so much ferocity that none of the criminals in the film seems potentially as dangerous as the hero himself. In spite of this excess, an essential element of the genre is apparent in these films too: violence on behalf of the rightful aims of society is morally supportable. That almost pathological element of contempt for the criminal that is always close to the surface of the detective's psychological makeup cannot simply be labeled as social maladjustment; it has to be understood in the context of the detective's professional commitment to destroying evil, a commitment always made prior to the beginning of the film but reestablished by the events of the film, the depiction of criminal violence.

Although the police detective, like the private investigator, solves crimes by intuitive or intellectual leaps that more conventional persons cannot make, he still uses physical means to track down his adversary. Much of his professionalism consists of his ability to use a gun, forcefully epitomized by the title of a minor 1970s genre film, *Magnum Force* (directed by Ted Post, 1973). He uses his fists and feet as well, since he must ultimately confront a desperate criminal who often prefers death to imprisonment. Besides, the killer has little to lose; the detective, recognizing this, takes on the ultimate commitment of his profession

208

as he goes after the killer and risks his own life. The police detective is rarely killed, but he is much more likely than the private investigator to be wounded or severely beaten.

THE PRIVATE DETECTIVE MYTH

Of all the major American film categories, only the private investigator film has a recurring mythic dimension that is present in almost all the notable works within it. The Western closely resembles it in the thematic and tonal thrust of a myth pattern, but the numerous categories of the Western prove that there is no one central myth present in all films of that genre. Both the Western and the private detective film readily employ myths because they are imbued with the same moral concerns found in equivalent patterns of other narrative forms traditionally containing a mythic dimension. For these moral concerns to operate plausibly in the fictional world of a particular film, they must reflect the sorts of activities and conflicts likely to arise in a given environment. For the Western, it is the loneliness implicit in the landscape, which is sometimes rural America but usually the uncharted desert and mountains where a man dependent on his inner strength must make his way. The private detective's world is urban America, where conflicts and passions are hidden beneath a veneer of sophistication. It is an indoor world where the worst traits of people, primarily greed, are depicted in intricate, sometimes almost indescribable plots.

209

Villains in the Western break the established codes of conduct, but they are rarely covert murderers, as in the private detective category. The usual obligation of a Western lawman or a lone rider of the West seeking revenge is to track down a known killer; the private detective, on the other hand, has to solve a puzzle—he must find out what happened and who did it rather than finding a runaway fugitive or known outlaw. Even when he begins with the relatively innocuous assignment of locating a missing person, as in Dick Richards's *Farewell, My Lovely* (1975), his investigation will eventually uncover murder and turn his major effort to the solution of that crime. And since the murderer in the urban setting is a familiar character—a neighbor, an executive, maybe even that most respectable of characters, the butler—he or she is always disguised as a normal, law-abiding citizen; thus, deception and fraud are the initial obstacles to the detective.

The character of the private detective resembles that of the Westerner not so much in what kind of person he is as in what he represents to us: the modern hero in search of an occupation. Few of us are ourselves detectives, and presumably none of us is a nineteenth-century Westerner, but many of us are soldiers, ministers, doctors, police, and lawyers. These professions, however, seldom afford possibilities for meaningful heroic action in the conventional sense of rescuing people or saving society; hence, the interest filmmakers have shown in the creation of the private investigator and the Westerner myths is easily understood. The two myths operate quite differently, but the world of each film genre is tangential to the real world. On the surface, both genres are realistic, but the best films of each are much more concerned with developing characterizations than with stressing a dramatic action or plotting a totally plausible series of events. Both are also premised on central characters who perform heroic actions at the appropriate time, and these actions are—to suit the modern taste—both physical and intellectual (or moral, in instances where the heroic act is dictated by virtue though not articulated).

Since he is seldom a man with any wealth but always operating in an environment where money is important, the private detective seeking clues rather than personal gain impresses us as a person of dedication, though we are often misled at first by his external toughness or his sleazy environment—his office and his friends. Somewhere in the course of his investigation, he will be offered a bribe—sometimes love rather than money—and he will refuse it. "I'm not corrupting you—you've been bought off before," a woman says (mistakenly) to Philip Marlowe in *Murder, My Sweet* (directed by Edward Dmytryk, 1944) when she senses his reluctance to accept her bribe. But she underestimates the hero's degree of integrity in this, the prototypical Marlowe film. His refusal reinforces the myth of incorruptibility common to the genre and which is effective in other films in proportion to the information we are given about the detective's urban surroundings. Were he not of modest means in the first place, the refusal of a bribe would not count for much; and it is therefore not surprising that the 1930s fee of $25 per day plus expenses lasted so many years into the post-World War II era of inflation: the private detective in the cinema simply forgot to raise his prices! Even more compelling a reason to accept the aura of incorruptibility is the nature of the criminal environment that dominates these films. Even when the major action is set against rather wealthy backdrops, as in Jack Smight's *Harper* (1966), the sense of corruption permeates the private detective's world. Most people in this world are crooks, but the private detective manages to separate himself morally and intellectually from the environment—though he always appears to remain among the devious and the dishonest. His worldly manner and his dubious associates conceal his true personality from all but his closest friends.

210

The style he adopts is his version in reverse of the disguise that murderers employ in order to pass as part of the establishment. The private detective plays the modern hero role as ironist, under-stater, deceiver in a righteous cause.

This aspect of the genre received its definitive treatment in the character of Sam Spade in John Huston's *The Maltese Falcon* (1941), where Spade looks and talks much like the dangerous and shady characters in his environment but at the end reveals himself as the most intense preoccupied moralist in all cinema. "Don't be too sure I'm as crooked as I'm supposed to be," he says to the woman he loves and is about to turn over to the police. But although Spade may be the best of his type, he is not essentially different from later ironists in the genre—though frequently the earlier private detectives were free of implicit moral evil, or only vaguely associated with corrupting influences.

Charlie Chan or Sherlock Holmes, of course, did not have Sam Spade's corrupt aura; those two had a different source of irony in their outer appearance which seemed innocuous and mild, hardly a match for the evil figures they went after. William Powell, who played Nick Charles in several Thin Man films (the best of the detective series), seemed so urbane and unfit for the world of crime that it always came as something of a shock to discover that once he was working on a case, he was highly competent, his wit expressing the usual brilliant insight into the criminal mind, his charm persuading police of their mistakes in following up the evidence. Although the tough-guy private investigator is certainly generic, it is not, therefore, antigeneric to cast unlikely types such as James Garner in Paul Bogart's *Marlowe* (1969), Elliott Gould as Marlowe in Robert Altman's *The Long Goodbye* (1973), and Jack Nicholson in Roman Polanski's *Chinatown* (1974) in the role; mildness of appearance is another of the traditional ironic guises of the American cinema hero, stemming probably from Douglas Fairbanks's role in *The Mark of Zorro* (directed by Fred Niblo, 1920).

Since the world depicted in the private eye film is characteristically evil, its surfaces always misleading, its truths undecipherable prior to investigation, it is no wonder that the hero himself must proceed by means of deceptions that involve both his assumed role and his actual integrity. People lie to him all the time, and he remains suspicious of everyone—aware that the least likely person may be guilty. Adopting the methods of the enemy, the detective is often seen breaking the law in minor ways (rifling desks, withholding evidence from the police), consorting with the underworld, buying or extorting information, beating up hoodlums, lying, informing, and in general following a pattern of activity similar to that of the social dregs he moves among. Yet

211

what distinguishes him from those around him is his moral sense. In some films such as *The Maltese Falcon*, the morality is even stated, though the tough pragmatic pose of the detective usually precludes his verbalizing his inner life. Where he does not defend moral principles verbally, the detective demonstrates his feeling for a somewhat abstract morality by dedication, even fanaticism, in striving to root out the criminal and, sometimes, some of his operatives (usually one or two on the lower rungs are particularly obnoxious and homicidal, and must be punished). The only ultimate scoundrel in the eyes of the detective, however, is the man at the top; the hero scorns the lower-echelon thugs he fights with along the way.

We excuse the methodology of the private investigator because we see no alternative to it. This is not the case in the police genre, where disreputable practices often are merely short-cuts, and standard procedures would work as well, if not as swiftly. But the private detective operates in a difficult world, unprotected by any public organization, always rushed for time, always in personal danger himself. His techniques are not just expedients; often they are desperate tricks of survival. Yet personal safety is hardly a guiding principle for such people; they continually risk everything in their solitary ventures, seeming to have a fairly charmed existence anyway, and their casual disregard of their own lives gives further meaning to their methods of searching for clues. Since they will use almost any means short of causing harm to innocent people in order to solve the case—and yet since they do hardly anything to provide for their own security (like waiting for the police before moving in on a killer)—they always manage to depersonalize their investigation. The search becomes a pursuit of objectified evil, never a mere vendetta, because the process involves each detective as an agent for a crucial social mission—the reestablishment of moral order. The agent himself is just a soldier fighting for this greater cause against the encroachment on society of some form of moral chaos.

This is not to suggest that detectives are without ego. They are proud figures, conscious of their own abilities and of the impressions of competence that they create. Yet they are essentially driven by feelings of hostility toward evil that make them less individual scourges than members of a profession idealistically committed to a certain moral norm. Bogart's Sam Spade is perhaps the only one to articulate the profession's code when he tells the murderess that if he did not bring in his partner's killer, it would be "bad all around, bad for every detective everywhere." There is a credo that private eyes follow but almost never talk about, a kind of oath to defend society, unwritten but binding all the same, and for that reason they emerge as American heroes.

But they are heroes with an abstract morality that operates on a mythic level. In real life, their business may be unglamorous snooping, private security, or bringing runaway children home. Even in the cinema their adventures seem, on the visual level, of little significance to a presumably normal world, but a world that is sometimes completely omitted from the film, and almost never more than glimpsed. It seems that we as audiences do not respond as much to the social significance of what we see in the film as to the heroic myth. In the encounter between the agent of the forces of moral order and the arrogant forces of disorder, we perceive, through the melodramatic fighting and the shooting, the endless basic struggle of abstract principles.

The narrative always contains a journey into darkness, a pattern that usually begins with a call for the services of the detective (but only about half the time is that initial request itself an honest one)—to check on a possibly cheating spouse or to find a missing person. As the innately suspicious detective begins to dig into the evidence, he uncovers layers of scandal or crime that usually lead to his being fired from the case or being offered a bribe to give up his search for the truth or simply threatened and beaten. Nothing, of course, will hinder the detective from solving the case and revealing the moral iniquities of those involved. The universal mistake made by his enemies and would-be corrupters is to assume from his appearance, language, or generally devious reputation that he can be bought, that indeed he operates on the same level of sensibility that they do.

The evil characters soon realize that an alien has arrived in their midst, and attempts are made again to silence him, sometimes outright attempts on his life. But the hero fearlessly, almost doggedly, proceeds with his search. In an allegorical sense, each investigation resembles a trip through an underworld or hell, not necessarily criminal but essentially decadent, perilous, and depraved. This symbolic journey into darkness in *Murder, My Sweet* begins with the opening imagery of Marlowe in a dimly lit room, his eyes completely bandaged. The hero of Alan Pakula's *Klute* (1971) begins his search by renting a basement apartment. In the older private detective films, the underworld was populated by low-life types who committed murder and personified greed, their other evils being hinted at by their appearances but not explicitly developed. The modern film, however, for commercial reasons is forced to deal in specifics about the kinds of evil that permeate the environment: thus much is made of alcoholism in *Harper,* drugs in *Tony Rome,* sexual perversion in *Klute,* and

213

incest in *Chinatown.* Along his path, the hero meets various derelicts, generally remaining untouched by their perverse personal habits, occasionally doing small kindnesses for them if they are not deceivers involved in the central plot.

In this allegorical subnormal world, many lures are set for the hero, who is simply not susceptible to them. Sexual enticement, for instance, seems standard in the genre, but until very recent years, the hero either shunned sex or accepted it only under vaguely implicit (never explicit) circumstances. The private detective still cannot spare a night while engaged in a case, and since modern "sophisticated" films are now usually required to introduce a sexually explicit sequence, the genre has to be stretched somewhat to accommodate an uncharacteristic interruption of the detective's search for clues. Harper, mauled in a fight that almost kills him, returns to his estranged wife for sympathy and love. In *Chinatown,* Polanski combines sex and plot action (extremely difficult to do in this genre) by having an important phonecall occur while the hero and his female client are talking in bed. In *Klute,* the hero has to be lured into bed by the prostitute-heroine he is trying to protect. On the other hand, the private eye usually seems to be sexually attractive to women and worldly wise in all such situations, especially when refusing an assault on his virtue.

In his allegorical trip through hell, the detective exhibits great courage and steadiness; he always seems to know the solution to the crime, perhaps because his instinct for perceiving people's true character beneath their facade is highly developed, and of course his intelligence is keen. He wades through distractions and dangers, emerging triumphant in the sense that he has for his own benefit solved the case. However, he is sometimes the victim of his own skills, destroying a relationship that was crucial to him at the beginning or was growing important in the course of his investigation. The pattern was clear in *The Maltese Falcon,* but earlier and later films have had it too. As Spade turns in the woman he loves, so Harper discovers that his friend is the murderer. The ending is cathartic in the Aristotelian sense, but even if the evil is found out, there is still not necessarily a happy ending. The rottenness uncovered in the long journey leads frequently to disenchantment or outright cynicism.

214

THE MALTESE FALCON
(1941)

Director	Cinematographer	Script
JOHN HUSTON	ARTHUR EDESON	JOHN HUSTON
Producer		Based on a novel by
HAL B. WALLIS		Dashiell Hammett
For Warner Brothers		

PRINCIPAL CHARACTERS

HUMPHREY BOGART	MARY ASTOR	SYDNEY GREENSTREET
Sam Spade	Brigid O'Shaughnessy	Kasper Gutman
PETER LORRE	BARTON MAC LANE	WARD BOND
Joel Cairo	Det. Lt. Dundy	Det. Tom Polhaus
GLADYS GEORGE	LEE PATRICK	JEROME COWAN
Iva Archer	Effie Perine	Miles Archer
		ELISHA COOK, JR.
		Wilmer Cook

Length: 100 minutes

215

No other classic of the American cinema has so decidedly lent its form to a genre as *The Maltese Falcon* did to the private detective film. Many earlier films helped establish the essential motifs and iconography still noticeable in recent examples, but until Sam Spade found his way through the intricate paths of *The Maltese Falcon* the crucial moral terrain of the genre had not been mapped. There were some very good detective films before this, especially the Thin Man series and a couple of the Sherlock Holmes films. But the strengths of such films reflected the genial or eccentric traits and quirks of their heroes encountering complicated puzzles that they would proceed to solve, not as an activity of professional or moral responsibility but as an expression of their skills or style of life. The two earlier versions of Spade's adventure, *Dangerous Female* (also called *The Maltese Falcon*), directed by Roy Del Ruth in 1931, and *Satan Met a Lady*, directed by William Dieterle in 1936, were within that format and now seem trivial. What John Huston, Humphrey Bogart, and a brilliant supporting cast brought to the genre in 1941 was the dark side of human nature, the confrontation with irredeemable evil, and the determination of the hero, no matter what the cost, to disclose the truth about the sordid experiences he has endured.

Most of the moral burden of the private detective film is placed on the hero, who functions in this regard as a source of moral awareness. His frequent professional experience with the criminal world prior to the beginning of any film in this genre makes the detective both suspicious of all relationships and cynical about human motivation. Typically, the detective adopts the mannerisms of the criminal characters he works among, and to judge by appearance alone we would associate Sam Spade with the worst of the type. Sophisticated criminals such as Gutman and Cairo attempt to hire Spade because they sense that his superb detective skills serve only his self-interest and can be readily diverted to illegal activities. The police, who also admire him, believe him capable of murder. Aside from his secretary, no one trusts him or suspects that his inner nature aspires to the knowledge of moral truth. The detective from then on was destined to work from a position of inner isolation to the establishment of a socially acceptable moral order in the world around him.

To imbue a whole genre with a moral sense required a model with the dramatic persuasiveness to make questions of morality seem inevitable to the narrative fabric. When at the end of *The Maltese Falcon* Spade declares his intention of turning over to the police the murderess, Brigid, with whom he has fallen in love, he presents a number of reasons for his decision, some of which he himself apparently regards as unimportant. But one reason, by its basic logic, firmly ties in to a code of ethics Spade argues for as operating within the entire value system of his profession. "When a man's partner is killed, he's supposed to do something about it," he states vehemently, speaking to the woman he loves but will send to prison for killing a man he disliked. To let her go, merely on personal grounds, would be "bad all around, bad for every detective everywhere." Spade does not suggest that such a code is simply a matter of personal belief, though as far as the cinema goes, he may indeed have invented it; rather, he indicates that the moral issue relates primarily to the nature of his profession, and in order to remain a professional he must follow the code to its logical conclusion—in this instance, sacrificing the woman he loves. Spade presents this imperative so forcefully that there seems no alternative, and it is this inevitability, the film's premises carried to their ultimate extension, that came to define the genre's moral dimension.

The issue of integrity that from then on was present in private detective films (usually dramatized by the attempt of one or more characters to "buy off" the detective) dovetailed with the development of the genre's premise that the true investigator is committed to his professional life above any other concerns—income, safety, or love. The cynical Spade seems the most unlikely of characters, at first, to create this generic concept of integrity; his literary antecedents come from the Dashiell Hammett-Raymond Chandler "hard-boiled school" of the 1920s. Yet his evident surface toughness, his disdain for his late partner's wife, with whom

he has had an affair, his lack of illusions, and his contempt for certain characters do not in any real way contradict his inner drive toward an almost spiritual goal. His higher aims lead him ultimately to ignore money, which everyone assumes he eagerly covets—the one thousand dollars he turns over to the police in the end may be tainted in that it was given to him by a criminal, but it was legally earned and belongs to Spade. Similarly, measuring his professional code against his personal feelings, he abandons Brigid.

From the premise of integrity stem other chief qualities of the genre associated with this particular film, perhaps most apparent in the hero's descent into the nether world of criminal life. The assorted criminals and perverts populating detective films prior to *The Maltese Falcon,* who commit isolated crimes for greed or revenge—motives common to the genre before 1941—suggest infrequent deviations from the normal world. The post-*Falcon* criminals have come to inhabit the total visual environment of the film, suggesting that the hero's descent occurs in a generally corrupt and decadent world (an allegorical dramatization of the real world) in which he himself symbolizes the main bulwark against depravity. The eccentric criminal types encountered by Spade—Brigid, Gutman, Cairo, and Wilmer—have long since been absorbed into the classic tradition of the cinema and have now become more lovable than sinister; but we must not forget Spade's own obvious disgust for their moral failure. All along he intends to bring them to justice, but equally apparent is his design to humiliate them as well, to make certain that no lingering claims can be made by some witness or participant to the equality of evil with the moral sense that Spade represents. Yet while manipulating events so as to provide demonstrations of the futility of evil, he often puts himself in grave danger. In the last sequence of the film Spade telephones the police to pick up the three male villains, explicitly warning them about the gunman Wilmer. Up to that moment, Spade has treated Wilmer as a teenage version of a 1930s James Cagney-type gangster, but Spade's handling of Wilmer is an act intended merely to dramatize the normal world's view of the despicable criminal; in reality, Spade is aware of the possibility that Wilmer might kill him. The point is that the detective-hero's descent into the nether world is based not on mere curiosity or casual involvement in a case, but on his hatred of evil and his desire to track it to its source, eventually to eradicate it, and thereby to cleanse the polluted environment of the film.

218

Therefore, the profession of the private investigator seems very much the equivalent of a calling to a life of self-sacrifice and commitment, resembling the life style of the medieval knight-errant. To perform well in his pursuits, the detective often adapts the disguise of one or another form of corruption for the purpose of gaining information or deluding the enemy, as Spade himself notes at the end. No matter what role he temporarily plays, the detective retains his identification with the moral order of the outside world he represents. Little is seen of this outside—presumably better—world in *The Maltese Falcon* or in any of the genre's major films, but its spirit is symbolized by the private eye's conviction that the discovery of truth is of ultimate value.

THE BIG SLEEP
(1946)

Director-Producer	Cinematographer	Script
HOWARD HAWKS For Warner Brothers	SIDNEY HICKOX	WILLIAM FAULKNER JULES FURTHMAN LEIGH BRACKETT Based on a story and a novel by Raymond Chandler

PRINCIPAL CHARACTERS

HUMPHREY BOGART Philip Marlowe	LAUREN BACALL Vivian Sternwood Rutledge	MARTHA VICKERS Carmen Sternwood
JOHN RIDGELEY Eddie Mars	CHARLES WALDEN Gen. Sternwood	ELISHA COOK, JR. Harry Jones
REGIS TOOMEY Bernie Ohls	DOROTHY MALONE Proprietress	CHARLES D. BROWN Norris the butler
BOB STEELE Canino		

Length: 114 minutes

219

The Philip Marlowe films taken together might in some sense constitute a category of the genre, but the diversity of characterizations of the hero probably preclude any meaningful grouping. In all of them the role of Marlowe is played with the same sort of sardonic wit, though it becomes less brilliant and more subdued with the passing years; in other respects, however, the one memorable portrayal is Bogart's in *The Big Sleep.* If this Marlowe lacks the intensity of his ancestor Sam Spade, it is perhaps the fault of the era, a postwar settling in of cynicism and weariness. Indeed, Marlowe's cynicism in this film establishes more firmly than ever before the essential defensive armor of the true private investigator about to embark on one of those dark journeys through the pits of human corruption.

Hawks's evident unconcern with the intelligibility of the plot line further contributes to the shaping of the genre by removing the private detective film from the whodunit, the popular amateur sleuth genre. Ever since the film appeared, it has not mattered how all the incidents connect, or whether every clue will lead (ever so indirectly) toward the solution of a crime. Rather, the emphasis falls on the violent and grotesque events encountered along the way by a hero ready for the worst and competent to evaluate each shifting element in the search for the ultimate meaning of the entire experience. It is not a formless structure,

though the plot line, as is always remarked by critics, is never satisfactorily clarified. The film provides us with a visual structure for the detective's search: between the first murder in the small house and the final violent shootout in the same place, Marlowe moves instinctively across a familiar psychological landscape, each incident a signpost indicating to him the direction to move toward a final comprehension of the journey.

And that final comprehension encompasses the discovery of at least the possibility of mutual trust within a world otherwise thoroughly abject and unredeemable. At the conclusion of *The Maltese Falcon,* Spade is left in splendid moral isolation, but desolate in regard to human contacts; in contrast, Philip Marlowe and Vivian Rutledge in the final shot of *The Big Sleep* look at each other with deep respect and affection. In one of its dimensions *The Big Sleep* projects a classic love story in which the hero rescues the heroine from encroaching degradation; in turn,

Vivian offers some hope to the cynical Marlowe, who engages in the detective's usual search for truth but never expects to find it embodied in a person. Marlowe wishes to solve a series of crimes, an ambition premised on the certainty that somewhere an objective truth exists, and that this truth is obtainable. In pursuit of this goal, Marlowe examines all the people he speaks to, but always with the assumption that they are lying to him. Lying appears to be the norm in Marlowe's jaundiced view of the world, and he resorts to it himself as a matter of convenience, as when he impersonates the effeminate book collector in the first stage of his investigation. Common sense, as it operates in the sordid world of Marlowe's experience, tells him that the truth cannot be reached through one individual speaking to another.

Thus, when Marlowe meets Vivian Rutledge, the spoiled, "wild" (Marlowe's impression of her reputation) daughter of a wealthy man, they can address each other only in ironic tones, sounding each other out indirectly—but at the same time establishing the grounds for their mutual attraction: cynicism, toughness, and overt disbelief in each other's honesty. Actually, Marlowe is immediately interested in her, appreciating the female counterpart of his own nature, but he will never trust her. She tries to hide her involvement in the complicated criminal events and plays the traditional generic role of the person who attempts to buy off the detective, and when Marlowe refuses to give up the case she goes to the district attorney with her complaint.

221

Throughout all this, their relationship manages to develop because Marlowe respects her character and her style. The restaurant sequence, in which Vivian and Marlowe inform each other of their mutual attraction, uses the slang of the racetrack— dialogue that seems thirty years later to be full of frankly sexual innuendo (with imagery reminiscent of Mae West's bawdy song of the 1930s, "Easy Rider"). Yet surely it was much less sexual to audiences at the time, though just as daring as it seems now. It is challenge dialogue—two people establishing their conditions for a possible future romance, speaking overtly yet obliquely so as not to commit themselves while in the process of bargaining and fixing their demands. Neither can trust the other at all, and so they cannot talk openly until the very end, when Marlowe forces Vivian to admit that her part in the plot was solely a matter of protecting her addict-sister. When Marlowe unmasks Eddie Mars as the real killer, he frees Vivian from the last need to remain secretive. He can finally trust her, and she no longer fears that his detective skills will destroy her family.

The Big Sleep contains more violence than most of its successors, with Marlowe receiving some of the brutality but causing even more. He kills the most vicious murderer in the film, Canino, while enraged (atypical of the genre, where most detective killings are either done from a distance or are unavoidable), firing repeatedly while the outmaneuvered Canino is unable to react quickly enough and dies with his own revolver in hand. Eddie Mars, at the end, is similarly outmaneuvered when he positions his gunmen outside his house but is forced by Marlowe, who is entirely aware of the situation, to leave first, and is thus mistakenly killed in the ambush set up for the hero. Nevertheless, Marlowe's typical traits are generically familiar: professionalism, coolness, absolute bravery, and a running wit, indicating a sense of the absurdity about him as well as a refusal to be put down by anyone—especially if that person holds a gun on him. Some of the scripting is careless, and four or five times Marlowe's tough ripostes have the effect of the teenage hood's "Oh yeah?" But for the most part the dialogue is briskly clever, with Bogart's delivery humorously capturing both Marlowe's brilliance and his compulsive talkativeness.

Typical of Hawks's films in general as well as of the detective genre, *The Big Sleep* tends to place a high value on style. Most of the style belongs to Marlowe and Vivian, but others have it, too: the two thugs who beat up Marlowe gain from the spectator, Jones, an accolade for professionalism, an opinion that Marlowe too seems to accept—albeit grudgingly. Jones himself has a kind of style that Marlowe approves of, for after making a joke about Jones's shortness that Jones objects to as being unfair, Marlowe acknowledges his error.* Later, after watching Jones poisoned by Canino and discovering that in the final moments Jones protected his girlfriend, Marlowe is much struck by this man's character, an impression that is a motivating influence in the revenge Marlowe later takes on Canino. Throughout the film, style indicates strength of character. Style reflects self-confidence, and those who have it are the only ones capable of ever divulging truth.

---

*The casting is worth a historical footnote to the genre. Elisha Cook, Jr. played Wilmer in *The Maltese Falcon*, where he was despised and often humiliated by Bogart as Sam Spade. Followers of the genre expect something similar on first seeing Jones, but Marlowe's apologetic response undermines our expectations and produces a new insight into the two Bogart roles.

HARPER
(1966)

Director	Cinematographer	Script
JACK SMIGHT	CONRAD HALL	WILLIAM GOLDMAN
Producers	Technicolor	Based on a novel
JERRY GERSHWIN	Panavision	by Ross MacDonald
ELLIOTT KASTNER		
For Warner Brothers		

PRINCIPAL CHARACTERS

PAUL NEWMAN	LAUREN BACALL	JULIE HARRIS
Lew Harper	Mrs. Simpson	Betty Fraley
ARTHUR HILL	JANET LEIGH	PAMELA TIFFIN
Albert Graves	Susan Harper	Miranda Sampson
ROBERT WAGNER	ROBERT WEBBER	SHELLEY WINTERS
Alan Taggert	Dwight Troy	Fay Estabrook
STROTHER MARTIN		
Claude		

Length: 121 minutes

223

Twenty years after Philip Marlowe entered the hothouse of General Sternwood's mansion and embarked on his exploration of the links between moral corruption and wealth, Lew Harper, a descendant of the archetypal Marlowe, discovers the same world and the same links but ends up without the sense of personal satisfaction of his predecessor. Marlowe at least helped Sternwood's daughter Vivian to move through her shield of decadent cynicism and emerge in a condition of hope. But twenty years later she has lapsed back into her debilitating decadence. (That is, Lauren Bacall—who also played Vivian Rutledge in *The Big Sleep*—appears in this film as the wealthy Mrs. Sampson, who, learning at the end of her husband's murder, cannot contain her glee as she calls for her daughter-in-law to announce the death and enjoy the girl's sorrow.) Like Marlowe, Harper is the completely devoted investigator, moving quickly from clue to clue, easily resisting the sexual invitations of the bored, self-indulgent young rich girl, playing many roles, adaptable to all situations, undismayed by a world of drug addiction, corruption, and murder; he is even beaten up a couple of times, for good measure. One interesting difference that marks the change of sensibility over two decades is that Marlowe starts out as a thoroughgoing cynic and finds some personal salvation in solving the crime. Harper is somewhat more trusting and discovers the depravity in those seemingly on his side, including his best friend, Albert Graves, a respectable lawyer, who has committed an almost motiveless murder. Harper's world is left in ruins. There is nothing in this environment worth retrieving, including the half-million-dollar ransom he merely drops at the door of the Sampson estate in the film's last sequence. The criminals are dead or arrested, and Mrs. Sampson, who received sufficient pleasure from the news of her husband's killing, will repossess the money.

The basic visual style of the film tends to intertwine the thematic strands of corruption and wealth. Establishing shots from a considerable distance present a luxurious environment, with images of wealth and beauty suggesting a placid and orderly life style. As we are drawn into the environment through the appearance of Harper—a disjunctive element in his dilapidated car—we note various tinges of moral disarray. Sampson, who is worth twenty million dollars, is killed in a filthy latrine on board a deserted freighter. The beautiful mountaintop temple on closer inspection is merely a hiding place for illegal Mexican aliens. The Sampson mansion, visually dominated by a magnificent swimming pool, is presided over by the spoiled young would-be temptress, Miranda, a failure even as a sexual lure. Inside dwell people who intensely hate each other. Under a sunlamp, the invalid Mrs. Sampson struggles to retain the semblance of her lost good looks (she is here a figurative descendant of General Sternwood in *The Big Sleep;* the analogy of needing artificial warmth to keep spiritually alive is striking). Her sarcastic remarks about her husband as she hires Harper to find him, and the fact that she speaks to the detective while draped in a towel, are an implicit overture that Harper refuses to pick up. Harper listens to her boast that she wishes only to outlive her husband and deflates her with the remark: "People in love will say anything." Later Harper effectively repulses Miranda in the grotesquely designed love-suite hotel quarters of her missing father. In contrast to visual displays of wealth that serve as facades to disguise internal decrepitude, the unpretentious appearance of Harper in his shoddy car, chewing gum, or even resorting to raiding his own garbage for yesterday's coffee grounds, seems wholesome and endearing.

Like his counterparts in the genre, Harper is conscious of his image and his ability to change it at will, to impersonate various types, to arouse anger or sympathy in someone else—all for the purpose of solving the mysteries he is involved in (a skill at impersonation also notable in Newman's recent portrayal of Harper in *The Drowning Pool,* directed by Stuart Rosenberg, [1975]). Sardonic and witty in the tradition of all the movie Marlowes, Harper is the first notable private detective in many years to be married and to be preoccupied with a personal problem. The problem, which is usually associated with the police genre and

almost never with private detectives, is the discontented wife who wants her husband to give up his career. Since Harper refuses to do so, she is in the process of divorcing him, while he keeps arguing for another chance. At one point, after a grueling fight in which he is almost killed by a gangster, Harper intrudes upon Susan, tells her he is quitting, and spends the night with her. Although he obviously loves her, he lets her know the next day that he will go back to work on his case. She cannot understand his passing up this last chance for reconcilement. "Why do you have to go back?" she asks. "Because it's not over yet," he answers, and her inability to comprehend her husband's vocation presumably dooms their relationship.

Professional dedication is at the center of the genre, and the failure of others to understand it morally isolates the hero. "What d'ya do this crummy work for?" inquires Miranda early in the film, but Harper realizes she is too stupid for an honest answer and responds with a comedy routine about working for the American way of life. But in the car ride at the end of the film, the issue is raised in another way by Albert Graves, his good friend, whom Harper discovers to be the murderer of Sampson. "You gonna turn me in?" Albert asks, after explaining the worthless nature of Sampson, and Harper answers, "Got no other choice." They muse on the failed hopes of their youth—Albert to become governor, Harper to become a great prosecuting attorney. Albert suggests that there is no point in turning him in, that the matter should be left alone for the sake of friendship and human fallibility. Harper tries to explain the nature of his commitment through one abstract sentence, which though it explains nothing in a literal way affords some insight into the entire genre. Talking about a period of "eight disgusting months" he had experienced in the recent past, he tells Albert of five or six weeks that followed that justified his dedication: "You wouldn't understand. . . . those five or six weeks I really felt alive." The film ends with a thoroughly ambiguous image in which the worldweary detective leaves Albert in the car and pauses on the threshold of the Sampson mansion seemingly disappointed that Albert did not shoot him down to prevent him from informing the police. Some viewers were left in doubt as to whether Harper would indeed turn in his friend, since the film ends with a frozen shot of the detective, hands half-raised in an ambiguous gesture. But as Harper himself says, there really is no alternative for a professional detective in this situation. The source material in Ross MacDonald's novel had no such ambiguity—the hero, in exactly the same determined style that Philip Marlowe used in similar situations, does what has to be done. The film's final ambiguity, though stylistically fashionable in the 1960s, does not truly satisfy the genre's implications, though neither does it negate them.

BULLITT
(1968)

Director	Cinematographer	Script
PETER YATES	WILLIAM FRAKER	ALAN R. TRUSTMAN
Producer	Technicolor	HARRY KLEINER
PHILIP D'ANTONI		Based on a novel
For Warner Brothers-Seven Arts		by Robert L. Pike

PRINCIPAL CHARACTERS

STEVE MC QUEEN	ROBERT VAUGHN	JACQUELINE BISSET
Frank Bullitt	Walter Chalmers	Cathy
DON GORDON	ROBERT DUVALL	SIMON OAKLAND
Delgetti	Weissberg	Captain Bennett
NORMAN FELL		
Baker		

Length: 114 minutes

The pressures on Lt. Frank Bullitt come from every direction. First Chalmers, the politically ambitious federal prosecutor, wants Bullitt to turn over to him a potential star witness, whom the policeman has been assigned to guard. Later, a police captain wants Bullitt removed from the case for conspiring to hide the fact from Chalmers that the witness who has been shot by the mob has died while in protective custody. Another captain, Bullitt's friendly commanding officer, gives Bullitt one day to catch the unknown murderers. The mob's hired gunmen follow him around waiting for him to lead them to the witness. And finally his girlfriend accuses him of having become completely callous because of his job, of living "in a sewer," of being unaffected by violence and murder.

The girlfriend's complaints, given in some detail about three-quarters through the film, point to the moral center of the narrative. Since Bullitt is by nature quiet and reserved, and since he seems destined to exist under continual harassment, he does not defend himself from the charges of growing insensitivity. Yet the thrust of the visual material does not direct us to her conclusion. Instead, we recognize the typical problem of the genre—his thoroughgoing professionalism places the detective hero beyond mundane personal considerations and ordinary police methodology. He is dedicated to solving the crimes and catching the perpetrators, not to explaining his actions or justifying his character. Presumably his success is his justification and his morality—he removes murderous individuals from society, a job he does with particular skill but with no overt probing of ethical issues attached to his behavior. From what we see of Bullitt risking his life, he does indeed seem concerned for others, but his concern is manifest in action, not in the explication of theory.

227

This professionalism surpasses the understanding of others in Bullitt's world. He is hardly a sympathetic character to those who argue with him, for his life resembles that of any person with a true calling: he seems overly committed, uncompromising, disdainful of those who do not understand, and annoyingly self-confident. Nevertheless, the genre is always highly supportive of true professionalism, and in this film the tendency is seen in a peculiarly ambivalent way: Yates's direction enables the two killers to operate in an almost admirable light because of their own professionalism. Two sequences in particular bear this out: in one, a white-haired, middle-aged killer appears in the hospital to finish the job on the witness; spotted by Bullitt, he flees through the hospital basement and manages to escape from the detective, a much younger man, but without Bullitt's coming off badly in any sense or carelessly letting him slip away. The killer is just extremely courageous and skillful in his own line of work. The other example occurs in *Bullitt's* most memorable sequence, the great car chase—perhaps the best one up to that time and not equaled since, outside of *The French Connection*. In this

sequence, the gunman and his driver are chased through the streets of San Francisco and out of the city by the relentless detective. There is some sensational stunt driving of both cars, indicating that the criminal and Bullitt are about equally proficient in this skill so important for each of their professions. The gunman and his driver never exchange a word during the chase, which demands the utmost concentration on both their parts—for as the fleeing car is being driven in a weaving pattern the gunman fires at Bullitt. All three participants are aware of the precision needed to survive this life-and-death struggle. Eventually Bullitt's skill proves slightly better than his opponents'; the driver of the fleeing car loses control and both gangsters are killed in the ensuing crash. The hero's excellence is enhanced by his ability to surpass his professional adversaries.

But professionalism in the genre is not merely a matter of exhibiting highly developed qualities of survival. If the detective hero did not use unorthodox methods and persistence in tracking down the criminals, not only would the villains escape, but more important, the illusions that shroud the events would never be dispelled. Ordinary investigators dwell on the surface realities and therefore cannot really defend society against the particularly subtle outrages of devious criminals. The real "heavy" in the film is Chalmers, not the murderers, for he is so intent on self-aggrandizement that he uses everybody for this end. His witness, Ross, will make him a nationally known figure in testimony before a Senate committee on organized crime, and Bullitt is assigned to guard Ross because Chalmers has learned that the detective makes "good copy" in the press. When Ross is killed, Bullitt knows that Chalmers will intrude in the matter and prevent him from finding the killers, who have also seriously wounded one of Bullitt's colleagues. He therefore conspires with the doctor on duty in the hospital to hide the fact of the witness's death, spiriting the body away to the morgue under a fictitious name and pretending to Chalmers that he still has Ross in custody. This unorthodox procedure produces the desired effect: it brings the killers out of hiding; it also arouses the wrath of Chalmers, who spends most of the rest of the film threatening Bullitt and trying to ruin him. Later, when Bullitt seems on the verge of success, Chalmers immediately switches tactics and tries to win him over with promises of great political rewards— though of course Bullitt's integrity cannot be challenged by such feeble considerations.

Bullitt discovers that the dead "star witness" was in fact an impostor, set up by Ross and made known to Chalmers in order to cover Ross's escape from the mob with a stolen two million dollars. The film concludes with a third chase, this time of the real Ross at the airport, where Chalmers tells Bullitt that he still needs Ross as a witness. But Bullitt's concern is simply to apprehend a dangerous criminal in a crowded airport. After Ross shoots an airport guard, it is inevitable that he himself will be shot down. Bullitt has performed well, but as the ending indicates, he remains morally isolated, with no one offering praise or being capable of understanding his achievement. The film ends with Bullitt returning to his girlfriend in the middle of the night, washing his hands, remaining silent.

KLUTE
(1971)

Director-Producer	Cinematographer	Script
ALAN J. PAKULA	GORDON WILLIS	ANDY K. DANIELS
For Warner Brothers	Technicolor	DAVE LEWIS
	Panavision	

PRINCIPAL CHARACTERS

JANE FONDA	DONALD SUTHERLAND	CHARLES CIOFFI
Bree Daniels	John Klute	Peter Cable
ROY SCHEIDER	DOROTHY TRISTAN	JEAN STAPLETON
Frank Ligourin	Arlyn Page	Goldfarb's Secretary
RITA GAM		MORRIS STRASSBERG
Trina		Mr. Goldfarb

Length: 114 minutes

230

John Klute is not an urban detective. He comes to New York from a small town in Pennsylvania, to investigate a missing-person case, and at the end of the film he leaves the city, in which he was not comfortable, to return to his occupation as a Tuscarora policeman. This fact largely explains the significant differences between *Klute* and the rest of the works in this genre. One other key aspect affecting the film's form is the shifting point of view, since half of the film is devoted to the story of Bree Daniels, a prostitute, and her attempt to establish a psychological identity. Her inner search provides the detective plot with the vital link between the victims and the murderer.

As a nonurban detective, Klute reveals a new perspective on the usual business of tracking down a murderer. His personal style is not ironic. In fact, he is the least humorous private detective in the entire genre. Like all the great investigators, he remains an intense observer from outside the environment of corruption that permeates the film—but he does not resort to the ironic wit of Marlowe or Spade as a means of distinguishing himself from the addicts, perverts, and pimps he encounters. Klute realizes all along that he is only a visitor to New York, that he need not stake out any permanent means of access to the subterranean world that he must visit for this one case. His telling comment on the lives of desperation that he views in the city might be understood by Marlowe and Spade, but they would never utter the words: "it's so pathetic."

This sensitivity to the pathos inherent in the decadent environment of the film, heightened by his unfamiliarity with the ways of the city, leads Klute to a personal involvement with Bree, who is facing a crisis in her life, trying to break away from prostitution

but afraid of facing an uncertain, uncontrolled existence. Unable to relate to people successfully except in her role as a prostitute, Bree falls in love with Klute but fears both his acceptance of her and his possible rejection. She therefore attempts to reject him first, but is thwarted by his essentially humane and selfless nature. For his part, he fluctuates between his sense of the pathetic in regard to her and a degree of objective disgust at what she does, though he quickly begins to feel protective toward her. Aware that she might become a possible victim of the murderer he is tracking, he refuses to leave her or even to argue with her. He patiently persists, and by the end of the film he overcomes much of her fear and takes her with him as he returns to Pennsylvania.

With all this, Pakula intensifies the texture of *Klute* beyond that of a standard private eye film; he does so in the most overt way by emphasizing a number of devices (such as snatches of conversation played back on a tape recorder by the killer) that tend to increase the ambiguities of the plot, and by switching the perspective on the action. Intertwining the two stories, Pakula sometimes follows Bree to her psychiatrist's office and at other times concentrates on the detective's search, or the killer's obsession with a tape of a night spent with Bree. Oddly enough, the killer himself is an outwardly reasonable man, submerging his psychopathic perversity beneath a veneer of kind concern—and, as often happens in the genre, the man paying the detective's bills. The complexity of Bree's story to some extent obscures the generic structure of the film, but this is really just a problem of first appearances. Underneath, the genre form is still holding everything together, as the competent detective traces through the moral morass that has stopped the police cold. (Toward the end of the film, a police expert on typewriter styles correctly names the murderer—but he admits that the police have no case, and, as usual for the genre, it is left to the private detective to arrange some plot to trap the killer.)

Klute himself is so quiet for a private eye, having none of the traditional patter or charm, that at first he does not appear to be anything more than a small-town cop taking on a private investigator's job as a favor to the missing man's family and because—as the killer himself notes early in the film before we identify the irony—"he cares." Caring is clearly the distinguishing trait of Klute's character, but he also has all the other skills: courage, daring (he chases a prowler on a dark rooftop and down some dangerous corridors without a moment's hesitation as to what might await him), the capacity to use his fists, and the cool competence that allows him to respond correctly to all situations. Of course his detective skills are of a high order, for he takes on the case only after a long, seemingly thorough police investigation has led to nothing; in fact, the police are not even aware of all three murders committed by the killer.

232

Since the dominant stylistic mode of the film is documentary realism—with the camera often going behind the backs of characters (observing them in the act of observing or following others) and acting performances geared to underplayed naturalism (much of Jane Fonda's Academy-Award-winning performance seems close to the level of improvisatory dialogue)—it is perhaps instructive to note the strength of the film's mythic dimension. To the detective's journey through the underworld of human depravity, Pakula has added the motif of human redemption through love. Bree is saved from herself by the strong, silent hero who constantly watches over her and modifies her destructive impulses. Still, the psychological effectiveness that his presence has on her is really determined by the genre's format, which gives the detective heroic stature. The surface realism makes the relationship between the detective and the prostitute plausible, while the genre's allegorical mode makes the rapid psychological development convincing.

DIRTY HARRY

(1972)

Director-Producer	Cinematographer	Script
DON SIEGEL	BRUCE SURTEES	HARRY JULIAN FINK
For Warner Brothers	Technicolor	R. M. FINK
	Panavision	DEAN RIESNER
		Based on a story by
		Harry Julian Fink and R. M. Fink

PRINCIPAL CHARACTERS

CLINT EASTWOOD	HARRY GUARDINO	ANDY ROBINSON
Harry	Bressler	The Killer
RENI SANTONI	JOHN VERNON	JOHN LARCH
Chico	The Mayor	Police Chief
JOHN MITCHUM	MAE MERCER	LYN EDGINGTON
De Georgio	Mrs. Russell	Norma
RUTH KOBART		
Bus Driver		

Length: 102 minutes

233

Two contemporary controversial issues tended to obscure the generic excellence of *Dirty Harry* when it appeared and made it, in spite of its overwhelming commercial success, a distasteful film to many of the more astute reviewers. One issue was the explicit violence, attributable to the fashion of the films of the 1970s; but violence can probably be artistically justified in this film for helping to establish the characterization of the hero in a milieu he comes to perceive as unbearably alien to him, even in light of his past experience of society's evils. The other issue negatively affecting the reception of the film is important to examine because it represents the sort of misunderstanding that occurs when a genre film—a film conceived in a special tradition—is interpreted without a clear impression of the implications embedded in the tradition. In this case, critics noted an unpleasant thematic motif that (considered out of its generic context) seemed dangerous to the spirit of a humanistic society.

At a point past the middle of the film, the police detective Harry Callahan succeeds in apprehending one of the vilest murderers ever depicted in the genre. However, in the process, he violates the court-established procedural rights of the arrested man, and the state determines immediately that the criminal must be released, for the evidence would surely be thrown out at a trial. The audience is as astounded as the hero is at the sudden turn of events, and from our perspective, the representatives of strict civil-rights procedure (the members of the district attorney's office) are insane. If Siegel were less of an artist, we might simply assume that he has personally taken the anti-intellectual populist side of an important social issue, whereby the public confuses civil rights guarantees with mere technicalities and legal quibbles. Typical of the hostility raised by the issue was Pauline Kael's comment: *"Dirty Harry is obviously just a genre movie, but this action genre has always had a fascist potential, and it has finally surfaced. . . . But since crime is caused by deprivation, misery, psychopathology, and social injustice, Dirty Harry is a deeply immoral movie."** Actually, what Siegel has done (regardless of his personal feelings on the civil rights issue) sharpens our perception of the moral nature of the genre.

The matter of procedural issues is really only Siegel's updating of the genre's traditional motif of third-party opposition to the detective's tracking of the criminal (as in Lang's *The Big Heat* and Douglas's *The Detective*). Representing the uncreative, methodical, second-rate group of citizens (here, typically, the hero's official superiors), the third party hates—and yet admires—the hero's abilities and tries to hinder his success. Thus, when Callahan realizes that his almost superhuman efforts at nailing the murderer have come to nothing, he reaffirms his total responsibility of ridding society of this force of evil and reestablishing society's control over the erratic, destructive elements that arise within it.

234

Inevitably, the genre dodges social issues; it remains at all times a genre in which the moral lines are drawn in the depiction of the initial situation. Here, a mass murderer kills citizens wantonly; he also abducts a girl and demands a ransom from the city itself. The killer, an extremely cunning monster, depraved rather than psychopathic, insists on promoting the conflict on the broader scale of man-versus-entire-city, assured that the civilized community does not know how to cope with him. Only Callahan is capable of combatting him rather than yielding to the diabolical possibility of a repeated pattern of such ransoms. Callahan's courage and hatred of evil are demonstrated at the opening of the film when, alerted to a robbery while in the middle of his lunch— he comes calmly to the rescue of society terrorized by sudden violence; his gun empty, he outfaces a wounded robber lying next to a loaded shotgun. We know, therefore, that the hero has the usual generic perspective on crime, and that the film will not require any further verbal articulation of why the policeman hates the criminal. The police superiors, too, oppose criminals— we are not to think of them as corrupt but as simply incapable of handling anything beyond the mundane. If they could catch the extraordinary criminal, there would be no need for the hero-cop.

*New Yorker, January 15, 1972, p. 81.

Nevertheless, it is typical of the genre that though the police detective is a loner tracking down the criminal and facing harassment from his superiors, he does take on the authority of the state; he is finally right in what he does. Yet Callahan throws his badge into the river that contains the murderer he has just shot. In *Dirty Harry* and other modern films of the genre, there is also a final realization that the hero must quit the force because in conquering opposition of the third party he has lost all respect for it. (The box office success of the film, however, brought Callahan back to the department in *Magnum Force* the next year, and this lesser film was an even greater commercial success than the first, thus suggesting, perhaps, a series of films and a "Dirty Harry" subcategory of the police detective category.)

The film engenders a consistent level of outrage on the part of the audience toward the brazenness of the killer and the society that cannot handle him. The characterization of the killer is fully developed, but hardly as a human villain: his abstract hatred for normality is by no means the usual kind of insanity of mass murderers. His ferocity symbolizes the rottenness that heroes like Callahan must root out, with enormous dedication and equivalent ferocity, in defense of the state. The two men's motives, in line with the genre, are no better established than this: they hate each other, and we are shown that they have cause to. At one point Callahan, thwarted in his attempt to rid San Francisco of the killer, begins to engage in psychological warfare by follow-ing the man he cannot legally arrest. The killer, in turn, with remarkable if unbelievable insight, hires someone to give him—the killer—a brutal beating so that afterward he can pretend that Callahan has entered into a personal vendetta.

At the end Callahan is vindicated, as he himself predicted, when the killer again asks for ransom, this time holding a bus-load of children. Callahan, disgusted with the authorities' impo-tence in the face of the threat, simply takes matters into his own hands, and the final showdown brings the killer to his inevitable doom. There is no reasonable qualm about fascist tactics when the matter in the end boils down to saving children's lives, but of course the film ought to be judged as a whole. Implicit in the earlier violation of the killer's rights was his potential to kill many people, including children. The police hero is instinctively aware of this kind of terror and responds quickly to it, while the plod-ders, the incompetents, the higher-ups talk of correct methodol-ogy. Correct methodology, according to the genre, always means the same thing—the ordinary procedures that are needed for ordinary criminals. The genre, however, always treats the extraordinary criminal and the heroic response of the one man able to see more clearly than everyone else and who ultimately brings everyone else to his perception, finally vindicated but remaining solitary in the very private world of his moral commit-ment.

236

CHINATOWN
(1974)

Director	Cinematographer	Script
ROMAN POLANSKI	JOHN ELONZO	ROBERT TOWNE
Producer	Technicolor	
ROBERT EVANS	Panavision	
For Paramount		

PRINCIPAL CHARACTERS

JACK NICHOLSON	FAYE DUNAWAY	JOHN HUSTON
J. J. Gittes	Evelyn Mulwray	Noah Cross
JOHN YELBURTON	DARRELL ZWERLING	PERRY LOPEZ
Hillerman	Hollis Mulwray	Lt. Escobar
		ROMAN POLANSKI
		Man with knife

LENGTH: 131 minutes

Chinatown is unusually interesting for a genre film; it proceeds in many respects from the major works of its tradition, but it is oddly textured by Polanski's macabre humor and the somewhat offbeat casting of Jack Nicholson as the Bogart-type detective, J. J. Gittes. The deviations from the conventional pattern are for the most part excellently done and serve to remind us that the power of the private detective myth is essentially unaffected by changes in its accouterments. The film is set in the 1930s, the decade before the time period of two famous Bogart portrayals, and the hero is not at all a denizen of the lower strata of society. His office is modern, with the look of prosperity, and he has two men as well as a secretary working for him. (Is this because he charges $35 a day instead of $25?) The car he drives is the opposite of Harper's heap, and when it is seriously damaged in an accident, the hero never mentions it again. Indeed, he seems something of a throwback to Nick Charles, though he lacks the urbanity and aristocratic manners of the hero of the Thin Man adventures; in language and capabilities he resembles Spade and Marlowe.

In spite of the new look Polanski gives the film, the sense of the seventies and its particular concerns (such as graphic violence, and corpses that look like corpses instead of the artful compositions of actors in repose that greeted Bogart in the 1940s), and in spite of the obligatory 1970s bedroom sequence, this film works in exactly the same pattern of dedication that all the great private eyes share. Some big fees are mentioned, and two of Gittes's clients hire him to work on the same case from different angles, but it is quite clear early in his investigation that Gittes is prepared to work for nothing, to work on his own time, to solve the complicated case that he has gotten involved in. The presumable surface motive for his dedication is that he has been fooled and that his curiosity or sense of pride dictates his following up on the case. However, Gittes also believes that the victim has not died an official, accidental death but has been murdered, and he senses a vast scheme to cheat the public on a bond issue that concerns a public utility, the water company. He never seems to show any hatred for evil or corruption, and *in that sense* the film is either ultimately something of a decline in the genre or a more sophisticated contemporary way of dealing with private eye morality, for what we see is a tireless investigator single-handedly, without help from the police or clients, fearlessly tracking down the elements of a multiple murder case and an enormous conspiracy of corruption. It is, of course, the same old journey through the vile dregs of life that all the private investigators since *The Maltese Falcon* have undertaken, but few have complained less or worked harder than Gittes.

In the tradition of recent Philip Marlowe films, this one does not present an absolutely unerring investigator; like the hero in *Marlowe*, Gittes is capable of mistaking the situation—in fact, he

237

238 makes a few mistakes that are indeed costly, though they are not
the kind that would lower our estimate of his skills. The film
opens with his turning over explicit photographs to a distraught
husband who has hired him to spy on his wife. This opening may
temporarily lower the hero in our esteem compared to the role of
supersleuth assumed by most private detectives at the very
beginning of an investigation: it is evident that Gittes's main
work is the usual business of real-life private eyes—spying for
suspicious spouses. Then he is hired by a wife to spy on her
husband (the head of the Water Department), catches the husband with a girl, reports to the wife, and later reads that the story
has made the front page of the newspapers. Next he learns that
he has been tricked into "getting the dirt" on the commissioner in
order to discredit the Water Department's stand on a bond issue.*
He properly resents being used, but his follow-up investigation
leads him to other revelations, particularly of the key scandal
regarding the city's water system.

Polanski's one major generic innovation in the film occurs at
the very end. The hero has made the traditional trip through the
underworld of depravity, culminating in his belief that the
woman he is attracted to is a murderess whom he must turn over
to the police (similar to the Spade-Brigid relationship in *The*

---

*After leaving the theater, we might realize that the premise is preposterous—
since the criminals could not plausibly suspect immoral conduct on the part of
the commissioner, except for the one criminal who could not have risked exposure of the woman involved.

Maltese Falcon, though Nicholson as Gittes probably does not feel any intense passion for the suspect). But just before the police arrive, a switch occurs, uncommon to the genre but hardly a new possibility: the woman turns out not to be a murderess after all, but indeed has an excellent justification for her dishonesty throughout the film. As a teenager, she was raped by her own father (the actual murderer in the film as well as the millionaire source of corruption in the matter of the water scandal—and played by John Huston himself). The child of that incestuous union is the one Gittes saw in the company of the commissioner early in the film, and thus the hero's mistakes, though apparently unavoidable, have been costly. Nevertheless, through skillful and persistent detective work he has solved the murder and uncovered the scandal, and at this point Polanski's innovation startles us into a deeper understanding of the genre's mythic pattern.

As Gittes confronts his rival and sometime friend, the police lieutenant, in the streets of Chinatown and in the presence of all those involved in the case, he tries to explain but is prevented by the general commotion—for, as usual in the genre, the police think that the private eye is the one to be arrested for withholding evidence. As the murderer sees his child leave with her mother, he attempts to stop her, for he genuinely loves the young woman. The mother shoots him in the shoulder and tries to escape, but the police, who have witnessed the shooting of a respectable citizen, kill her as she drives off. Gittes is overcome by the suddenness of the events; there seems to be no sense in explaining the murders or in revealing the scandal, since the evidence would not be substantial without the mother. He then walks off, dazed; the murderer, spiritually destroyed but physically free from legal restraints, walks off too, and the film ends. Our sense of justice is injured for a moment; it seems futile. But the truth that Polanski has grasped about the genre is that it is not essential for justice to be served. The genre, after all, is not concerned with justice but with the search for moral truth. The only one who really cares about the moral truth, in most private eye films, is the hero himself. Polanski is probably artistically correct in this insight— the lonely hero is the only one capable of a final understanding, and that is the essential matter, not the broadcasting of that truth to the representatives of the civilized world, when the only ones left for that message are the police.

Coming as a totally unexpected event, the ending seemed to critics to be another example of the contemporary cinema's moral ambiguity, but the film is in no real sense ambiguous. The trail of depravity and its subsequent mysteries are solved as we leave the underworld at the end. What we are spared—in retrospect—is the kind of ending we saw in *The Big Sleep*, where Philip Marlowe is ready to explicate the incredibly complicated series of events at the end of the film. But who would believe him? In probability, five minutes after that film ended, Marlowe would be arrested himself. This assumed unraveling of impossibly intricate events is common in many intrigue narratives. An increasingly complex series of episodes may culminate only in one private understanding of the moral cosmos of the narrative. There is always a final truth, but there is not always a representative of the normal world, aside from the hero, capable of perceiving it.

240

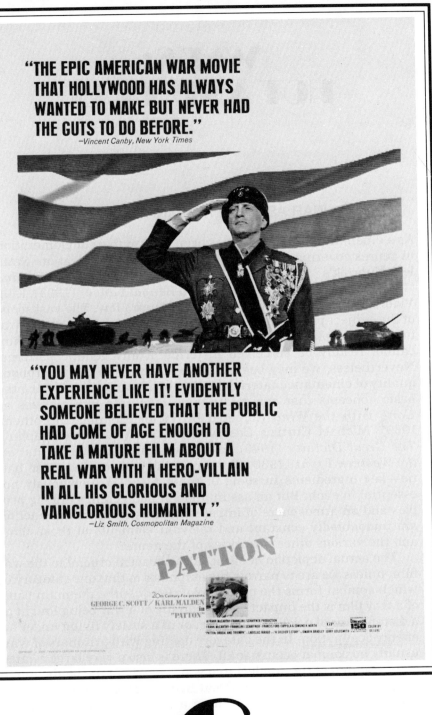

WARS:
HOT AND COLD

WAR AS AN ATTITUDINAL GENRE

As a cinematic subject, war has been treated in a conglomeration of genres covering any historical period of any civilization: Stanley Kubrick's *Spartacus* (1960), Otto Preminger's *Exodus* (1960), Henry Hathaway's *Lives of a Bengal Lancer* (1935), King Vidor's *War and Peace* (1956), to name just a few. The vast scope of the subject precludes definitions based on action, characterization, theme, place, or tone; indeed, the portrayal of war in film cannot readily be perceived in terms of any generic patterns. Nevertheless, we may begin to give structure to the amorphous quality of cinematic material dealing with war by considering the basic concepts that can relate such disparate film classics as *Gone with the Wind* (directed by Victor Fleming and others, 1939), Michael Curtiz's *Casablanca* (1942), Charles Chaplin's *The Great Dictator* (1940), and Lewis Milestone's *All Quiet on the Western Front* (1930). Romance, intrigue, comedy, and battle—key ingredients in some of these films—are obviously not essential in each. But an assumption of belligerency among peoples and an atmosphere of impending or existing military action are undoubtedly constant and relevant elements of these films and the various other categories of the genre.

The actual depiction of battle does not seem crucial to the war film, unless we are to narrow the emphasis to that one category in which combat forms the central plot. Frequently, the main point of a war film is the impact on civilian life of a war being fought at a distance, or of a soldier on leave, or of a society living under an enemy occupation. In the category dealing with prisoners of war, usually no combat occurs at all. There is also a very large related category, that of the "undeclared war," in which the belligerents, usually the United States or Great Britain, opposing the USSR or China, engage in espionage; here a nation's armed forces are replaced by surrogate warriors from the CIA or the KGB. Spying is included in the overall genre of the war film because it expands and illuminates the moral issues involved in one nation's hostility toward another: that of the human impulse to use force to control another people's destiny.

The war film is therefore the most difficult of all genres to define, even though the idea of war is obvious enough. The formlessness of the genre derives from the fact that the subject incorporates attitudes toward war, responses, preparations, results, aftermaths, and so on; the narrative representation of war frequently does not dwell on the most overt visual aspect, warfare itself, but on the conceptual materials that really give character to the genre. For this reason, the battle film, though numerically the dominant category of the genre, is among its least distinguished manifestations. Furthermore, since many of the most famous films related to the genre, such as *Casablanca*, cannot sensibly be excluded from a meaningful discussion of how the cinema has handled the subject of war, any fruitful attempt to define the genre must be extended to include any national conflict. We then become aware of the superiority within the genre of many noncombat films—particularly in regard to such categories as prisoner-of-war films and resistance-to-occupation films.

Since in qualifying the conditions of the genre we do not insist **243** on the actual depiction of warfare, it is logical to include those films that use the subject of war as a background for comedy, romance, adventure, or anything else. This is no farfetched extension of a sensible definition, for the history of film is replete with examples of the genre that require situations of war in order to establish the vitality of human conflicts and problems not themselves war-centered. Indeed, the genre was developed in exactly this way in the films of D. W. Griffith, who was particularly adept at mixing such otherwise incongruous themes as love and battle. No one can dispute Griffith's status as a master of the battle scene, achieving the highest imaginable level of pictorial realism. (His 1911 fifteen-minute film, *The Battle*, tends to make most modern-day war epics look like low-budget films.) Yet even in his monumental war films such as *America* (1924), Griffith gave primary emphasis to personal stories of romance, courage, deceit, and so on; the splendid battle scenes provide the environment for personal stories of characters responding to crises, of personalities taking shape in perilous times. The Griffith heritage leads to films like *Gone with the Wind*, in which the idea of war— much more than the actual depiction of war—affects the decisions and life styles of the leading characters.

Yet although there is a grand heritage of the war film, there is still no evident cohesiveness within the genre. The reason may be that, in comparison with the main character types of the other major genres discussed in this book, the character most readily identifiable with the war genre, the military figure, is less central to the war film than the Western hero is to the Western, the star performer to the musical, the figure of terror to the nightmare world, the criminal to the crime film, or the investigator to the detection film. Obviously, war as a broad topic is not so immediately referable to an individual as are the topics of other genres. Similarly, the broad thematic implications of war do not necessarily suggest physical environments (aside from the special case of battlefield encounters); they tend to move toward disparate abstractions. This of course is another reason for the difficulty in specifying a definitive model for the genre.

If the genre is definable at all, the similarities among its categories are to be sought neither in its iconography nor in its patterns of narrative. War films can be perceived as a genre only in terms of a certain kind of atmosphere. This atmosphere does not evolve from an actual war, since films without combat scenes (such as *Casablanca*) or films that take place largely during peacetime (*The Great Dictator*) make up a prominent part of the genre's tradition. Rather, the source of atmosphere lies in an oppressive sense of impending disaster on a grand scale (for instance, an invasion, a massive loss of life, or a more generalized loss of liberty), a concern that is usually not made explicit except in those films that take place within a combat area. The psychological depression caused by war may have more to do with the threatened loss of a way of life than with the possibility of the loss of life itself.

In any case, the core of the genre does not develop directly from the physical disasters of wartime but rather from the attitude of characters confronted with the situation of war, present or impending. This attitude manifests itself in a generalized opposition to the *spiritual* force represented by the enemy—that is, the heroes are motivated to defend their side against an oppressive or totalitarian enemy, usually depicted only from the heroes' point of view, if depicted at all, as a source of abstract evil. Interestingly enough, the personified enemy may not in himself be frightening—he may in fact be a comic fool, as is Ernst Lubitsch's Hitler in *To Be or Not To Be* (1942) or Chaplin's Hitler (Hynkel) in *The Great Dictator*—and yet he may still represent the atmospheric threat that causes the good characters to respond in a manner recognizable to the genre. However, the threat is never adequately embodied by one person, even in a serious depiction of a tyrant; the enemy must represent not merely a potential military defeat for the good side but an eventual crushing of the human spirit in favor of the establishment of some universal, if only vaguely suggested, evil.

Since the enemy symbolizes a spiritually evil force, the genre tends to base significant action on the premise of any good person's response to the oppressive atmosphere of the war situation; hence, even a small battle can represent a whole war. The platoon sent out on a mission to destroy an enemy bridge is really fighting the war in miniature. Similarly, the courageous action of Chaplin's Jewish barber in *The Great Dictator*, passionately pleading for peace to an audience of millions while impersonating Hynkel, represents every good man's affirmation of liberty against the overwhelming threat of totalitarianism. In the war film, the generalized situation of war or impending war creates the need for, first, a generalized attitude of opposition and, ultimately, a specific response that affirms the commitment to the "right" side at great personal risk.

Thus, the spy film is a category of war films when the spying is carried on by different nations, but becomes a category of crime films if carried on, for instance, between rival companies or gangs. The prisoner-of-war film, removed from the location of battle, represents an extension of the battle by some former participants motivated to escape to rejoin the battle; but when the enemy guards become, in certain film comedies, lovable eccentrics, then such films lose their generic identity in relation to war. Similarly, films concerning peacetime preparations for an anticipated war or films that take place in occupied countries belong to the war genre if the attitudes of the main characters express their preoccupation with the eventual expulsion of the enemy. But films dealing with the rehabilitation of soldiers after a war are not of this genre, unless the previous situation of war and the consequent attitudes of the characters are carried into the present and determine the ongoing nature of their problems.

245

WAR AS PROPAGANDA

Of all the major American genres, only the war film has been a consistent outlet for propaganda, that is, for the delivery of a social message with a predetermined point of view rather than a message evolving entirely from the dramatic conflicts portrayed on the screen. In war films, even the good ones, characters will frequently and unashamedly express their views on what they stand for and against, and this cinematic phenomenon occurs whether or not a country is at war at the time of production of a given film. In time of war, of course, screen depictions of the enemy are even more negative and stereotyped than the depiction of the same enemy will be years later. The motion picture industry recognizes a certain moral duty in an era of national emergency, and is, so to speak, drafted into the war effort. In wartime the public will sometimes respond unfavorably to the depiction of the enemy in anything resembling human terms; even the Lubitsch and Chaplin portrayals of Hitler as a comic villain rather than as a source of real evil met with complaints of bad taste from some reviewers. Thus, it is no wonder that many films made during a national conflict take on an aura of intolerable one-sidedness later. The accepted attitudes of a wartime society may become the cynical jokes of a disillusioned peacetime world viewing history in retrospect.

Because the war film, by tradition and possibly by nature, is so susceptible to propagandistic uses, it becomes extremely difficult for a filmmaker to shape its thematic import: the film tends to take its theme ready-made from the prevailing public view of war at the time of its production. It would, for example, be as difficult today to make a prowar film for general theatrical release as it was to make an antiwar film in 1943. John Wayne's unhappy experience as director of *The Green Berets* in 1968 (espousing the same heroic war values as his earlier, noncontroversial film, *The Alamo* [1960]) appeared at a time when the best that could be said about the Vietnam War—during that election year—was that we ought to get American troops out of Vietnam as soon as possible. The *New York Times*'s review of *The Green Berets* was typical of most: "so unspeakable, so stupid, so rotten . . . false . . . vile and insane . . ."*

Yet it is not exclusively, or even primarily, external values that affect a filmmaker's presentation of the relevant themes. The subject of war, with its violent denial of humanistic premises about the worth of individual life, demands certain basic explanations along with its presentation. Merely to say that war is stupid or unnatural may not suffice to explain its prevalence as a continuing human activity throughout history. While certain emotional factors of a given era determine its portrayal, war could not be an important genre in terms of quantity of films if most of its cinematic depictions were negative or pacifist. In fact, most films on the subject support war as a necessary aspect of national life, with all its individual tragedies recognized—and sometimes extolled—for the ennobling effect they have on those remaining alive. No one has demonstrated this better than John Ford in *They Were Expendable* (1945), a saga in which the squadron manning the PT boats of the Second World War suffers enormous casualties and personal losses in the process of developing into a highly efficient fighting unit; the necessary individual sacrifices made for the group effort dramatize the theme of

246

*Renata Adler, June 20, 1968, p. 49.

strength in union, whereby the mutual dedication of all men endows each with a portion of nobility and heroism.

The propaganda content of most war films, then, is a justification of the way society goes about the ugly business of conducting a war that must lead either to victory or to terrible defeat—defeat that would mean conditions worse than those endured in combatting the enemy. Although there are plenty of well-made minor films like Allan Dwan's *Sands of Iwo Jima* (1949) and Raoul Walsh's *Objective: Burma* (1945) or almost-forgotten films that celebrate war, films of this type that are still acceptable today only partially condone the aspect of battle; the emphasis in such films falls on the gallantry of individual soldiers who have to do their best under dreadful conditions (William Wellman's *The Story of GI Joe* [1945]), or those whose glory is to die in defense of others (John Farrow's *Wake Island* [1942] and Tay Garnett's *Bataan* [1943]), or those who carry on courageously on the home front (William Wyler's *Mrs. Miniver* [1942]).

The largest category of war films is comprised of battlefield situations (on sea or land) describing the pressures on soldiers, the relationships, fears, hopes, and values amid the continual violence and imminent perils of the environment. The very act of delineating a group under battle conditions tends to create sympathy for their hardships and respect for their procedures of survival. Even a professed critic of war like Samuel Fuller seems to create prowar themes in such films as *The Steel Helmet* (1950), *Fixed Bayonets* (1951), and *Merrill's Marauders* (1961), if for no other reason than that the perspective is narrowed to the immediate concerns of life, death, and heroism. Another aspect of the glorification of war is the depiction of successful strategy. A war film that details the intricate problems of taking a well-defended enemy position (or of an entire invasion, as in the epic *The Longest Day* [directed by Ken Annakin and Bernhard Wicki, 1962]) creates an appeal similar to that of a big caper film: for all that planning to go awry would seem a huge waste of effort, and in any case would leave us with no alternative point of view to support. A film about a failed attack does indeed deliver an antiwar message about the futility of military effort, but few such films have been made. However, there have been a few memorable films about the corruption of leadership, including Stanley Kubrick's *Paths of Glory* (1957) and Robert Aldrich's *Attack!* (1956).

A more impressive type of war propaganda film—apparently much more conducive to real art—uses the threat of war to rally support for an ideology or to warn about the dangers of complacency. We find in this diverse category works by major filmmak-

247

ers like Frank Capra in his anti-Nazi, home front film, *Meet John Doe* (1941), and Alfred Hitchcock in the warning message communicated by *Foreign Correspondent* (1940) and, more allegorically, by *Lifeboat* (1944). Often neglecting such quality, critics generally relegate the film supportive of war values to the lowest level of the genre; we should also remember that *Casablanca* belongs to this category. *Casablanca*, like hundreds of lesser films produced in a climate of war preparedness, patriotism, and potential disaster, explicitly seeks to affirm that aspect of the humanistic tradition that calls on people to sacrifice selfish interests for a higher national cause—in other words, to join the war.

Other kinds of propaganda film also flourish in a war era. The virtues of home front activities during periods of mobilization (the domestic wartime film represents a large, but not distinguished, category, marred frequently by the intrusion of sinister spies), or battlefield virtues such as courage against great odds, are thematically quite obvious in the conception of many minor films. In Zoltan Korda's *Sahara* (1943), the idea of strength through unity is described in terms of a small group of Allied soldiers from different countries, led by Humphrey Bogart through a North African desert; when the group is attacked by German soldiers, its unity enables it to wipe out an immensely larger number of the enemy. One other type of war propaganda film worth noting serves to rouse support for an Allied nation normally not considered a peacetime friend. During the Second World War, the favorable depiction of Russia, very effective in Curtiz's *Mission to Moscow* (1943), became, a few years later, a source of considerable embarrassment to the film industry. The American cold war films that began to be made in the late 1940s were an attempt by the industry to atone for its past errors—but this is the danger with propaganda: the anti-Russian films of the 1950s are now more annoying to watch than the pro-Russian films of the 1940s.

Within the general classification of films presenting a favorable if qualified image of certain aspects of war are two categories readily identifiable by their narrative patterns: the prisoner-of-war film and the special mission film. The first category, relatively rare in America, tends to develop plots in which the prisoners carry on their war campaign through a peculiar method of subversion, most explicitly stated in John Sturges's *The Great Escape* (1963): they practice a form of harassment of their guards—their continual efforts to escape preoccupy the prison administration and undermine the enemy's self-confidence. The intellectual game of planning escapes on the one side and thwarting the anticipated attempts on the other manages to demonstrate the spiritual superiority of the prisoners even when they are recaptured. In *The Great Escape,* the mass exodus of Allied prisoners torments the German command, destroys its orderly procedures, and in large measure psychologically defeats the whole system of German prison internment—even though a great number of recaptured prisoners are brutally executed. The escape, in other words, may in itself be considered a successful military campaign regardless of the outcome.

Prisoners lead a fairly drab existence, naturally, and the problem of maintaining a decent level of daily living is part of the iconography of the genre. Following the precedent set by the one overwhelmingly powerful work in the category, Jean Renoir's French film *La Grande Illusion* (1936)—perhaps the greatest of war films but, unlike the traditional prison-camp films that came after it, thoroughly antiwar—most of the memorable American examples, including the best of the category, Billy Wilder's *Stalag 17* (1953), contain a good deal of comedy. The activities of prisoners, who also happen to be soldiers, promise little in the way of cinematic possibilities without the sense of an impending escape. Reduced to putting on theatricals in drag (which comes from Renoir's film) or preoccupying themselves in bartering for hard-to-get goods (Bryan Forbes's *King Rat* [1965]), the men are driven to escape attempts by the very tedium of their life style. Yet for more than reasons of morale, as we see in David Lean's well-known British film *The Bridge on the River Kwai* (1957), the urge toward escape seems essential to the prisoners' own conception of their identity as soldiers.

249

Almost as consistently structured as the prisoner-of-war category, the special mission category preserves its narrative pattern in a variety of situations. In its common 1940s manifestation, the special mission was usually devised when some urgent, unexpected problem or opportunity arose. A small group of fighting men would then volunteer for the particular dangerous assignment of solving the problem. More recent films, even when set during the Second World War, resemble the format of a big caper film, featuring the careful recruitment of special forces and their intensive training, and concluding with a highly detailed depiction of the mission (for example, Aldrich's *The Dirty Dozen* [1967]).

Men engaged in special missions exhibit two obvious characteristics: physical toughness (sometimes seen as a rather crude attitude toward the physical reality of their surroundings) and—almost paradoxically—romantic sensibility. They harbor illusions about what they are doing and why. We are probably beyond the point where, in the 1940s films, whole platoons stepped forward on the first call for volunteers to fly behind enemy lines. Nevertheless, the other extreme—hustling a reluctant group of imprisoned criminals into joining a special squadron, as in *The Dirty Dozen*—does not seem to be the only alternative. It is always possible to appeal to the romantic nature of some individuals who can be convinced of the moral rightness of their side's position.

A special mission group may also be made up of soldiers of fortune—a better term than mercenaries (soldiers who fight in other countries' wars for purely monetary reasons). They are therefore not ordinarily considered heroic, but when they seem to be there for a higher cause, heroism becomes a possibility. In Fuller's *China Gate* (1957), the film begins with a dedication to the "gallant" French stand against the Communist threat in Indochina, but it really concerns a special force eventually headed by an American, Sgt. Brock, who successfully leads his men through the jungle and destroys the enemy's chief munitions stockpile. In his squadron is an American volunteer fighting because "there are still a lot of live Commies around" after the Korean War. Although the grand cause of these men reflects a now-repudiated cold war mentality, the fact that they espouse *some* cause, perhaps viable at that time, explains, if it does not justify, the violent actions in which they participate as part of their professional undertaking of this dangerous and treacherous assignment.

250

When we view a war film, we cannot evaluate the propaganda content objectively since so much of it is shaped by the circumstances of a particular era. But even though the issues of a past era are no longer our issues, we can still respond to the sense of commitment that motivates the hero in such a film. The perilous journey to the castle—the source of the enemy's strength—is the mythic base for much of the war genre's continuing claim on our interest. With variations on such an eternal theme, audiences are likely to continue to accept the genre's adventure stories and its archetypal dimension without too much concern for the propaganda that helped structure the film in the first place.

THE ANTIWAR FILM

"When it comes to dying for one's country, it's better not to die at all," says the soldier-hero of *All Quiet on the Western Front*, to the patriotic dismay of an entire high school class preparing to enlist in the army. Notwithstanding romantic illusions about valor, liberty, and righteousness, the ultimate realities of war are death and desolation. Glamorized war films get around these realities by focusing on the heroic exploits of combat, but the same imagery applies to both prowar and antiwar films. The infantry advance across no man's land may be viewed as exhilarating or futile depending on the context of the film.

The complementary alternative to the glamorized war film, the antiwar film is equally propagandistic in format, but it is generally easier to appreciate because it appeals to a much more socially respectable point of view than the prowar film does. Since its function as propaganda is usually inoffensive, we tend to perceive the antiwar film favorably, simply as a war film rather than as a message film. In other words, we generally comprehend the idea "war is hell" merely as a statement of the obvious—though always worth restating—and we evaluate it only to the extent that the film sets forth interesting evidence to document the truism. This may indeed be the world's oldest humanitarian concept, and yet we have not gone one step further toward acting on its premise than we had when it was stated in the *Iliad*. What the *Iliad* demonstrates so convincingly, and what all antiwar battle films tend to duplicate (from Chaplin's *Shoulder Arms* [1918] to the present), is the fact that for nonwarring nations certain admirable, heroic, and spiritually uplifting virtues can never show themselves—that only battle and its pressures may bring out the best in individuals, even while bringing out the worst in the activities of nations. This explains the paradox of certain pacifist films that end up advocating the necessity of military action as a duty to mankind that ranks higher on the scale of human values than personal religious conviction (as demonstrated, for example, in Wyler's *Friendly Persuasion* [1956]). Forced to confront the choice between the individual's beliefs and society's needs, the American film rather persistently portrays the hero sacrificing his pacifism to do what the nonpacifist community requires for its salvation. Furthermore, such films can manage to support both attitudes in terms of romanticizing the nature of self-sacrifice; a hero reluctant to participate is an even greater hero when his ultimate capitulation to the war effort results in great personal success in battle. This result is notable in the appealing story of Sergeant York, both in his real life and in the famous Howard Hawks film of 1941.

251

Nevertheless, such ambiguities within one category of the antiwar film cannot negate the overall lessons of compassion conveyed by the 1930s examples, any more than the 1950s and 60s' indictments of the military leadership's arrogance and stupidity could be blunted by the high adventure of that period's antiwar cinema. While establishing a pervasive tone of compassion in *All Quiet on the Western Front*, Milestone popularized the image of the doomed soldier advancing through the shell-swept field toward either death or temporary shelter in some new trench. Eventually, the film suggests, death awaits all but a handful of lucky ones. The motif of the replacement of troops by others fated to repeat the pattern is visualized in *All Quiet* by a dead soldier's decent pair of boots, passed on to a comrade; the comrade is killed in turn and the cycle is repeated. Another major concept of the antiwar film—that soldiers are the same in all armies—lifts the theme of compassion beyond the nationalistic level of mere political propaganda. Milestone's film, for instance, is about German soldiers fighting French soldiers, instead of taking the point of view of the Allies in the First World War. One famous battle sequence shows the young German hero trapped for a time with a dying French soldier he has wounded, the similarity of their predicament uniting them in our mind and effectively projecting the unpredictable, certainly uncontrollable, element of mass warfare.

The major tradition of the antiwar film operates mainly in a realistic mode that serves to deglamorize the romantic elements associated with fighting for a cause, for freedom, or for the attainment of noble or heroic ends. A second prevalent tradition of the antiwar film employs an iconoclastic approach to debunk heroic warfare. The infliction of horrible, excessive damage by our troops on a civilian population is depicted in George Roy Hill's *Slaughterhouse Five* (1972). Another type of debunking film calls to account incompetent or corrupt leadership, as in Nicholas Ray's *Bitter Victory* (1958). Relatively few films have tried to satirize the concept of soldier as hero within the realistic mode as in Blake Edwards's *What Did You Do in the War, Daddy?* (1966). More subtly, the projection of a hero's image in Arthur Hiller's *The Americanization of Emily* (1964) deflates the whole notion of heroism. In this film, the pragmatic main character, an aide to an admiral and also a virtual con man and a coward, ends up after a series of misadventures as the first man to land on Omaha Beach during the Allied invasion of Normandy; his assumed death makes him a posthumous hero, and he shows up undaunted later on. Films of the 1960s began to portray war as a kind of ongoing madness, with visual imagery that suggested a widely dispersed insanity; this trend culminated in Mike Nichols's not very successful film adaptation of a popular novel by Joseph Heller, *Catch-22* (1970).

In the realm of antiwar films depicting the madness of national combat, one of the most impressive statements, because it is entirely unpretentious as propaganda, remains the Marx Brothers classic, *Duck Soup* (1933), directed by Leo McCarey. Most of this film is devoted to the kind of cold-war diplomatic idiocies that lead countries into "hot" war, including spying and minor diplomatic insults. The announcement of the start of hostilities turns the film into a musical satire on jingoism and super-

252

patriotism. On the battlefield, the brothers' cowardice, ineptitude, and anarchic violence devastate their own side, including commander-in-chief Groucho's machine-gunning his own men by mistake and casually trying to cover up his blunder when it is pointed out to him. It is not merely zaniness that *Duck Soup* conveys, but a deeply felt distrust of political bombast and tyrannical manipulation of nations into inextricable antagonism. The film to a certain degree satirizes the rise of German Nazism in the early 1930s, but its real impact belongs outside history.

One of the most dramatic methods of intensifying the antiwar theme is designing the action to stress the total destruction in the aftermath of a war. This can be done in a realistic setting, but with the advent of the atomic bomb, creating the possibility of an utterly demolished world, the industry began to produce some science fiction films with a war-related source. The idea of confronting the horror of wide-scale nuclear explosions has for various reasons not often succeeded in its cinematic versions, perhaps because the essential literariness of the concept works against effective cinematic realization. In Stanley Kramer's *On the Beach* (1959), a gloomy mood is evoked by the images of a society awaiting its unpreventable annihilation by radioactivity. However, there is a static visual orientation built into a film originating from, and featuring, a theme. When a racing-car driver, played by Fred Astaire, crashes his car to epitomize the despair of the world, the audience no doubt wishes that he had instead danced himself to death so that we could be given some relief from the prevailing and unifying mood of doom.

Other holocaust films with clever formulations, including James Harris's *The Bedford Incident* (1965), Sidney Lumet's *Fail-Safe* (1963), Ray Milland's *Panic in the Year Zero* (1962), and Ronald MacDougall's *The World, the Flesh and the Devil* (1958), seem intended to serve as war-warning films; the next world war, so the message in these films communicates, will entail weaponry that man cannot control (a science fiction motif). *The World, the Flesh and the Devil* makes good cinematic use of the always-effective science fiction image of the deserted metropolis, and *The Bedford Incident* employs some traditionally interesting submarine footage, but so far only one American science fiction film has moved beyond the limitations of its propaganda base (warning of the obvious devastation of nuclear bombs) to the level of an artistic war film: Kubrick's *Dr. Strangelove, or How I Learned To Stop Worrying and Love the Bomb* (1963). There might seem to be an obvious connection between the success of this film, compared to others of the type, and Kubrick's willingness to depart from the realistic mode so stolidly insisted upon in other war-warning films. Of course Kubrick's horror is delivered

253

in a comic mode, which also helps to account for the peculiar effectiveness of a propaganda film that does not attempt to gain audience identification through some tragic personal story. In any case, it remains the high point of the cinema of atomic cataclysm, and among the most dramatic antimilitary statements in the entire war genre.

WAR IN THE AIR

A type of battle film that is distinctive because of its setting, the air war drama has always held a peculiar fascination for the moviegoing public. The essential relationship between man and machine, perceived mainly in their frequent mutual destruction, creates an awareness of combined skill and luck that may account for the endurance of this category. The pilot personifies a kind of hero whose ability, great as it may be, does not assure him of success, and with some slight turn in his luck all his skill may come to nothing. The Red Baron is at last shot down by the least

254   pretentious of rivals (most recently in Roger Corman's *Von Richthofen and Brown* [1971]). The element of luck, which makes the pilot-hero conscious of the chanciness of his life, leads to fatalism on the one hand and a willingness to accept voluntary, near-suicidal missions on the other.

The original nature of air warfare emphasizes a potential for personal heroism not granted to ground troops in most situations. The use of planes for combat and bombing in the First World War became an extraordinarily exciting cinematic possibility a decade later, as evidenced by the first major American film on the subject, Wellman's silent classic, *Wings* (1927). In this film the planes appear (from our perspective in history) rather flimsy—in fact, an element of heroism seems to be involved in merely climbing into the cockpit. Even in Second World War films, with larger planes, we are always reminded of the possibility of running out of fuel over the ocean or of the engines failing. The potential disaster implicit in using the aerial machine itself was small, however, in comparison to the deadly menace of antiaircraft fire from the ground or those endless lines of Japanese Zeroes suddenly appearing on the horizon to attack the solitary bomber. One of the great recurring visual images, the parachuting flyer helplessly tossed by the winds to a landing behind enemy lines, emphasized the precarious nature of man dependent on readily destructible mechanical implements of war. The crashing airplane became the ultimate cinematic symbol of wartime sacrifice both in those instances when it was not possible to bail out or when, as in Hawks's celebration of courage, *Air Force* (1943), a heroic flyer determined to attempt a crash landing and salvage his plane.

Since in American films the profession of flying demands both courage and fatalism, we can only expect that the pilot will be a romantic. His romanticism manifests itself in his devotion to his duty, his tendency to immerse himself in the life of his squadron (much emphasis is placed on camaraderie), and his taking upon himself the responsibility for the lives of others. Thus, the hero must risk his own life before those of any of his fellow pilots, and the death of another will create guilt. In Hawks's *The Dawn Patrol* (1930), the high level of casualties suffered by the daily dawn patrols suggests a common guilt on the part of the survivors though it is not overtly referred to. Brand, the commanding officer, suffers most, having to live with his responsibility for sending out the planes on the orders relayed to him from a distant command post. When Brand is relieved and his job is taken over by the squadron leader Courtney, the cycle of guilt becomes the dramatic center of the film. Courtney no longer can fly missions but must himself send younger, inexperienced flyers on assignments that he knows will end in their death—he must now make the decisions for which he had criticized Brand. In the 1938 version of *The Dawn Patrol,* directed by Edmund Goulding (a lesser film in other ways but the epitome of the genre's romanticism), the torment of the men in command relates very much to the antiwar message, for here the depressing sense of futility of the incessant air strikes is mitigated only by the men's courage, whereas with Hawks the task done well has in itself a certain redeeming merit.

255

The romantic spirit of the later version of *The Dawn Patrol* is best revealed by the suppressed emotional suffering of Courtney (played by Errol Flynn). The dramatic episodes culminate in Courtney's being forced to send young Scott, newly arrived and totally unprepared, on an almost hopeless assignment, in spite of the protests of Scott's older brother, who is Courtney's best friend. The predictable result is the death of the younger brother witnessed by the older brother, and Courtney's acceptance of his role in this tragic event. "What a rotten war," Courtney says at one point, but his cynicism is totally romantic (otherwise he would simply desert or rebel). When the time comes for the assignment of a suicide flight over the enemy's munitions depot, naturally Scott—as the senior flying officer—volunteers, and naturally the guilt-ridden Courtney as commanding officer gets Scott drunk and takes his place. The expiation is completed when Courtney accomplishes his mission and is intercepted and shot down by the Red Baron. The German ace and the tragic hero exchange mutual gestures of respect as Courtney plummets to his death.

The "rotten war" theme is introduced earlier in the film: a German flyer, after scoring a kill, is shot down by Courtney and captured. When he is brought to the Allied airfield he is treated as a comrade by his enemies. The theme, however, has no particular social effect; it functions primarily to reinforce our sense of the pilots' courageous romanticism, a willingness to sacrifice themselves not so much for a country or a cause but for a romantic ideal of service—perhaps a realization that though life itself is "rotten" their deeds, at least, overcome its inherent deficiencies by their avowal of a glamorous fatalism.

WAR AS BACKGROUND

A large category of war films relegates the actual conflict to the background; such films emphasize either a personal relationship during wartime or a theme that requires the atmosphere of war without the peculiar turmoil that preoccupies the thoughts of people imperiled by actual fighting. Sometimes the subtlety of the association between the action of a war and the action of a film has left critics unable to recognize its connection with the genre. It is, for example, difficult to perceive Chaplin's *Monsieur Verdoux* (1947) as a war film, and yet the film's core is the bitterly cynical analogy Chaplin makes at the end between the murderer and the state engaged in war: "Wars, conflict—it's all business. One murder makes a villain; millions, a hero. Numbers sanctify!" But that is an extreme case; much more typical is the film with a visually tangential tie-in: the battle is geographically determinable (if not necessarily portrayed), with characters moving toward their fated rendezvous with war, as in John Huston's *The African Queen* (1952). The exile film, though separately identifiable, generally partakes of this broader classification too. Another common form of the war background film is the depiction of men in military service, waiting around for the inevitable involvement. Even when the men are unaware of the impending outbreak of war, the audience readily sees the dramatic irony of their situation, as handled in Fred Zinnemann's *From Here to Eternity* (1953) and Preminger's *In Harm's Way* (1964).

More common than the anticipation of war is the background presence of war while in the foreground a drama is played out with reference to the events of a particular time. War as a shaping device for dramatic conflicts pervades *Gone with the Wind,* and nowhere is the point more clearly developed that even from a distance, the consequences of the event cannot be evaded, and no matter how self-absorbed a person is, that person cannot ignore

256

the encroaching disasters that preoccupy everybody else. The love story in any film with a war background seems to take on new meaning from the precarious position of the lovers, who face an uncertain future. Discovering love at a time when life itself may have little meaning—for instance, during a soldier's leave—presents quite different problems from those of an ordinary romance. In Walsh's *Battle Cry* (1955), a tough marine falls in love just prior to a combat engagement, a change that leads him to decide to desert; only the active intercession of his lover prevents him from going through with his decision. The fact that war cannot be postponed or denied creates divided allegiances for the soldier-lover, but generally he accepts the inevitability of his profession and goes back to war after his romantic interlude—though in Frank Borzage's *A Farewell to Arms* (1932) the soldier later deserts to rejoin his lover. In some films the departure of the hero, leaving behind his lover or his family, is made poignant by the expectation of his death, as for instance in the unusual Astaire-Rogers biography-musical, *The Story of Vernon and Irene Castle* (directed by H. C. Potter, 1939).

The musical, of course, does not contribute much to our understanding of the war genre. The most thematically satisfying example is the British film *Oh! What a Lovely War* (1969), directed by Richard Attenborough. Anthony Mann's *The Glenn Miller Story* (1954) managed to develop some of the poignancy of the doomed lover because the audience at the time the film was released was well aware of the facts of the musician's death. The truth seems to be that the Hollywood musical's best approach to war, even during the Second World War, was simply to depict performers in uniform on a three-day pass carrying on in the usual tradition of musicals—while there just happened to be a war going on—so that Gene Kelly's and Frank Sinatra's time for romance would be limited (as in George Sidney's *Anchors Aweigh* [1945]).

257

Perhaps the most successful type of war background film is the comedy war film. In the silent era, the unheroic figures of Charles Chaplin and Harry Langdon in uniform were enough to establish the incongruities of military life for the natural misfit. As a subject of perpetual interest, supplying an infinite number of variations on military routine and inanity, war provided excellent material for most of the famous comic teams, including Laurel and Hardy and Abbott and Costello. There is another comic tradition, more realistically presented, that develops from the silent war film, particularly from King Vidor's *The Big Parade* (1925) and Walsh's *What Price Glory?* (1926). In such films, the war is not merely a background but a present reality of the fighting men's lives. Nevertheless, even though people are killed in the battle scenes, this tradition of the comic war film manages to deemphasize the sense of horror and threat by the persistently comic behavior of the main characters. In Edwards's *Operation Petticoat* (1959), which takes place in the Pacific battle zone, convivial horseplay develops into a battle of the sexes when a group of women officers is transported on a submarine. Some later films employ a good deal of black comedy within a battle environment to point out the comparative levels of insanity, as in Robert Altman's *M*A*S*H* (1970), where the constant bloody surgical operations are played off against the surgeons' determined efforts to create a life style unaffected by the war that surrounds them.

VICTIMS OF WAR

The noncombat films dealing with the effects of warfare rather than the preparations for it usually concentrate on the conditions of war victims, civilian or military. These films are not necessarily antiwar in spirit, for even on the subject of postwar casualties, the emphasis may fall on overcoming the physical and psychological problems relevant to rehabilitation (as in Zinnemann's *The Men* [1950]) or the more generalized difficulties of readjustment to civilian life (Wyler's *The Best Years of Our Lives* [1946]). Postwar films that handle the theme of readjustment generally direct our attention away from the facts of war; the past is not part of the dramatic reality of the present, and for this reason the category of the returning veteran is often not significantly a part of the war genre but of some other immediately recognizable genre, as are Stanley Donen and Gene Kelly's *It's Always Fair Weather* (1955) and Walsh's *The Roaring Twenties* (1939).

Films that deal with the aftermath of battle in terms of the damaged military hero's coping with his new life are not necessarily affirmative. Edward Dmytryk's life-aboard-ship adventure, *The Caine Mutiny* (1954), portrays the declining mental stability of a naval captain, whose petty tyrannies reflect the pressure of too many battle situations; he finally reaches the point where he must be relieved of command. The ensuing court-martial ratifies the act of mutiny while at the same time vindicating the honorable career of the captain prior to his breakdown. A more emotionally emphatic portrayal of the military victim occurs in Dalton Trumbo's *Johnny Got His Gun* (1971), in which the totally dismembered victim—blind, deaf, and dumb, and apparently completely shut off from the world—manages to make some meaningful communication from his hospital bed, expressing his desire to offer himself as an exhibition of the horrors of warfare.

258

Although the antiwar theme appears to dominate the film, its negativism is mitigated by the personal struggle of the victim, which elevates his endeavor to a symbolic account of mankind's indomitable will to survive.

Another type of war victim, though one infrequently depicted on screen, suffers the psychological effects of his experience later on when returning to a normal civilian environment. Perhaps the most interesting example occurs in John Frankenheimer's black comedy, *The Manchurian Candidate* (1962). The damage done to a prisoner of war, a combination of then-fashionable "brainwashing" and perennially fashionable hypnosis, results in his turning into an assassin programed to kill on response to certain signals. Although the film operates primarily in the realm of political satire of extremism, it managed to popularize a new horror of modern-day warfare: the threat of a destroyed mind, undiagnosed and concealed behind an apparent surface normality. Previous films about shell-shocked heroes or psychological cases (such as Mark Robson's *Home of the Brave* [1949]) always left the victimized soldiers in an overtly abnormal condition, with society eager to provide the necessary help and rehabilitation.   259

Perhaps the most important category of the wartime victim film depicts life in a conquered country. Although a more fully developed category in the European cinema, the subject of occupation often appears in American films, though the United States has not had an occupying army on its continental territory in two hundred years. Thus, such films require an act of imagination about a topic not truly conceivable to the American national consciousness, and are therefore set in a foreign locale (Norway, Russia, France). The emphasis, however, may be effectively aimed at an individual's personal plight, which stands for the tragic consequence of an entire country, as successfully dramatized in George Stevens's *The Diary of Anne Frank* (1959).

The most interesting of the Second World War occupation films center on a beleaguered band of patriots courageously carrying on a campaign of sabotage against the established Nazi regime. Even though the Resistance films always show the patriots causing more casualties than the German occupying army, the patriots are still the victims of the conflict, and their members from time to time are caught and killed. If in the 1940s films of this category, the Nazi command was stupid, brutal, and arrogant, the general sympathy for the patriots began to spread toward the Germans in later decades. In Frankenheimer's *The Train* (1964), the conflict between the German authority figure, Colonel von Waldheim, and the French Resistance fighters is dramatized in terms of a trainload of great paintings that are to be removed to Germany prior to an allied invasion of Paris. An intelligent and cultured man, Colonel von Waldheim is driven to desperation by the clever strategies of the Resistance, strategies that eventually destroy him; but he represents a much more recognizably real character than the Nazi command villains depicted in films made during the Second World War such as Irving Pichel's *The Moon Is Down* (1943) and Fritz Lang's *Hangmen Also Die* (1943).

EXILES AND ISOLATED HEROES

Exiles inhabit a personal universe. The exact place of their exile is important only for understanding the particular circumstances that led them to where they are when we encounter them in a film. They may be found in any sort of place, urban or rural; but the choice is always based on expediency—whether they stay for a short time or forever has little to do with the particular locale, for they do not commit themselves to that place. The essence of this category is that the site of exile represents any place *away* from the place, or more commonly, person, the exile has voluntarily abandoned, fled from, or lost. Viewed in relation to the genre of war films, the exile becomes a victim of wartime crisis, uprooted by events not of his making.

Although not a particularly extensive film genre, it is almost the very oldest narrative genre. It takes its roots from Cain's exile in Genesis—not, probably, from Adam and Eve's, since they would have preferred to remain in Eden and left under a threatened punishment. However, the main sources of mythic structure in the narrative tradition of the exile probably stem from Greek war myths about heroes like Philoctetes and Achilles. Perhaps most notable is Odysseus, who does not want to go to war, yet who not only serves as a prototype of the myth—which entails both the exile and the return from it—but also presents himself as the romantic epitome of the type.

A person in exile must exhibit certain romantic traits. Even in antiromantic, classical Greece, a distinction is drawn between an involuntary exile like Odysseus and a recluse like Calypso, his sea-nymph captor for seven years, who appears contented permanently apart from civilization. In war films, the exile generally exists in a state of brooding alienation, but always with a submerged patriotism—for the right side, if not for the flag-waving that symbolizes the right side. His opposition to the wrong side (such as Rick Blaine's opposition to the Nazis in *Casablanca*) has been effectively neutralized at the beginning of the film by his exile's role; after all, he is immediately identifiable to everyone in his environment as a man without a country. This

260

position guarantees him a degree of safety while others are endangered; the enemy will usually tolerate an exile while tracking down collaborators or subversives. Thus, the exile's adopted role as an outsider or observer, indifferent to political concerns and national hostilities, is accepted by the enemy and is generally an outward sign of moral indifference.

Yet in truth the exile communicates something else to us: he stands for the potential hero who, when fully aware of his own strength and the necessity of action, can be counted on to burst his bonds. One version of this myth is that of Samson, the once-mighty warrior, his strength impaired, imprisoned in his enemies' land. Because Samson symbolizes a fallen hero in spiritual shackles, the role of the exile has to be played by a hero type whose world-weary outward appearance disguises inward strength that can be drawn upon at a critical time. Bogart's characterization of Harry Morgan in Hawks's *To Have and Have Not* (1944) is a perfect example of the romantic exile determining to join the war against fascism at precisely the moment he is most needed; Bogart's role as the dilapidated riverboat captain in *The African Queen* has similar meaning within the genre when he participates in the destruction of a German warship. Surface indifference to great events merely reflects the hero's internal conflict, which, when resolved, enables him to give up his disguise and become the civilian warrior-hero.

The environmental isolation of the exile relates closely to the spiritual isolation of another kind of potential hero common to the war genre: the reluctant warrior. This type frequently appears as a pacifist figure, though not always overtly so. In any case, he always ignores or underestimates his own capacity for heroic activity on the battlefield, sometimes, as in Huston's *The Red Badge of Courage* (1951), because his potentiality for cowardice obscures his potential for heroism. In such films, a certain point ultimately arrives when the proper choice must be made, not merely for the sake of survival, but because human decency demands affirmative action. This moment of affirmation exactly climaxes that development in the career of an exile.

Coming to the defense of his country or the community that requires his help, the reluctant soldier shows his kinship with the exile through his abandonment of a self-designed identity (as a coward, a pacifist, or an uninvolved bystander) in favor of a group-approved identity—one that actively partakes of the great ideals of the wartime society. Both identities may in fact be equally romantic and subjective views of where truth and morality can really be found within the environment of war. Exile films always avoid the examination of the national issues that created this environment, for the internal conflict of the isolated hero—

261

which may indeed reflect moral uncertainty—is played against an external military conflict representing freedom and oppression as clear alternatives. In the war genre, exile and isolation mean moral indifference. The return from exile reestablishes moral commitment as a primary social value.

SPIES AND SECRET AGENTS

The great popularity of the spy film and its affinity to the detective film make it difficult to distinguish from some of the more significant American categories of adventure melodrama. Spying is one of the few categories to exhibit similar patterns in American and European films: it has both wide appeal and international status as a fitting occupation for the modern hero. Still, relatively few important spy films have been made in this country. Alfred Hitchcock, however, has chosen to work in this category several times, creating perhaps one masterpiece per decade and giving the spy film lasting artistic stature.

262

The great commercial success of the British James Bond films in the 1960s probably provided a dubious model for the category, resulting in too many carelessly designed films and an unusual number of silly parodies. Without a major artistic example of the spy film in the early and mid-1960s, the sheer proliferation of such films solidified certain minor motifs into mythic patterns, leading to countergenre films within the category. At the moment, the dominant recognizable form is still that of the James Bond films, replete with modern-day technology and incessant gimmickry. Actually, the spy myth suggests moral uncertainty and our fragile contemporary existence, in contradistinction to James Bond's wonderful weapons and unflinching sense of purpose. For the modern spy film to incorporate the Bond-type traits with the older aspects of indecision and subtle dangers is to risk internal disorder. Small wonder that many spy films exhibit not merely uncontrolled inconsistencies but also an element of self-conscious parody, as if they must proclaim their own ridiculousness before the audience proclaims it for them.

By its nature, the profession of espionage imposes great responsibilities and great dangers. For someone to accept this kind of career, he or she must have rare abilities and presumably enjoy the challenge; financial rewards do not seem to be the inducement. We can assume that a professional spy believes in the rightness of his government's involvement in the spying episode. Some attempt is often made at the beginning of the film to establish the importance of the particular spying mission, but this expository material used to be much more convincingly portrayed in the 1940s, when our country was seriously engaged in a war of actual survival and, later, a cold war in which survival again seemed an impending issue. Disillusionment with cold war tactics, along with a general cynicism toward the CIA, has led to greater difficulties in establishing plausibility and loyalty in spy films, but at the same time it has brought out the inherent moral dilemma of the spy: the discrepancy between what may be a good enough ultimate end and the means used to achieve that end. It is the oldest moral problem in philosophy, and it is articulated in what most people seem to regard as the best American spy film made after the Second World War, *North by Northwest* (1959). Hitchcock has the following exchange take place between his hero Thornhill, a citizen forced into complicity with a CIA plot, and the Professor, the representative of the CIA:

"I don't like the games you play, Professor . . ."

"War is hell, Mr. Thornhill—even when it's a cold one."

"If you fellows can't lick the [enemies] without asking girls like her to bed down with them and fly away with them and probably never come back alive, maybe you better start learning to *lose* a few cold wars!"

263

If the spying assignment were not at least potentially crucial, the work of most spies would degenerate into mere theft on foreign soil. On the other hand, if a spy's means of obtaining information were not illegal or unethical, there would be no danger and probably no story. Thus, the underlying tension stems from the spy's degree of awareness, his qualms about his methods, and ultimately his doubts about the whole system. James Bond has no qualms, and his personality consequently borders on fanaticism and sadism (or complete cynicism). But the human— as opposed to the Bondian superhuman—spies sometimes suffer enormous misgivings, as in Martin Ritt's *The Spy Who Came in from the Cold* (1965). In this film the British Secret Service agent Leamas encounters a series of disillusioning events, culminating in a somewhat fantastic repudiation of everything his organization stands for. The film opens as he watches one of his under-agents shot down while attempting to cross from East to West Berlin. Back in London he listens to his chief, referred to throughout merely as Control, expound on the philosophy of modern-day spying, admitting that agents in the free world must and do adopt the most vicious practices of Communist spies; the only distinguishing aspect is the belief that the free world's cause is just. Control himself does not seem to place much faith in his own agency's moral superiority, but Leamas at this point has not yet reached disillusionment with his profession.

Leamas pretends to be a defector for the purposes of the Secret Service plot to discredit Mundt, the top Communist agent in East Berlin. Leamas's job is to drop false clues to his interrogator Fiedler, Mundt's second-in-command, who hates his superior and will therefore eagerly follow the clues in preparing a case to expose Mundt. Since Mundt is a nasty Nazi-like type and Fiedler a likable man, Leamas's task seems morally straightforward. But at the official hearing before an investigating panel of the East German hierarchy, Leamas's London girlfriend is produced as a witness and innocently undermines Leamas's testimony; thus, Leamas, discredited as a witness, undermines Fiedler, who is arrested on the spot as Mundt triumphs. Mundt turns out to be London's double agent. Leamas, escaping with his girlfriend, realizes that he was used by his own organization to destroy Fiedler and save Mundt, just as his girlfriend was used by London to discredit him. The final twist of the plot is the shooting of the girlfriend as she tries to climb over the Berlin Wall, just as Leamas reaches the top of the wall. Leamas, evaluating the degree of betrayal that his own organization has shown toward him, refuses to escape, despite the pleas of agents on both sides of the wall. At the end of the film, Leamas jumps back into East Berlin, virtually forcing the guards there to kill him. It is the ultimate image of the modern spy's renunciation. Few spy films are as explicitly antiespionage as this one, but most of the better ones do present heroes who have some misgivings. In this category, failure to respond with some inkling of self-doubt about a person's occupation suggests moral insensitivity, a blindness not easily forgiven if the film visually presents the materials that describe moral uncertainty.

One common method of dramatizing the moral issue at the heart of this category is to introduce the spy's counterpart: the representative of the foreign government. Often also a spy, but sometimes just the administrative head of a totalitarian governmental agency, this person (sometimes a woman) is the mirror image of the hero in terms of abilities and responsibilities. Generally, however, a major difference emerges quite early: the Communist is ruthless in his or her dedication while the hero has his doubts. If the hero and the enemy equivalent are equally ruthless, as in the Bond films and their innumerable imitations, we have a film totally given over to surface plotting, with quite a number of corpses certain to follow. But such films, though numerically now the majority in the spy category, are not the best spy films. To be capable of artistic expression on more than the surface level of flying fists and bullets, the spy film must take its shape from the inherent tension produced by the conflict of means and ends.

Often the story line of the spy film will call for a third party to symbolize the nature of the hero's predicament; very likely, the pattern will call for the spy to encounter a woman and become involved with her. Forced by the nature of his assignment to "use" the woman, the spy's loyalties become divided. Sometimes he faces the choice of sacrificing either his love or his mission, though the solution in the film rarely carries out the logic of either alternative: somehow, the ingenious cunning of the spy will lead him to complete his task and keep his woman too, but the complexities of this final turn of events are seldom explored in the wildly active conclusions typical of such films. (For example, if the spy is to leave a foreign country the woman often must defect, but her situation cannot be terribly complex itself or it would distract us from our involvement with the hero's dilemma.)

The central interest in most spy films is the espionage itself. If something is to be stolen, the hero must either sneak inside territory controlled by the enemy (for instance, to photograph missile plans) or else ingratiate himself through some disguise that will place him in the proximity of the object. In the latter case, his deception attests to his skill, but it increasingly complicates his relationships with others, for in the better films he gets to meet some likable people on the other side, who must eventually be destroyed or ruined by his deception. Also, he might discover romance while pretending to be something quite different from what he really is. Role playing is often the major achievement of the master spy in the cinema, as it undoubtedly is in real life. In one of the chief variations on the spy plot, the assignment is sometimes to uncover a master spy from the other side who is known to have succeeded in establishing himself within the governmental agencies that employ the hero. In such cases, the films usually have the hero engage in a deception to find the deceptive foreign spy. Although this spy is usually native-born, though in the employ of the foreign enemy, the issue of treason is usually too complex for the genre to explore. One film that does probe the moral complexity of the issue of treason is Hitchcock's *Topaz* (1969), perhaps the most brilliant (and surely the most difficult) of modern spy films. In *Topaz* the problem of loyalty to one's country is handled in the context of other loyalties—to friends, family, and ideals—any of which may conflict with others; therefore, given the deceptive nature of espionage, the spy's betrayal of some person or cause is virtually inevitable.

Structurally related to espionage and counterespionage is the spy film that relies on infiltration of the enemy spy ring in an

265

enemy-controlled or neutral country. On dangerous ground, virtually unprotected by his organization, the hero-spy must play a completely disreputable role—he must give up his old identity and become an entirely different person. His motivation for doing this in ordinary spy films is the usual unspecified fanaticism, a belief in his own cause at least to the point of intellectual blindness. Yet conceivably, the infiltration idea, with its built-in suspense situations, offers the best of possibilities for the examination of the mentality of the person who, for pay, honor, or whatever else, sacrifices his own identity to pretend totally to be someone else. The one notable American film success in this category is Hitchcock's *Notorious* (1946). The motivation in this instance is very carefully established: a nonprofessional spy, the daughter of a traitor who herself has led a dubious life, insecure and drifting, is talked into helping an American Secret Service agent to spy on a Nazi sympathizer. Her motive is apparently not so much a chance to make up for her father's crimes as to reclaim her own life. To fulfill her mission, her American contact, the Secret Service agent, seems to acquiesce in her marrying the man she is spying on. She is in fact in love with her contact and he with her, but they cannot trust one another enough to stake everything on an honest appraisal of their feelings, so she goes through with the marriage. She has, in other words, given over her life to the service of her country, but not for an abstract cause; she hates what she is doing, but she has no real life to return to. Hitchcock develops the horrible aspect of her deceit by making her husband, the Nazi, a truly likable character, ultimately left to pay his fellow Nazis with his life for having been tricked into marrying a spy. The film is less about the procedures of spying than about the moral rot involved in this occupation.

266

HELL'S ANGELS
(1930)

Director-Producer	Cinematographers	Script
HOWARD HUGHES	TONY GAUDIO	HOWARD ESTABROOK
For United Artists	HARRY PERRY	HARRY BEHN
	E. BURTON STEENE	Based on a story by
	Portions in Technicolor	Marshall Neilan and
	and Wide Screen	Joseph Moncure March

PRINCIPAL CHARACTERS

BEN LYON	JAMES HALL	JEAN HARLOW
Monte Rutledge	Roy Rutledge	Helen
DOUGLAS GILMORE	LUCIEN PRIVAL	JANE WINTON
Captain Redfield	Baron von Kranz	Baroness von Kranz
JOHN DARROW		
Karl Arnstedt		

Length: 135 minutes

Hell's Angels, like the other two classic antiwar films released in the same year, Milestone's *All Quiet on the Western Front* and Hawks's *The Dawn Patrol,* deals with the inherent tragic irony of war that forces men into heroic but futile actions that lead them to death. The alternative to heroism often is mere cowardice, a temporary avoidance of the inevitable tragedy awaiting everyone engaged in warfare. For this reason, prudent self-interest designed to preserve one's life is never presented as a viable alternative even in those circumstances supportive of the cynical attitudes of men under the stress of a probable doom.

In *Hell's Angels,* the first examples of heroic choice are given to the enemy, the German crew of a zeppelin sent to bomb London during the First World War. Attacked by the Royal Flying Corps, the zeppelin needs to gain altitude quickly—the only means of preventing the shooting down and capture of a valuable airship. Ordering everything portable thrown overboard, the captain himself cuts the cable of the observation car beneath the airship, sending a young crew member to his death—a painful but essential decision. Nevertheless, the RFC is about to overtake the zeppelin when a German officer steps forward and grimly tells the captain that there is only one more thing to do. The officer, without asking for volunteers, strides through the zeppelin, hypnotically attracting followers; then, one by one, the men jump overboard to a frightening death. Typical of the film's outlook, the zeppelin is destroyed anyway, after the valiant sacrifice of these men, by a British flyer who crashes his own plane into the airship. The stunning footage of the collision and the zeppelin aflame and

268

falling to earth captures perfectly, in an overwhelming image, the terrifying sense of waste and death in an incident essentially meaningless except for the mutual sacrifice of heroic flying men on both sides.

The ambiguity that lies at the heart of most antiwar films is in the manner in which bravery and noble actions seem to counter the thematic issue of war's futility. Hughes shares these ambivalent attitudes with his audience: as a result, all the wasted lives and the ravages of war are almost balanced by the inspiring spectacle of men facing the worst and accepting their fate. At the end of *Hell's Angels*, a prisoner, refusing to wear a blindfold, is executed by a firing squad; he appears for only a few seconds, scorns his executioner's attempt to blindfold him, and is shot down without complaint. The whole event takes less than a minute but gains the admiration of the few witnesses. Although such a death gains no military victories, we are made to feel, somehow, that the antiwar film may indeed be inwardly structured primarily to make us approve of those small gestures of defiance and courage that define our humanity. There are undoubtedly things more important than life itself, but of all cinematic genres virtually only the war film—and in particular, the antiwar film—continually demonstrates this ideal.

The particular form of honor developed in *Hell's Angels* is self-sacrifice to the war effort. (Issues of freedom are not even peripheral in most First World War films since the United States is not always involved; indeed, it is not a belligerent in any of the three famous 1930 antiwar films.) The Royal Flying Corps suffers great casualties not in the name of some magnificent ideal but because the war must be fought and this is the required procedure. Stoical resignation, the code of the flyer, is challenged in the film by Monte, who fluctuates between indifference to the war and a more active opposition to it in very basic terms: "I want to live." His older brother Roy, a traditional, reliable sort, is a member of the same RFC squadron, serving to keep a rein on the antiwar effusiveness of Monte. Roy's girlfriend, something of a vamp as played by Jean Harlow, seduces Monte, calls Roy a prig, and readily takes up with a third flyer, but the personal story does not amount to much, nor does it essentially characterize the two brothers, who function mainly in regard to their generalized responses to the issue of self-sacrifice.

The central incident of the film develops from Monte's growing doubts about his own character. He expresses the fatalism inherent in his work: "Somebody always gets it on the night patrol. . . . I'll get it sooner or later—we'll all get it!" Referring to his fellow flyers as fools for carrying on this murderous war ("What are you fighting for? Patriotism? Duty?"), Monte begins to wonder whether he isn't a coward after all. To test himself, he volunteers for an extremely dangerous mission, and Roy quickly volunteers too: they are to fly in a captured German plane behind enemy lines and destroy a munitions dump so that a large-scale ground attack will have a chance of success the following day. (The plot resembles that of *The Dawn Patrol*, and occurs elsewhere in the category of special assignments.) Later that night, a drunken Monte wants to get out of his commitment, but is dissuaded by his brother.

Immediately after the two successfully destroy the dump, Baron von Richthofen and his squadron, the "flying circus," descend upon the brothers' plane. The ensuing fight memorably recreates the air war in some unsurpassed filming, ending in the inevitable victory of the Red Baron. The brothers, however, survive their plane's crash for one more ultimate test of courage. As prisoners of war, they are told by the German commanding officer that they will be shot as spies unless they reveal the plans for the imminent ground attack. Monte falters. He convinces Roy that he cannot face death given the chance to avoid it, even at the cost of many of his fellow soldiers' lives. But Roy, unshaken in his commitment to the hero's code, secures a gun from the German commander by saying he intends to kill his "compatriot" (they have not disclosed their relationship) and commit treason himself. His purpose, however, is to prevent Monte from talking. He shoots his brother, who in his death agony concedes that it is better to die than to betray his side; Roy is then executed. The film

269

remains consistent in its ironic point of view: heroes on both sides die in the futile endeavors of meaningless combat. At the same time, the perhaps deeper irony of such films remains a disturbing possibility: it is only within the realm of war's futility that consummate acts of self-sacrifice become ennobling human gestures. The question of whether the personal nobility of a hero redeems the horrible war around him is never overtly raised in films such as *Hell's Angels*.

GONE WITH THE WIND
(1939)

Directors	Cinematographers	Script
VICTOR FLEMING	ERNEST HALLER	SIDNEY HOWARD
GEORGE CUKOR	RAY RENNAHAN	BEN HECHT
SAM WOOD	JOSEPH RUTTENBERG	DAVID O. SELZNICK
	WILFRED CLINE	VICTOR FLEMING
Producer	LEE GARMES	Based on the novel by
DAVID O. SELZNICK	Technicolor	Margaret Mitchell
For MGM	Reissued 1967 in	
	70mm Metrocolor	

PRINCIPAL CHARACTERS

VIVIEN LEIGH	CLARK GABLE	LESLIE HOWARD
Scarlett O'Hara	Rhett Butler	Ashley Wilkes
OLIVIA DE HAVILLAND	THOMAS MITCHELL	HATTIE MC DANIEL
Melanie Hamilton	Gerald O'Hara	Mammy
BUTTERFLY MC QUEEN	RAND BROOKS	HARRY DAVENPORT
Prissy	Charles Hamilton	Dr. Meade
CARROLL NYE		
Frank Kennedy		

Length: 220 minutes

The glory of the collaborative craftsmanship of the American studio system, *Gone with the Wind* has seldom been associated, either by the industry or by writers on film, with the war film genre but rather assigned to the amorphous category of historical or costume romance. Yet *Gone with the Wind* incorporates a whole range of economic, social, and philosophical problems confronting the South during the Civil War and its aftermath. And it does so with a still-unsurpassed vividness in detailing an entire society's plight apart from the battlefield, even though the events consistently focus on the personality of Scarlett O'Hara, an aristocratic heroine determined to ignore the widespread wartime disaster until it envelops her and permanently affects her attitudes. The second half of this film saga deals with the defeated South's attempts at reconstruction, and in particular Scarlett's reestablishment of her place in that society; but the spiritual and psychological damage sustained in the just-concluded war is accurately shown to have irrevocably altered the gracious life style of the southern aristocracy. The generally acknowledged visual splendor of *Gone with the Wind*, therefore, is not merely pictorial; it functions profoundly in terms of the theme implicit in its title: the beauty inherent in the physical possessions (the land and the mansions) and the life style of the southern aristocracy is destroyed, with both good and bad results, by a war stemming from the moral flaws of that society.

The key structure of *Gone with the Wind* is the relationship between the main characters on the home front and the background forces of war—not dramatized battlefield conflicts but the reported events, the military casualties, and the physical ravages inflicted on place and property. To judge Scarlett or the other major characters without considering this context is to turn *Gone with the Wind* into a mere romantic period piece about a selfish woman given to tantrums when frustrated in her attempts to control the men in her life. Within the film's context, however, Scarlett's personality—and those of other major characters—achieves another dimension because it parallels the collective consciousness of her society. The facades of splendor and charm are everywhere: Scarlett's beauty enables her to disguise certain serious faults of character—dishonesty, extreme conceit, and rapaciousness; her father's magnificent estate, Tara, operates through the labor of devoted but completely dependent slaves; the charming manners of southern gentility often conceal an arrogance and an ignorance that confuses role playing with reality. Indeed, the only great reality of the time is the Civil War, a lost cause from the start—as Rhett Butler, the film's representative realist, notes at the beginning of the film—but the South's obstinate self-aggrandizement leads society to its ruin. At the moment of the South's climactic military defeat, Scarlett refuses to admit to herself that Tara is doomed; under Rhett's protection she flees invaded Atlanta to return to her family's home, leaving the city on fire and the aristocratic way of life it represents completely wrecked.

271

The moral blindness of this society is represented by Scarlett's narrow perception of the world she lives in. Throughout the film she pursues a vain ideal of possessing Ashley Wilkes, an intellectual, refined, dispassionate member of her own class, though it is

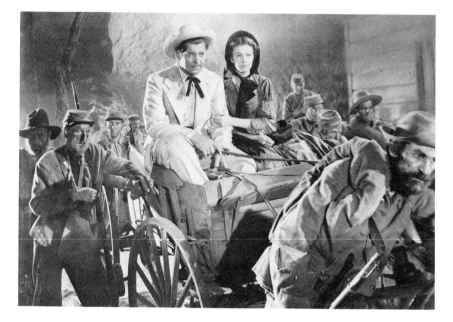

272

clear from the beginning (to her father and to Rhett) that she and
Ashley are not suited for one another, that he does not return her
love—indeed, that he is incapable of the emotional vitality that
characterizes her—and that he will remain faithful to Melanie, the
woman he marries early in the film. Although the Civil War
begins shortly after we are introduced to the characters, much of
the film is concerned with Scarlett's selfish preoccupations with
Ashley, rather than with the devastation inflicted on the society
she belongs to. Thus, the discrepancy between our view of her
central situation (a young woman caught in a war that is about to
destroy her way of life) and her own perception of her situation (a
woman thwarted by frustrating circumstances from marrying
the man she wants) develops the film's pervasive irony.

The visual contrast between the issue of survival looming in
the background and Scarlett's determined policy of self-interest
in the foreground is shown most memorably in a group of
sequences pertaining to the birth of Melanie's child. Scarlett had
married Melanie's brother without any affection for him, and
then conveniently had become a widow after he contracted pneu-
monia while in the army (an event that in itself is a commentary
on the unheroic and futile wastefulness of war). While in Atlanta
staying with Melanie, whom she despises for having won Ashley
in spite of what Scarlett perceives as an essential dullness in
Melanie's character, Scarlett performs volunteer services in a
military hospital, not because she shares Melanie's concern for
the wounded but because it is an activity that society expects

from women of their status. The visual impact of the suffering soldiers in the drastically understaffed hospital establishes the film's basic motif of the disasters of war; the horrible reality upsets Scarlett, who determines to go home to rural Tara, which she assumes is a haven from the war encroaching on the Atlanta region. Her plans, however, are interrupted by the ironic predicament of Melanie: Melanie, about to give birth, cannot receive any medical attention, and thus Scarlett is required by Dr. Meade to remain in Atlanta, at some personal risk, to look after a woman whom she dislikes and who will give birth to the child of the man she thinks ought to be her own husband. When the time for Melanie's delivery is at hand, Scarlett must go to the hospital herself to persuade the doctor to assist Melanie, but he tells her that he cannot possibly abandon the many injured soldiers under his care. In the memorable visual image after Scarlett leaves the hospital, the camera pulls back to reveal the wounded soldiers lying about the depot in the street; the immensity of their number, increasing as the camera moves farther back and Scarlett attempts to weave her way through what seems to be a large proportion of the Southern army, symbolizes the massive suffering that surrounds any individual's personal grief in a time of national disaster.

273

The general motif of national disaster, however, functions not so much as a theme but as a context for other themes. In the wake of the tragedy of Atlanta, people are given different kinds of opportunities to draw on their inner strengths and to perform heroically, in a sense partially redeeming their lives of excessive privilege and indifference. Scarlett, who had never done anything useful for anyone, faces up to the emergency and—suppressing her inclination to flee—admirably delivers Melanie's baby. Later, at Tara, threatened by a marauding Yankee soldier, she is able to summon enough courage to kill him. (Others are not as capable of responding to situations of distress: Scarlett's father loses his mind through a successive series of misfortunes culminating with the death of his wife.) Perhaps the best example of a character confronting the realities of war and rising to meet them is Rhett Butler, who abandons his own selfish and cynical ways at the very time when the South stands on the verge of defeat; even though he knows that the cause is lost, he enlists in time for the final defense, fully expecting to be killed for his gallant effort, but still feeling the necessity of some gesture of idealism for himself and his country.

The second half of *Gone with the Wind* traces the rise in the economic fortunes of its heroine, who determines to rebuild her father's wrecked estate and does so, driven by the experience of poverty and the loss of status she suffered in the early days of the

South's defeat. The war has created Scarlett's obsession with accumulating money; this in turn leads her into another loveless marriage, which gives her the opportunity to discover her excellent business sense. Although she persists in nurturing her infatuation with Ashley during her second marriage and widowhood, Rhett, who is actually the ideal match for her, finally gets her to marry him. This marriage ends in disillusionment as Rhett abandons her, just at the time when she has begun to see that she really wants him. As a representative figure of the Old South, Scarlett demonstrates her society's aggressive determination to overcome the economic and physical destruction of the war; but in her achievement we also note the disappearance of the South's luxurious gentility, a life style made attractive by the visual style of *Gone with the Wind,* though self-destructive in its own time and ill-suited for the realities of the new era that followed.

274

TO BE OR NOT TO BE
(1942)

Director-Producer	Cinematographer	Script
ERNST LUBITSCH	RUDOLPH MATE	EDWIN JUSTUS MAYERS
For United Artists		Based on an original story by Melchior Lengyel and Ernst Lubitsch

PRINCIPAL CHARACTERS

JACK BENNY	CAROLE LOMBARD	ROBERT STACK
Josef Tura	Maria Tura	Lt. Sobinski
FELIX BRESSART	LIONEL ATWILL	STANLEY RIDGES
Greenberg	Ravitch	Prof. Siletsky
SIG RUMANN	TOM DUGAN	CHARLES HALTON
Col. Erhardt	Bronski	Dobosh

Length: 99 minutes

In *To Be or Not To Be* Lubitsch brings the style of the comedy of manners to the subject of war and proceeds in his typical way to deflate mankind's preposterous pretensions. Nevertheless, the ominous Nazi shadow stalks throughout the film: Poland is bombed and occupied by a totalitarian force, Gestapo executions are ordered, and the underground movement fights back. The comedy does not cover up the terrors of war, but instead approaches them in a new way, suggesting that in the long run, because the inane ideology of Führer worship can attract only stupid people, the opponents of tyranny will prevail. At one critical moment, Josef Tura, impersonating a Gestapo spy at Nazi headquarters, is placed in a room with the newly discovered corpse of the real spy. The Nazis expect Tura to crack under this psychological game and confess his impersonation, but with great aplomb Tura, though he is an amateur at spying and astonished by his situation, manages to outwit the continually credulous Germans and convince them that the corpse is really the impostor. The cloddish Germans have the power, but the Resistance fighters escape to continue their operations in exile.

Almost all war films are restricted thematically to the issue of war itself, which of course defines the activities that the characters engage in. *To Be or Not To Be,* however, brilliantly evolves from the abstract problem of the relationship of art and reality, yet settles so firmly onto the visual level of the wartime situation—Warsaw under Nazi occupation—that Lubitsch's philosophical perspective never seems to obtrude upon or hinder the comic development of the plot's contemporary dramatic conflicts. **275** What is the social function of the artist? What identity must he assume when he is forced to abandon temporarily his function as artist? Questions like these hardly seem the stuff of farce and melodrama, but they provide a dimension to this film that no other Resistance film shares.

The plot concerns a theatrical company trying to preserve the Polish underground from the tyranny of the German oppressors. Throughout the film, role playing and theater settings dominate the action because the conflict arranges itself in terms of which side will control the appearances of reality. The professional performers are better at the craft of illusion-making than the Germans, and win out since the conflict seems to consist of the staging of a series of illusions. The Nazi mentality is nonartistic, incapable of perceiving the substance behind the appearance, and is therefore manipulated by the skills of the acting troupe—in particular, those of Josef Tura, the extremely egocentric artist, who in normal situations would have nothing to do with mundane reality. The personification of the ham actor that Jack Benny carried over from his famous radio program to his role as Josef Tura, featured performer in the Warsaw troupe, is perfectly represented by his delivery of Hamlet's introspective soliloquy, "To be or not to be . . . ." Whatever the precise existential import of Shakespeare's lines about Hamlet's evaluation of his future identity and action, Tura's interpretation never gets past the phrasing of the question, for a member of the audience always walks out at that point, jolting the actor's otherwise impervious belief in the

276

greatness of his performance. Lubitsch not only explodes the pretentiousness of Tura's acting style (magnificently pompous and solemn) and mocks Shakespeare's abstruse metaphysics, but he also focuses on the *idea* behind the theme that the artist can "descend" to the real world under the encroaching pressure of an emergency. This idea holds that the world of art may indeed become the self-contained preoccupation of the artist divorced from the ordinary concerns of humanity. Tura's world—ridiculously irrelevant to us as outsiders—is wholly the contemplation of the art and the artist (himself) merged together.

For Tura, the shattering experience occurs when, reciting the soliloquy again, he sees the same spectator walking out on him. The fact that Germany is marching on Poland presents, for this ham, no immediate threat to his self-contemplation and therefore strikes him as only of minor interest. Later, however, informed of the need to work decisively to save the lives of members of the underground, Tura cooperates in staging a hoax on Professor Siletsky, the master Gestapo spy who has gathered a list of current underground members from unsuspecting exiled Poles flying with the Royal Air Force. Masquerading as the German officer, Col. Erhardt, Tura learns that a copy of the list is secured at Nazi headquarters; after Siletsky discovers the hoax and is killed trying to escape, Tura impersonates him to retrieve the documents. Lubitsch complicates the plot with discoveries and surprises, but always at center stage we find the undoctrinaire Tura, risking his life for the Resistance, a cause which he supports without real emotional conviction. Tura can be emotionally stirred only by his egotistical imagination, as indicated by his repeated efforts to get people to praise his acting ability. Disguised as Siletsky, he asks the real Col. Erhardt, the buffoonlike commanding officer, if he knows of that "great, great Polish actor, Josef Tura." The reply—for which Lubitsch was roundly criticized in the press for including in this 1942 film—was "What he did to Shakespeare, we are doing now to Poland." More than the real danger to his life, more than the increasing suspicion that his wife may be having an affair with the man who walks out on his Hamlet soliloquy, Tura is shaken by the negative comments on his acting.

The film ends with a series of farcical events resulting from an impersonation of Hitler by a member of the troupe. The foolish loyalties of the Germans are parodied in their unquestioning obedience to their supposed leader to the extent of jumping from a plane at his command. In the last sequence the actors, having escaped to freedom in England, are once again performing *Hamlet*, and inevitably as Tura begins his soliloquy he once more loses a spectator. Thus, returning to the world of art after defeating an army of occupation—an irrelevant interlude in his life—Tura is able to concentrate again on what truly matters: getting through Shakespeare's lines without an interruption.

277

CASABLANCA
(1942)

Director	Cinematographer	Script
MICHAEL CURTIZ	ARTHUR EDESON	JULIUS J. EPSTEIN
Producer		PHILIP EPSTEIN
HAL B. WALLIS		HOWARD KOCH
For Warner Brothers		Based on the unproduced play *Everybody Comes to Rick* by Murray Burnett and Joan Alison

PRINCIPAL CHARACTERS

HUMPHREY BOGART	INGRID BERGMAN	CLAUDE RAINS
Rick Blaine	Ilsa Lund Laszlo	Capt. Louis Renault
PAUL HENREID	CONRAD VEIDT	SYDNEY GREENSTREET
Victor Laszlo	Maj. Heinrich Strasser	Señor Ferrari
PETER LORRE	S. Z. SAKALL	MADELEINE LEBEAU
Ugarte	Carl	Yvonne
DOOLEY WILSON		
Sam		

Length: 102 minutes

278

The exile Rick Blaine—charming, detached, mysterious, and amiable even in his alienation—is perhaps the most admired personality ever portrayed in the American cinema. He seems entirely conscious of his image, which is the deliberate creation of a man who wants to appear a certain way both to preserve his privacy and to establish his public facade. As his sardonic companion, the police prefect Captain Renault, points out several times in an attempt to stick pins in the image, Rick Blaine underneath it all is a sentimentalist, a romantic. Exiles generally are romantics, whose detached or indifferent attitudes can be appealed to by those in need of help. *Casablanca* is typical of the category in tracing the development of the exile's progress back into the community of civilized men through an emotional appeal to his essentially romantic nature.

Exile presupposes an abstracted setting; that is, the hero can dwell in the crowded city or the African jungle, but his isolation will remain complete wherever he goes because the sentence of exile is self-imposed and the spatial restraints are merely the portable shell that he carries everywhere. The city of Casablanca is exceedingly crowded, decadent, vulgar, and desperately in need of air conditioning; no one there wants to be there—except Rick, who seems to be running a prosperous, locally famous nightclub with a back-room casino. Everyone else is awaiting means of travel to Lisbon, from where they can get to the United States. Admired not only by his fiercely loyal employees but by

everyone in town, Rick operates his club with independence and aloofness, exhibiting a slight touch of scorn for both his customers and his business (he calls it a saloon). The city is presented as a place of shady operations, its biggest business the buying and selling of visas to emigrants fleeing war-torn Europe. The theme of refugees in transit supplies the political undertone to the whole film, since the hero insists that he is now apolitical, though his credentials indicate that a few years prior to the beginning of the film he had certain commitments to fight against the fascists in Spain, Ethiopia, and France. No one else claims political neutrality aside from Rick and Capt. Renault, the apparent top official in Casablanca and the representative of the Nazi-collaborating Vichy government in France. Although Casablanca, being in French territory, is unoccupied and theoretically neutral, it favors the Nazis as a matter of political expediency. But since the city is filled with refugees and has an active underground, there is no doubt where the populace stands, and in one rousing sequence, the singing of the "Marseillaise" drowns out an attempt by a group of Nazi officials to sing a German song.

Curtiz continually reinforces this sense of place in images of a city filled with pressures, potentially explosive, and populated by transients. The police round up suspects, shoot at criminals, close down cafés, and, through Capt. Renault, participate thoroughly in the corruption of the time. And it is very possible that Rick has settled in Casablanca because of all the turmoil and tumult, for his majestic serenity, his indifference to money schemes, and his obvious integrity create by visual contrast precisely the romantic notion of himself that all romantic heroes strive for. No wonder that everyone—from Laszlo, a bulwark of moral commitment, to Ferrari, overlord of illegal activities in the city, to Ugarte, a murderer, to Renault, the hedonistic petty tyrant of the city—seems to admire Rick. The admiration is evoked largely by his projected image of mystery and disinterestedness. He makes few claims, even indirect ones, for moral superiority, but he radiates that quality nevertheless. The one crucial act he performs before the middle of the film, however, is meant to suggest a typical, though impulsive, willingness to get involved on occasion with the infinite number of troubled people he encounters. A young newlywed about to barter herself sexually to Capt. Renault in return for visas for herself and her husband (the husband will never, of course, be told what she is willing to do for him) is saved by Rick's intervention. Her husband is permitted to win a small fortune at the casino table when Rick gives the sign to his croupier; this action thwarts Capt. Renault, who is first outraged, then amused when he discovers Rick's tactics. This hero's gallant nobility reveals that under his stylized and hardened shield, his romantic nature can still be penetrated.

280

The plot of the film incorporates a principal generic trait of movement away from exile—in other words, a return to an aspect of civilization presumably renounced by the romantic, for good cause, in the past. Now, if the cause was good, though it was deeply personal, the return implies a sacrifice of that cause, a personal loss accepted for some even greater cause—a true romantic trait. The overpowering effect that this film generates in audiences, whether they have seen it several times or are seeing it for the first time, testifies to our own deepseated desire to do something of the same kind—and perhaps we all would, if we could devise and project a heroic image comparable to Rick's. Having no such image, we might fear that our sacrifice would simply appear foolish—or not even be noticed by the world at large.

Rick achieves greatness and nobility with his sacrifice. His lost love Ilsa has briefly reentered his life and arrived at the point of leaving her famous husband, the freedom fighter Victor Laszlo, for Rick. Much of the middle part of the film relates, partly by flashback, the frustrated love affair that Rick had with her in Paris, culminating in Ilsa's abandoning him on the eve of the German occupation. It was this affair that turned Rick into an exile, but his cynicism is finally dissolved in his determination to help the cause of freedom by getting Laszlo out of the country with letters of transit. He makes Ilsa go with her husband, reminding her that the personal entanglements of three people "don't amount to a hill of beans in this crazy world" (a somewhat ungraceful line for an otherwise sparkling screenplay). It is the inherent requirement of the category that something precious be sacrificed to symbolize the hero's awakening to the needs of the larger community. When Ilsa and Victor fly off to continue their fight against fascism, using the letters of transit that would have guaranteed a safe escape either for Victor alone or for Ilsa and Rick together, we know that Rick, who now faces probable imprisonment, has forever renounced his personal exile. This sacrifice is so powerful a heroic action that it wins over the arch cynic, Capt. Renault. When Rick shoots the Nazi major who attempts to intercept the departing plane, Renault has one of the cinema's greatest moments—a chance to redeem all his corruption with one magnificent sentence. When his police run to him for orders on what to do about the major lying a few feet away, Renault pauses, glances at Rick, who a few moments before had forced him at gunpoint to participate in Laszlo's escape, and rises to the occasion; instead of arresting Rick, he wryly smiles: "Major Strasser's been shot—round up the usual suspects."

The film ends with Renault and Rick walking through the airport fog, making plans to leave Casablanca together. Their cynicism and their mutual suspicion have turned to respect for each other's capacity for commitment to the morally right side despite personal interests. They have gone beyond alienation and self-absorption. Bound together by their new knowledge of themselves, they are no longer exiles.

PATHS OF GLORY
(1957)

Director	Cinematographer	Script
STANLEY KUBRICK	GEORGE KRAUSE	STANLEY KUBRICK
Producer		CALDER WILLINGHAM
JAMES B. HARRIS		JIM THOMPSON
For United Artists		Based on a novel
		by Humphrey Cobb

PRINCIPAL CHARACTERS

KIRK DOUGLAS	RALPH MEEKER	ADOLPHE MENJOU
Colonel Dax	Corporal Paris	General Broulard
GEORGE MACREADY	WAYNE MORRIS	RICHARD ANDERSON
General Mireau	Lieutenant Roget	Major Saint-Auban
JOSEPH TURKEL	TIMOTHY CAREY	
Private Arnaud	Private Ferol	

Length: 86 minutes

282

Kubrick, in *Paths of Glory,* adds a new dimension to the tradi-tional antiwar film: the cruelty and inhumanity of commanding officers toward their own troops. In the story of a disastrously con-ceived First World War field attack by the French on an impreg-nable German position, and a subsequent coverup by the high command that necessitates the execution for cowardice of three innocent soldiers, the film relentlessly details the horrors of mili-tary injustice set against the background of the physical horrors of battle. Although directly within the heritage of *All Quiet on the Western Front,* this film does not suggest that the deaths of soldiers have any redeeming value of heroism or nobility. All the deaths are senseless from the point of view of the dying men, who will not get to play the role of heroes. Thus, the message delivered by the film is bleaker than that of any of its famous predecessors.

A greatly admired work, *Paths of Glory* seems seriously flawed in one major respect—its theme develops in very clearly defined good-bad contrasts, and the dialogue articulates the prob-lem of injustice in such compelling terms that only complete villains—the generals—could fail to be won over to the victims' side. The theme, reinforced by the visuals, is certainly presented with stylistic consistency. For example, cutting between the bat-tlefield and command headquarters, Kubrick will first show sol-diers either in trenches or advancing very slowly on the battle-field, stressing their confinement, the miserable physical conditions, and the sense of the individual submerged in the mass; then, in contrast, he shows the extraordinarily luxurious salons of the commanding officers; the voluminous space empha-

sizes the class difference that dominates the structure of an army. The execution of three soldiers, chosen by lot to represent the supposed cowardice of the entire attacking force, is carried out directly in front of the generals' magnificent chateau. When Colonel Dax, the heroic spokesman for justice, goes to make his last plea for mercy for the doomed soldiers, the sequence showing the men in their cells is punctuated with shots of the ball in the chateau; there, the music and the casual unconcern of General Broulard heighten our awareness of the disparity between the conforts of those controlling the military hierarchy and the sufferings of those serving it.

Indeed, Kubrick goes out of his way to shape our point of view in the unfolding tragedy. Dax is first presented as a conscientious leader of men who objects strenuously to the disastrous plans of General Mireau, the chief villain. Mireau, needing a dramatic military victory for personal advancement, expects to lose an enormous number of men in taking the German position, Ant Hill. As a courageous and obedient soldier, Dax leads the charge, attempting to inspire his men, though he regards it as either a lost cause or one that will in any event not justify the tremendous cost of victory. But the casualties are so great that his men falter and cannot proceed, whereupon Mireau, from the safety of his own position, orders the battery to fire on his own troops. Infuriated but checked by the battery officer's refusal to fire without written orders, Mireau later determines to execute hundreds of men but finally agrees to court-martial just three as symbolic sacrifices. The trial sequence is brief, the conclusions of the judges predetermined, and the restrained but legally valid defense made by Dax (a lawyer in civil life) is not given serious consideration.

Yet Kubrick's film cannot be deemed simplistic merely because the thematic development is stacked so heavily against the inhumane generals—Mireau, who orders the executions, and Broulard, who permits them. *Paths of Glory* has a contending point of view presented in the visuals, though it lacks a spokesman comparable to Dax to lend it any emotional validity. The generals are proponents of military structure—the regulations, orders, chains of command that they inherently believe represent a reasonable and perhaps even spiritual morality. War is absolute chaos, mere senseless massacre, and the only purpose one finds in it is the possibility of order itself. "The men died wonderfully," Mireau says in admiration of the three men he destroyed. True, the sacrifice of lives for the establishment of orderly procedures and hierarchical structures dehumanizes the generals, yet from their side it seems that no other way of life can hold armies or societies together. Broulard's comment, "Soldiers are like children—they need discipline," is typical. We have no doubt where Kubrick stands in relation to the problem, but it is necessary for us to see the generals' side to appreciate the fact that they have both principles and commitments.

When Dax threatens to reveal Mireau's gross error in attempting to turn the cannon on his own retreating men, Broulard's response is to get rid of Mireau—not, as Dax had expected, to rescind the death penalty for the three soldiers. Broulard's discovery of Mireau's irrational behavior leads him to decide to destroy his associate (whom he was helping to promote) because he knows that Mireau represents a weak link in the hierarchical chain. His decision represents an unusual moral perspective for the war film. Broulard turns on a fellow general of his own class, without any bitterness, apparently only for the reason that Mireau can no longer be trusted to function properly in a pressure situation. Broulard could, perhaps, have simply granted reprieves to the soldiers, silenced Dax, and ignored Mireau. But cynic and tyrant that he is, Broulard "sacrifices" Mireau by telling him that a court of inquiry will be summoned. Thus, the hierarchy perpetuates itself by removing its misfits and minimizing scandal to the outside world, which is not able to judge the issues properly.

The subsequent offer of Mireau's position to Dax is not at all out of character for Broulard, who recognizes talent in his humanistic opponent. Dax may be shocked at the cynicism he recognizes in the offer because he is still staggering from Broulard's failure to stop the execution. In this sense he fails Broulard's test of the good commanding officer—one who will bury his personal feelings to maintain the integrity of the military institution. Kubrick's antiwar theme propounds the rottenness of that institution and its inevitable injustice. The point, of course, is that at the heart of the war machine there is no heart at all and no ideal but self-perpetuation.

NORTH BY NORTHWEST
(1959)

Director-Producer	Cinematographer	Script
ALFRED HITCHCOCK	ROBERT BURKS	ERNEST LEHMAN
For MGM	Technicolor	
	VistaVision	

PRINCIPAL CHARACTERS

CARY GRANT	EVA MARIE SAINT	JAMES MASON
Roger Thornhill	Eve Kendall	Phillip Vandamm
JESSIE ROYCE LANDIS	LEO G. CARROLL	PHILIP OBER
Clara Thornhill	Professor	Lester Townsend
JOSEPHINE HUTCHINSON	MARTIN LANDAU	
Housekeeper	Leonard	

Length: 136 minutes

285

North by Northwest is perhaps the most visually stunning example of the spy film. Its mixture of comic style and the serious probing of deceitful identities has been copied by others, but the combination seldom fits the philosophic perspective of a filmmaker the way it does Hitchcock's. This spy category is concerned with the reactions of the unwilling spy, the person caught up in circumstances that require him to perform a certain action or carry a message that he would not normally do if he had matters under his control. Hitchcock had done this before, most memorably in *The Thirty-Nine Steps* (1935), where the emphasis was wholly upon the responses of the main character to the complexities of the situation which suddenly enveloped him. In *North by Northwest* the hero, Roger Thornhill, snatched from a successful career in advertising, is continually astonished and infuriated at the events that push him along a course of disaster, and the dramatic emphasis is divided between his physical reactions and his verbal protests against what is happening.

To get an innocent person to serve the dangerous purposes of a government engaged in espionage, some strong threat must usually be held over that person. In *North by Northwest,* Thornhill is mistaken for a CIA agent by the enemy spies on the one hand, and on the other is assumed to be a murderer by the police (after he was photographed pulling the knife out of the victim of a murder he witnessed at the UN). Behind the scenes are the real CIA agents, who know the truth of the matter but intend to use Thornhill as a diversion from their real spy, Eve Kendall, who has infiltrated the enemy group. Thornhill must pursue the spies and simultaneously avoid the police. As a CIA pawn for most of the film, he rages against what he considers everyone's tendency to misunderstand his reasonable explanations; later, when he learns that the CIA is behind his troubles, he bitterly reflects on the despotism of that organization but agrees to cooperate with it to save Eve's life. His cooperation, however, is short-lived, for he goes ahead single-handedly to save her at a point where the CIA seems willing to sacrifice her—as they were prepared to sacrifice him earlier. Hitchcock makes no great point of the mission that is preoccupying the CIA (it may or may not be the equivalent of the "vital secrets" of *The Thirty-Nine Steps*); very little of the objective is even hinted at. Furthermore, just as in that earlier film, and as in *Notorious* (1946) and *Topaz* (1969) as well, Hitchcock makes at least one of the enemy faction thoroughly charming. The enemy spy leader Vandamm, as played by James Mason, is cultured, calm, reasonable, and projects no plausible threat to the safety of the United States.

286

To Hitchcock, the predicament of a man caught between two spy organizations, the CIA and Vandamm's mysterious group, is both comic and tragic. With his usual visual wit—superbly toned in this film—Hitchcock leads his hero on an extended chase through unusual environments, responding to a series of emergencies with courage, intelligence, and some luck. But the constant comedy, even the self-conscious comedy of Thornhill's recurring encounters with the spies, does not deter the filmmaker from presenting the growing disaster of Thornhill's life. Thornhill, played by Cary Grant in one of his most impressive roles, starts out as an extremely self-assured, successful, charming— but selfish and perhaps tyrannical—executive. Kidnapped by the even more polished Vandamm, he can only consider the whole affair a great mistake, something that can be talked over between sophisated gentlemen, for his great ability lies in promoting himself (his choice of profession was not made by chance) as a likable, reasonable man. But his overture is returned by an attempt to kill him—Vandamm's men get him drunk and send him off in a car on a winding, hilly road. When he crashes into a

police car and is thereby saved (though arrested for drunken driving), he again assumes that he can convince others of the seriousness of his predicament. Thornhill cannot see himself in unusual circumstances because his entire life has been lived in environments favorable to him. The culmination of his difficulties with new environments (all of which are traps) is the famous sequence that takes place on an open country road next to a cornfield. He comes for a final reasonable discussion with the man he has been seeking—the man who can give him back his identity—but actually he has been set up for assassination. The sequence has been justifiably studied as a masterpiece of cutting and of pure visual cinema; it should also be noted, however, that much of the effect grows out of the film's entire context up to that point—for what happens to Thornhill, as his hopes fade and as an increasing element of fear enters the situation, is that for the first time he begins to understand the nature of his vulnerability. The city man in the rural locale, isolated and open to an attack from any direction, manages to avoid death because he really is highly competent, even though the attack comes from a startling new direction, the air.

For all the film's comedy, the profession of spying is not let off lightly. Eve Kendall's willingness to have Thornhill killed to protect her identity as an agent, though she is attracted to him and knows he is innocent of anything, is not glossed over. Thornhill's disdain for the methods of the CIA is supported not only by its callousness but by its decision-making process: a group of distant management figures sits in committee, estimating gains and losses in human terms.

Thornhill is one spy whose character improves through the adventures he undergoes. When he finally learns of the game he has unwittingly played, he determines to save Eve at a real risk to his own life. He goes after the enemy spies in the self-parodying locale of Mt. Rushmore, with its gigantic heads carved into the mountain which reflect his own sense of the ambiguous nonsense and high seriousness involved in the whole enterprise. At the ultimate moment, when everything seems in jeopardy and Roger and Eve find themselves close to plummeting off the great stone face of a president, he proposes to her, and when she asks about his first two marriages, he says, "My wives divorced me. . . . I think they said I led too dull a life." His self-mockery at that moment is one indication of a new awareness. We have first seen Thornhill rushing through a New York crowd and dictating to his secretary, expressing within a few seconds his indifference to the crowd, his secretary, the elevator operator, his girlfriend, and a stranger whom he tricks into giving up a cab. When he becomes the reluctant decoy in an espionage situation he gradually grows to the point where he can become personally involved with the life of another while risking his own, through his own free choice. In *North by Northwest* the spy achieves freedom, moving from the position of a mere operative to an agent working independently of the agency. The cold war fought here between professional spy organizations without apparent ideologies is seen as mechanical and indifferent to human values, but it serves to provide heroes with an arena equivalent to that which we find in battle films.

DR. STRANGELOVE

Or How I Learned To Stop Worrying and Love the Bomb

(1963)

Director-Producer	Cinematographer	Script
STANLEY KUBRICK	GILBERT TAYLOR	STANLEY KUBRICK
For Columbia		TERRY SOUTHERN
		PETER GEORGE
		Based on a novel
		by Peter George

PRINCIPAL CHARACTERS

PETER SELLERS	GEORGE C. SCOTT	STERLING HAYDEN
Group Capt. Lionel Mandrake	Gen. "Buck" Turgidson	Gen. Jack D. Ripper
President Muffley	KEENAN WYNN	SLIM PICKENS
Dr. Strangelove	Col. "Bat" Guano	Maj. T. J. "King" Kong
PETER BULL	TRACY REED	JAMES EARL JONES
Ambassador de Sadesky	Miss Scott	Lt. Lothar Zogg, Bombardier

Length: 94 minutes

289

Within the cinema of cataclysm, no film has ever achieved a greater emotional impact than Kubrick's black comedy about man's irresistible urge toward self-destruction. Its one genuine moment of joy occurs at the end, when the fanatic Major "King" Kong straddles the nuclear bomb as it heads for its Russian target; when it strikes, it will trigger the doomsday machine set to devastate the entire earth. Although science fiction cinema is usually reassuring, the science fiction war film seems premised on disaster stemming from the incompetence of military meddling in the political affairs of society. The ending of *Dr. Strangelove* is the ending of civilization, and in no conceivable way can the survivors look forward to any future—except for the ex-Nazi mad scientist whose name occupies the prominent place in the title. To him, making eugenic arrangements for the underground life of the next hundred years provides an opportunity for a glorious scientific experiment. However, watching the film for the first time, audiences cannot really be sure that a happy ending won't be pulled off: they think that the incredibly horrendous alternative to a happy ending has to be implausible, even though the theme and plot develop in strict consistency with the irrational behavior they are witnessing. The dramatic question—can the holocaust be prevented?—is answered negatively, and with the relentless logic of the best of science fiction.

In one important sense *Dr. Strangelove* appears antipathetic

to the antiwar catastrophe category: its satirical approach. Although George Méliès, the father of science fiction cinema, constantly satirized his materials, the rigidly straitlaced tradition of Anglo-American science fiction films isolates *Dr. Strangelove* (though the tradition of the science fiction novel of course includes satire). What remains distinctive about *Dr. Strangelove*'s comedy is the way in which the intricate details of disaster are worked out in realistically ordinary locales, familiar from many banal films but enlivened here by the vitality of a collection of insane but unconfinable leaders from the military, political, and scientific worlds. Kubrick's vision of the world as a lunatic asylum is premised on the completely plausible assumption that sooner or later events will get out of hand and that we, the inmates, will bring about our own annihilation. This credible line of development is convincingly established through the characterization of men victimized by their own narrowness, men whose responses are shaped by abstractions, vague premonitions, or colossal daring—such as the willingness of General Buck Turgidson to accept twenty million casualties for the opportunity to knock out the enemy by striking first (a view that seems to have been held or contemplated by some real-life military strategists during the cold war). This film's leaders are all high-comedy types familiar in satire rather than believable individuals, but catastrophe films seldom achieve even the plausibility of stereotyping.

The ordinariness of the settings transforms the broader elements of the comedy into meaningful social satire. In a nondescript room, General Jack D. Ripper, the commanding officer of a nuclear strike force base, confides, to an exchange officer of the RAF, his one-man conspiracy for involving the United States in a war with Russia. In another commonplace cinematic setting, aboard a bomber heading toward its destination in Russia, we observe the kind of solemn procedural business recalled from countless films about the Second World War, updated somewhat in the light of modern technology but essentially identical to sequences from the bomber attack films of thirty years ago. What is new in each locale, of course, is the vivacious insanity of those presiding over the impending cataclysm. The major sequences for the unwinding of the plot occur in the underground War Room in the Pentagon, where the President and his military advisors and the Russian ambassador convene in an emergency session to discuss their alternatives in the few minutes left to them. The only visual element of interest is the traditional giant wall map of the world, which an American general insists is top secret and should not be opened in the presence of the Russian ambassador. The film ends with the Russian ambassador achieving the level of patriotic insanity attributed to him by the general by secretly taking pictures of the map with a disguised miniature camera, while civilization goes up in an atomic cloud.

291

Kubrick structures his plot by intercutting among these three primary settings; the comedy carries each sequence on its own, and the developing tension links each area of action with a sense of story line progress. The real progress is not, however, in the plot, which is fixed at the beginning and takes on only one additional facet in the middle (the discovery that Russia's retaliatory device is a doomsday machine impossible to shut off); the whole dramatic development is formulated around a simple question of whether "our" nuclear bomber can be shot down in time to prevent its triggering "their" nuclear war machine. Yet we are not really far removed from the small-scale disasters of the 1930s dawn patrols or infantry charges, which featured an unyielding exchange of casualties for no conceivable military advantage. Since the point of the antiwar film is that both sides lose in all wars, the truth of the history of the First World War is reasonably projected to the scale of a Third World War in *Dr. Strangelove*. The film's bitter irony reflects mankind's inherent weaknesses from a modern-day perspective.

PATTON
(1970)

Originally subtitled *Lust for Glory*

Director	Cinematographer	Script
FRANKLIN J. SCHAFFNER	FRED KOENEKAMP	FRANCIS FORD COPPOLA
Producer	Deluxe color	EDMUND H. NORTH
FRANK MC CARTHY	Dimension 150	Based on factual material from
For Twentieth Century-Fox		"Patton: Ordeal and Triumph"
		by Ladislas Farago and
		"A Soldier's Story" by
		Omar N. Bradley

PRINCIPAL CHARACTERS

GEORGE C. SCOTT	KARL MALDEN	STEPHEN YOUNG
Gen. George S. Patton, Jr.	Gen. Omar N. Bradley	Capt. Chester B. Hanson
MICHAEL STRONG	CARY LOFFIN	MORGAN PAULL
Brig. Gen. Hobart Carver	Gen. Bradley's driver	Capt. Richard N. Jenson
KARL MICHAEL VOGLER		
Field Marshal Erwin Rommel		

Length: 170 minutes

292

As spectacularly filmed as many of the battle sequences are in *Patton*, for many viewers the most memorable sequence occurs before the titles, when General George S. Patton appears in front of a massive American flag that completely fills the wide screen, salutes, and begins to address his troops prior to leading them into battle overseas. The troops are never shown, as the camera continuously relates Patton to the patriotic symbol behind him. His first words manage to encapsulate his entire public personality: "I want you to remember that no bastard ever won a war by dying for his country. He won it by making the other poor dumb bastard die for his country." The blunt diction should not obscure the Shavian humor, that continual thrust through the rhetoric of the noncombatant's concept of honor, that characterizes the hero's philosophy. Like George Bernard Shaw, whom he refers to once in the film, Patton adopts a public role: he wants to appear extremely toughminded, realistic, hard-driving, and inevitably successful in the great cause of national survival, for as he says later, "I don't want these men to love me, I want them to fight for me." Of all generals the most willing to use obscenities, Patton is also the most cultured—a military scholar, a brilliant, daring strategist, even a poet, and so self-confidently articulate that he can improvise speeches in French. Within the genre, military heroes in command positions may be dislikable and dogmatic, yet the ultimate victory of these commanders carries with it the justification for their previous actions. Not so in *Patton*, for

battle and inevitable victory are virtually an extension of the hero's personality; but since our comprehension of the war is filtered through his imagination, we must evaluate this controversial portrait of the modern hero in terms of his interpretation of events and his reasons for responding to them in his inimitable way.

The ambiguity that audiences detected in George C. Scott's characterization of Patton originates in the script's concept of the romantic warrior encountering the depersonalized warfare of the twentieth century. "Compared to war all other human endeavors shrink to insignificance," the general asserts, a remark that suggests not the horror but the exaltation of war. The film appeared at a time when the antiwar approach was the only viable form of the genre, and yet in spite of its touches of the "war is hell" theme, *Patton* presents a hero peculiarly at home in battle situations. "You love it," his conventional friend General Bradley tells him, almost as a criticism. Thus, the problem arises of the film's attitude toward its central character, but it seems clear that no single attitude was ever intended, that the material essentially concerns the ambiguity of *our* response to Patton. We see him always within a wartime context, performing as an unorthodox leader isolated by his frequent, forcefully expressed, and original opinions on how things ought to operate in a continual series of crisis situations. Although his is obviously not an endearing personality, the peculiar standards of the crisis context modify our possible disapproval of his manners because we know that his intuition is better than the standardized procedural systems urged by more tactful but less imaginative leaders.

The film depicts all the worst aspects of the general's character, everything from vanity and crudity to a sometimes cruel hostility toward those who fail to achieve his level of perception regarding the press of events. Yet in all important ways, Patton retains a reasonableness under pressure that certifies an inner nobility of character. The film elaborates on the circumstances underlying the otherwise indefensible actions of the man, particularly the famous incident in which he slaps and insults a hospitalized soldier who admits to being a victim of "nerves." To Patton, this psychological condition is merely a mode of cowardice. And since his genuine pride in his soldiers' courage and achievement attests to his spiritual association with them—they are the physical, he the intellectual, attribute of a unified mechanism—he needs to remove the weak cog from the machine. Yet whatever the truth of this historic incident, the film's context makes Patton's action justifiable. Patton is outraged that the hospital's wounded patients, whom he considers heroes, must abide the presence of a soldier who is merely afraid to continue in battle. Modern-day psychology does not permit the kind of rage Patton exhibits, but if the general's psychology is out of step with the times, he himself is conscious of another kind of example that his action sets for his troops: his own conduct, as part of his public role, is aimed at boosting morale, encouraging bravery, exhorting ever greater efforts, and achieving victory. Disruptions of the mass psychological conditions he establishes can only lead to demoralized troops, and thus his ultimate ends justify his means because he always works within a wartime crisis situation.

Throughout the film, the controversial style of Patton is played off against two probable alternatives, defeat and death. The film begins with a scene of carnage, a position abandoned by a defeated American army, leaving behind its casualties to be looted by the natives. Patton's job as he assumes command, then, is to shape an army to confront the Germans, who have so far shown the upper hand. There is never any doubt that Patton sincerely suffers for the deaths and the wounds of American

294

soldiers, that he is a religious man in his rather profane way. (When asked by a clergyman if the story is true that the general reads the Bible frequently, Patton wittily sizes up the audience, some of whom expect him to play his tough, obscene role, and answers, "Every goddamn day.") Having his soldiers' best interests as well as his own at heart appears natural in him, for war is his whole life. "I feel I am destined to achieve some great thing," he says at the low point in his career, prior to his greatest success. He is not merely a successful strategist, an overpowering leader, but an artist with a calling to his profession. And true to his art, to his personal vision of how war ought to be conducted, he attempts to control the elements of his medium and to force his creative vision upon everyone else. Therefore, while the continual justification is that without his unorthodox methods his troops would face greater losses, the truth is that he alone is capable of comprehending the total vision of what is going on.

The extravagance of his character ought not to deflect from the element of greatness about him, but no doubt his emphasis on personal military bearing (from carrying ivory-handled pistols to wearing a third star before Congress officially approves it), his belief in reincarnation (always as a warrior), his practice of shooting his pistols at attacking airplanes, his turning of a world war into a series of personal rivalries (against the German Rommel and even against an ally, the English general, Montgomery), and his recommendation at the end of the war in Europe to immediately declare war on Russia—all suggest a combination of eccentricities that cast suspicion on his stability. Yet Patton, in spite of his romantic sensibility, is also a realist. Having proven his capacity to win, as he always claimed he could, he sees that with the end of battle he has become functionless. The next large-scale war, he knows, will be strictly automated and, he notes sadly, will require no heroes and no real generals. What Patton accomplished in the Second World War was to inject the personal element—his vision—into a conflict that was already becoming mechanized. Without that personal element, the warrior-artist is replaced by an instrument of destruction, and war to Patton loses all meaning without the sense of heroic achievement. Some of the genre's chief thematic strands are woven together in this film—if war is a necessary evil, it needs heroes to shape its events in a humanly meaningful way, and it provides opportunities for those of real conviction or courage to achieve a greatness unattainable in the ordinary world at peace.

295

BIBLIOGRAPHY

INTRODUCTION

Flynn, Charles, and Todd McCarthy. *The King of the B's: Working Within the Hollywood System.* New York: Dutton, 1975.

Jacobs, Lewis. *The Rise of the American Film, A Critical History.* New York: Teachers College Press, 1968.

Kaminsky, Stuart. *American Film Genres.* Dayton, Ohio: Pflaum-Standard, 1974.

McConnell, Frank D. *The Spoken Seen: Film and the Romantic Imagination.* Baltimore: Johns Hopkins University Press, 1975.

Pye, Douglas, "Genre and Movies." *Movie* 20 (Spring 1975), 29–43.

Sabchack, Thomas. "Genre Film: A Classical Experience." *Literature/Film Quarterly* 3 (Summer 1975), 196–204.

Schrader, Paul. "Notes on Film Noir." *Film Comment,* Spring 1972.

Solomon, Stanley J. "Film Study and Genre Courses." *College Composition and Communication,* 25 (October 1974), 277–83.

Tudor, Andrew. *Image and Influence, Studies in the Sociology of Film.* New York: St. Martin's Press, 1974.

———. *Theories of Film.* New York: Viking Press, 1974.

CHAPTER 1
THE WESTERN AS MYTH AND ROMANCE

Bazin, Andre. "The Western, or the American Film, *Par Excellence,*" and "The Evolution of the Western." *What is Cinema,* vol. 2. Berkeley: University of California Press, 1971.

Calder, Jenni. *There Must Be a Lone Ranger, The American West in Film and in Reality.* New York: Taplinger, 1975.

Cawelti, John G. *The Six-Gun Mystique.* Bowling Green, Ohio: Bowling Green University Press, 1971.

Fenin, George N., and William K. Everson. *The Western from Silents to the Seventies.* New York: Grossman, 1973.

French, Philip. *Westerns, Aspects of a Movie Genre.* New York: Viking Press, 1974.

Kitses, Jim. *Horizons West, Anthony Mann, Budd Boetticher, Sam Peckinpah: Studies of Authorship Within the Western.* Bloomington, Ind.: Indiana University Press, 1970.

Nachbar, Jack, ed. *Focus on the Western.* Englewood Cliffs, N.J.: Prentice-Hall, 1974.

Tuska, Jon. *The Filming of the West.* New York: Doubleday, 1976.

Warshow, Robert. "Movie Chronicle: The Westerner." *The Immediate Experience.* New York: Atheneum, 1970.

Wright, Will. *Six Guns and Society, A Structural Study of the Western.* Berkeley, University of California Press, 1975.

CHAPTER 2
SINGING AND DANCING: THE SOUND OF METAPHOR

Croce, Arlene. *The Fred Astaire and Ginger Rogers Book.* New York: Dutton, 1972.

Greene, Stanley, and Burt Goldblatt. *Starring Fred Astaire.* New York: Dodd, Mead, 1973.

Hodgkinson, Anthony W. " 'Forty-Second Street' New Deal: Some Thoughts About Early Film Musicals." *Journal of Popular Film* 4 (1975), 33–46.

Kobal, John. *Gotta Sing, Gotta Dance, A Pictorial History of Film Musicals.* New York: Hamlyn, 1970.

Kreuger, Miles, ed. *The Movie Musical from Vitaphone to 42nd Street.* New York: Dover, 1975.

McVay, Douglas. *The Musical Film.* New York: A. S. Barnes, 1967.

Scheurer, Timothy E. "The Aesthetics of Form and Convention in the Movie Musical." *Journal of Popular Film* 3 (Fall 1974), 307–24.

Stern, Lee E. *The Movie Musical.* New York: Pyramid, 1974.

Springer, John. *All Talking! All Singing! All Dancing!* New York: Citadel Press, 1966.

Taylor, John Russell, and Arthur Jackson. *The Hollywood Musical.* New York: McGraw-Hill, 1971.

CHAPTER 3

THE NIGHTMARE WORLD

Baxter, John. *Science Fiction in the Cinema.* New York: Paperback Library, 1970.

Butler, Ivan. *Horror in the Cinema.* New York: Paperback Library, 1970.

Clarens, Carlos. *An Illustrated History of the Horror Film.* New York: Capricorn Books, 1967.

Dillard, R. H. W. "Even A Man Who Is Pure at Heart." *Man and the Movies.* W. R. Robinson, ed. Baton Rouge: Louisiana State University Press, 1967.

Evans, Walter. "Monster Movies and Rites of Initiation." *Journal of Popular Film* 4 (1975), 124–42.

Film Journal 2 (1973). Special issue on the horror film.

Gow, Gordon. *Suspense in the Cinema.* Cranbury, N.J.: A. S. Barnes, 1968. 1968.

Huss, Ray, and T. J. Ross, eds. *Focus on the Horror Film.* Englewood Cliffs, N. J.: Prentice-Hall, 1972.

Johnson, William, ed. *Focus on the Science Fiction Film.* Englewood Cliffs, N.J. Prentice-Hall, 1972.

Sontag, Susan. "The Imagination of Disaster." *Commentary* 40 (October 1965), 42–48.

CHAPTER 4

THE LIFE OF CRIME

Alloway, Lawrence. *Violent America: The Movies, 1946–1964.* New York: Museum of Modern Art, 1971.

Baxter, John. *The Gangster Film.* New York: A. S. Barnes, 1970.

———. *Hollywood in the Thirties.* New York: A. S. Barnes, 1968.

Bergman, Andrew. *We're in the Money: Depression America and Its Films.* New York: New York University Press, 1971.

Everson, William K. *The Bad Guys, A Pictorial History of the Movie Villain.* New York: Citadel Press, 1964.

Gabree, John. *Gangsters, from Little Caesar to the Godfather.* New York: Pyramid, 1973.

Kaminsky, Stuart M. "*Little Caesar* and Its Role in the Gangster Film Genre." *Journal of Popular Film* 1 (Summer 1972), 209–27.

Karpf, Stephen L. *The Gangster Film: Emergence, Variation and Decay of a Genre.* New York: Arno Press, 1973.

McArthur, Colin. *Underworld U.S.A.* New York: Viking Press, 1972.

Warshow, Robert. "The Gangster as Tragic Hero." *The Immediate Experience.* New York: Atheneum, 1970.

CHAPTER 5
THE SEARCH FOR CLUES

Baxter, John. *Hollywood in the Sixties.* New York: A. S. Barnes, 1972.

Cauliez, Armand Jean. *Le Film criminel et le film policier.* Paris: Editions du Cerf, 1956.

Everson, William K. *The Detective in Film.* Secaucus, N.J.: Citadel Press, 1972.

Gregory, Charles. "Knight Without Meaning? Marlowe on the Screen." *Sight and Sound* 42 (Summer 1973), 155–59.

Higham, Charles, and Joel Greenberg. *Hollywood in the Forties.* New York: A. S. Barnes, 1968.

Shaheen, Jack. "The Detective Film in Transition." *Journal of the University Film Association* 28 (1975), 36.

Solomon, Stanley J. "The Private Eye Genre: Huston's *The Maltese Falcon.*" *The Film Idea.* New York: Harcourt Brace Jovanovich, 1972.

Steinbrunner, Chris, and Otto Penzler, eds. *Encyclopedia of Mystery and Detection.* New York: McGraw-Hill, 1976.

CHAPTER 6
WARS: HOT AND COLD

Fearing, Franklin. "Warriors Return." *Film Quarterly* 1 97–109.

Hughes, Robert, ed. *Film, Book 2: Films of War and Peace.* New York: Grove Press, 1962.

Isenberg; Michael. "An Ambiguous Pacifism: A Retrospective on World War I Films, 1930–38." *Journal of Popular Film* 4 (1975), 98–115.

Jacobs, Lewis. "World War II and the American Film." *Cinema Journal* 7 (Winter 1967–68), 1–21.

Jeavons, Clyde. *A Pictorial History of War Films.* Secaucus, N.J.: The Citadel Press, 1974.

Jones, Ken D., and Arthur F. McClure. *Hollywood At War.* New York: A. S. Barnes, 1973.

Kagen, Norman. *The War Film.* New York: Pyramid, 1974.

Lyons, Timothy. "Hollywood and World War I, 1914–1918." *Journal of Popular Film* 1 (Winter 1972), 15–30.

Morella, Joe, Edward Z. Epstein, and John Griggs. *The Films of World War II.* New York: Citadel Press, 1973.

Shain, Russell E. "Hollywood's Cold War." *Journal of Popular Film* 3 (Fall 1974), 334–50.

INDEX OF FILMS

NOTE: Letters in **boldface** refer to film distributors. Full names and addresses can be found in the List of Film Distributors, p. 304. Some films are available from more than one distributor, but only one is listed for each film.

299

301

303

LIST OF FILM DISTRIBUTORS

AB Audio Brandon Films
34 MacQuesten Parkway South
Mount Vernon, New York 10550

CV Cinema V
595 Madison Avenue
New York, New York 10022

FI Films Incorporated
440 Park Avenue South
New York, New York 10016

HCW Hurlock Cine-World
13 Arcadia Road
Old Greenwich, Connecticut
06870

Im Images Film Company
2 Purdy Avenue
Rye, New York 10580

Ivy Ivy Film
165 West 46th Street
New York, New York 10036

Ja Janus Films
745 Fifth Avenue
New York, New York 10022

Kil Killiam Collection
6 West 39th Street
New York, New York 10016

RBC RBC Films
933 North La Brea Avenue
Los Angeles, California 90038

Roa Roa's Films
1696 North Astor Street
Milwaukee, Wisconsin 53202

Sel Select Film Library
115 West 31st Street
New York, New York 10001

Sw Swank Motion Pictures
393 Front Street
Hempstead, New York 11550

Tw Twyman Films Inc.
329 Salem Avenue
Dayton, Ohio 45406

UA United Artists
727 Seventh Avenue
New York, New York 10019

Un United Films
1425 South Main Street
Tulsa, Oklahoma 74119

U/16 Universal 16
445 Park Avenue
New York, New York 10022

WB Warner Brothers
4000 Warner Boulevard
Burbank, California 91503

GENERAL INDEX

Abbott, Bud, 257
Air wars, 254–56, 267–70
Aldrich, Robert, 23, 247, 249
Allegory, 37–40
Allen, Woody, 117
Altman, Robert, 21, 258
Anderson, Broncho Billy, 12
Annakin, Ken, 247
Antiwar films, 250–54, 267–70, 282–85, 289–91
Astaire, Fred, 62, 63, 64, 66, 70, 71, 73, 77, 79, 83, 84, 86–90, 160, 253
Atomic monsters and mutants, 127
Attenborough, Richard, 257
Autry, Gene, 22

Bacall, Lauren, 223
Bacon, Lloyd, 66, 68, 72
Battle films, 242, 243, 254–56, 267–70, 292–95
Beatty, Warren, 171
Benny, Jack, 275
Benton, Robert, 192
Berkeley, Busby, 69, 71–73
Berlin, Irving, 86
Big caper films, 159, 160, 166–68, 171
Biographies:
    criminal, 159–60, 167–68, 174–77, 181–84
    musical, 66, 102–05, 257
    Western, 14–15
Blondell, Joan, 81, 82–83
Boetticher, Budd, 21, 23, 37, 48, 50
Bogart, Humphrey, 29, 162, 212, 215, 219, 248, 261
Bogart, Paul, 211
Borzage, Frank, 257
Brando, Marlon, 70, 77, 197
Brecht, Bertolt, 106
Brooks, Mel, 12
Browning, Tod, 124, 128

Cagney, James, 29, 162–66, 168, 174, 181, 188–89, 197
Capra, Frank, 248
Catastrophe films, 127

Chaffey, Don, 127
Chandler, Raymond, 216
Chaplin, Charles, 159, 173, 242, 244, 251, 256, 257
Chevalier, Maurice, 73
Clive, Colin, 133
Cocteau, Jean, 129
Codes of behavior, in Western films, 13–14, 48–51
Comedy, 2–3
    in big caper films, 160
    in horror films, 132–33, 139, 149
    in war films, 257–58, 274–77, 289–91
Communal relationships, in Western films, 22–23
Conceptual genres, 3
Cook, Elisha, Jr., 222 n
Cooper, Gary, 14, 22
Cooper, Merian C., 124, 127
Coppola, Francis Ford, 5, 67, 167, 194–97
Corman, Roger, 128, 254
Costello, Lou, 257
Courtship-romance musicals, 66
Crawford, Joan, 14
Criminal films, 159–98
    big capers, 159, 160, 166–68, 171
    biographies, 159–60, 167–68, 174–77, 181–84
    concealed criminals, 159
    criminal values, 166–71
    organized crime, 159, 166, 167, 177–81, 187–90, 194–98
    prisoners, 159, 171–73, 184–87
    public image of gangsters, 191–94
    swindlers and con men, 159, 168–69
    sympathetic gangsters, 159–60, 162–66
    thieves, 159–60, 166–67, 170
    urban settings, 26–29, 161
Criminal investigation films. See Police investigation films; Private detective films
Croce, Arlene, 85–86, 90
Cronyn, Hume, 172–73
Crosby, Bing, 70
Crosland, Alan, 72

305

307

309

ILLUSTRATION CREDITS CONTINUED

A 6
B 7
C 8
D 9
E 0
F 1
G 2
H 3
I 4
J 5